The New
Oxfordshire
Village Book

THE VILLAGES OF BRITAIN SERIES

Other counties in this series include:

Avon*

Bedfordshire*

Berkshire*

Buckinghamshire*

Cambridgeshire*

Cheshire*

Devon*

Dorset

Essex*

Gloucestershire*

Hampshire*

Herefordshire*

Hertfordshire*

Kent

Lancashire*

Leicestershire & Rutland*

Lincolnshire*

Middlesex*

Norfolk*

Northamptonshire*

Nottinghamshire*

Powys Montgomery*

Shropshire*

Somerset*

Staffordshire*

Suffolk

Surrey

East Sussex

West Sussex

Warwickshire*

West Midlands*

Wiltshire

Worcestershire*

*Published in conjunction with County Federations of Women's Institutes

The New Oxfordshire Village Book

Compiled by the Oxfordshire
Federation of Women's Institutes from notes
and illustrations sent by Institutes in the County

Published jointly by
Countryside Books, Newbury
and the O.F.W.I., Oxford

First Published 1990
© Oxfordshire Federation of Women's Institutes 1990

Countryside Books
3 Catherine Road
Newbury, Berkshire

ISBN 1 85306 090 9

Cover Photograph of Harwell Village
taken by Joyce and Peter Millward

Produced through MRM Associates Ltd, Reading
Typeset by Acorn Bookwork, Salisbury
Printed in England by J. W. Arrowsmith Ltd, Bristol

Foreword

Oxfordshire is mainly a rural area with pleasant market towns and attractive villages for visitors to explore. The rivers Thames and Cherwell and Oxford Canal offer a variety of water sports and holiday facilities.

The Oxfordshire Way, Ridgeway, Thames Path and numerous well marked footpaths cater for those wishing to walk, and the new motorways and high speed rail services bring this very interesting county within easy reach of many. Whilst travelling in the area one becomes very aware of the abundance of different building materials available locally over the centuries, from limestone and marl to flint and the lovely silvery blue bricks which were produced around Watlington and Henley.

The county has its share of stately homes. Blenheim is obviously a must for many, but the smaller houses, some still used as family residences, are a joy for the visitor.

With the coming of the motorways a number of our villages have been subject to new and 'in-fill' housing, bringing new folk to live in the community. This has inevitably changed the face of village life but the central core of the village remains, with the older inhabitants and the new working together.

I know that our members have enjoyed compiling this book and sincerely hope that visitors and residents alike will, after reading their efforts, view Oxfordshire with new eyes.

From the open countryside with wonderful views around the Ridgeway, through the Thames-side villages to the edge of the Cotswolds there is much to see and enjoy.

May you return again and again – it is a welcoming county.

Joyce Millward
County Chairman 1985–1990

Acknowledgements

The Oxfordshire Federation of Women's Institutes wishes to thank all Institutes whose members have taken part in this book by providing profiles and drawings of their villages.

Thank you, too, to the following:

Dr. Kathleen Burke (Long Wittenham)
A. R. Dufty (Kelmscott)
John Gieve (Chipping Norton)
Gerald Howat (North Moreton)

Finally, a special thank you to Nancy Gieve, the co-ordinator of the project.

County of
OXFORDSHIRE

Shiplake Lock

Adderbury

'Recent' Adderbury history – for it dates from Saxon times and its mellowed parish church of St Mary the Virgin was started in the early 13th century and largely completed by the 15th century – is of its importance as a Royalist stronghold in the Civil War. The most dramatic episode in village history concerns that war – when the vicar of Adderbury, the Rev Dr William Oldys, was shot by a Parliamentarian soldier outside the church gate. The church has close links with New College, Oxford and was beloved of Sir John Betjeman.

Adderbury House has housed troops from wars as far apart as the Civil and Second World Wars. In the former war Henry Wilmot, 1st Earl of Rochester and Prince Rupert of the Rhine were Royalist cavalry commanders there; in the second, King George VI visited his troops in 1942. During the 17th century the house was home to John Wilmot, 2nd Earl of Rochester (1647–80), a fine lyrical and satirical poet and a notorious Restoration rake.

Owned at various times by Dukes of Argyll, Adderbury House was in the possession in the 19th century of Major Larnach. When his Adderbury-trained horse *Jeddah* won the Derby at 100–1 and also won at Ascot to complete the 'blue ribbon' of the Turf, the Major gifted the building of the village Institute. This was opened, in great ceremony, in 1898. Seldom have winnings been more happily invested! The Institute has been the setting of countless village events since then, ranging from early instruction and sewing meetings to the present-day Theatre Workshop productions, meetings of the over sixties, jumble sales and Scout meetings.

The village name Adderbury has had several changes of spelling (it was Eadburg in the Domesday Book). There was an abbess of a priory in Thanet, St Eadburg of the Silver Pen, who lived from about AD 700 to 740, though it is uncertain whether this St Eadburg had local connections as there were at least seven Royal ladies of this title in Mercia. However, the abbess, who had charge of 600 women, was considered an ideal patroness by Adderbury ladies of the WI in the 20th century, as her educational aims in the 8th century were their ideals too! Their strikingly beautiful banner, designed by Miss Janet Blunt, incorporates these pictorial themes.

Miss Janet Blunt figures prominently in village history. Daughter of an Indian Army officer who settled his family in Adderbury in 1892, she

Adderbury House

wrote down from word of mouth Morris dance tunes which had for generations been handed down from father to son. Miss Blunt died in 1950 at the age of 91 and it was only the timely intervention of her former maid that saved the manuscripts from the bonfire. It is to these same tunes present-day Morris dancers cavort at their annual Day of Dance around the village inns and on the green on the last Saturday of April, each year. Generously, they are also shared and taught throughout Oxfordshire.

The village green, with its majestic spreading chestnut tree, once held court to visiting magistrates who meted out punishment to miscreants, by way of whipping stool, ducking stool or the stocks. The latter (removed in 1885) were within the memory of one of the earliest members of the WI at its foundation in 1920.

Adderbury has, since 1969, been several times winner of the title Best Kept Village of North Oxfordshire and twice taken the Winner of Winners class. It is clear the judges find its blend of warm honey-coloured stone, beautiful manor houses and cottage gardens brimming over with flowers, incomparable.

Appleford 🦢

About a mile and a half due east of Sutton Courtenay, on the south bank of the river Thames, is the village of Appleford. As you approach the village the eye is taken upwards to the Wittenham Clumps with its crown of trees and below it the spire of the church. If you look to the right, the bulk of Didcot power station commands the view across the fields.

As its name suggests there was once a ford in the village, which made it a good place for a settlement since earliest times. The history of Appleford dates back to the Saxons and the church of St Peter and St Paul originates from then. Nothing is left of the original building, but part of the chancel contains remains from the 12th and 13th centuries and the font is Norman. It has always been a chapelry, with no vicar of its own, but for 500 years has been part of the living of Sutton Courtenay. At the expense of Walter Justice, the church was heavily restored in 1885–86 when the square tower and spire were added.

The village is bounded on its western side by the railway. The halt was closed in 1849 but rebuilt in 1934 and is still in use, linking Appleford to Didcot and Oxford.

Close by the railway line, on its western side, is Bridge Farm, the former home of Mr Arthur Napper. In 1968 a collection of pewter plates and domestic ironware was discovered in Mr Napper's fields. Dating from Roman times, this is known as the Appleford Hoard and is housed at the Ashmolean Museum, Oxford. Other evidence has shown that a Romano-British settlement existed here and two large collections of Roman coins were also ploughed up.

At the centre of the village is the 'Nap' or green. On its north side is Orchard House. This was once the home of Edmund Bradstock, Appleford's principal benefactor. In his will dated 1607, money and land was left to found a village school as well as charities for the aged of Sutton Courtenay and Appleford. These are still administered by the Bradstock's Trust. Sadly the school closed in 1961. It is remembered by the name 'School Lane' and modern houses stand in its place.

East of the village and close to the church is Manor Farm. Part of its buildings are very old and it was probably the grange of Abingdon Abbey. Interestingly, the field immediately south of the farm is exceptionally large and has never been divided by hedges. East of the churchyard is the ancient footpath to Long Wittenham.

The path to the church porch is lined with beautifully shaped yews and the churchyard is very well kept. In it can be found the tombs of the Justice family (as well as six memorial tablets within the church). A prominent Appleford family, the Justices are mentioned in the parish registers from 1548. Other prominent families included the Steeles, Whicheloes, Carters, Reynolds and later, the Pullens.

While the Pullens were at Manor Farm, six or seven skeletons were found, buried in shallow graves, by farm workers. These were thought to have been soldiers who fought in a local skirmish during the Civil War.

The most interesting character to have lived in Appleford appears to have been John 'Jockey' Faulkener. He is interred in Appleford churchyard in an unmarked grave. John Faulkener died in 1933 at the age of 104. He rode his first race at eight years old and his last, in 1903, at 70! Aged 18 years he won the City Bowl at Salisbury and 74 years later watched his grandson win the same race.

John Faulkener had two wives and 32 children, the eldest of whom was the same age as his second wife. His name was Jimmy; he also in turn became Britain's oldest jockey, beating his father by a short head, marrying three times and having 33 children.

During the last 20 years the village has seen many changes. Not only has the village school disappeared, but many of the old cottages as well.

The old thatched cottages in Main Road (once called Littleworth), the terrace of cottages built in Napoleonic times and the Black Horse – Appleford's other public house, have all been replaced with modern houses as have the two fields, one called Chambrai Minor and the other in Church Street.

The pre-war cricket pavilion has been skilfully converted to a village hall which stands in the recreation field, and provides a meeting place for village activities. Sadly, the village stores and post office closed in 1988. Very few of the villagers work in the vicinity, but the village spirit remains.

Appleton & Eaton ✍

The village of Appleton, with which the smaller village of Eaton has long been associated, stands on rising ground 100 ft above the river Thames, which is its western boundary.

Woodlands, known as Besselsleigh Common and Appleton Common, still partially cover its eastern and southern boundaries. The Saxon name for the village was Earmundslea or 'Edmund's clearing'.

One can still receive an impression of its old character and charm as a considerable number of stone houses remain standing in the centre of the village, from the Tavern Inn to Charity House Farm. Modern housing exists along the roads in and out of the village, and in recent years a considerable amount of in-filling has taken place. The population of the village is now approximately 1,000.

Unfortunately, most of the inhabitants work away from the village, but there is a village shop and post office, a butcher's shop, a greengrocer's/market garden, and a woodyard making garden funiture and fencing. All these businesses are owned by village people. There is a saddler's shop also, which serves the surrounding area.

The White family have a workshop in the village and for four generations have practised the rare craft of bell hanging. Their fame has spread countrywide and they service church bells throughout an extensive area. The family form the core of the bell ringers of the ten bells in the 15th century church tower. The 4th of March is celebrated as the bells' birthday to commemorate the installation of the original peal of six bells in 1818. Peals are rung during the day by visiting ringers and a grand dinner in the village hall ends the celebrations.

Church Lane, in the centre of the village, leads down to the 12th century church of St Laurence. A modern primary school has been built in the old manor orchard in the lane, and on the right is the manor pond and tithe barn. The church has a Norman arcade and nave, and has grown during the centuries by additions and restorations, but it is still a homely little church with a feeling of peace and cosiness.

The manor house, which also dates from about 1190, has a moat. This house too has been enlarged and improved by succeeding generations of owners. It is still lived in as a family home. Mabel de Appleton was the first known owner in 1212, followed by the Fitzwarins. A branch of the Fettiplace family, who were important landowners in the Thames valley area, lived in the manor in Tudor times, and after them came the Southby family in 1684. They remained at the manor until 1880. Monuments to both these families are in the church, and they left charitable bequests to the village – one of which was the distribution of sixpences to poor people attending church on Ash Wednesday and Good Friday.

The lane leading down to the river from Badswell Lane has an ancient well, known as Badger's Well. The water of this well, according to village legend, was a sovereign cure for eye ailments. Before good roads were made this lane was the way by which goods were conveyed for transportation by river.

Another interesting house in the village is The Close, which was originally a plague house. The Thames valley was severely hit by the Black Death in 1348, and many houses were burned down to clear the infection. Those in authority gave the owners the framework for a new home, ie beams, fireplaces etc, and the owners completed the work with lath and plaster or stone.

There are two working farms in the village and two large farms at Eaton.

Ascott-under-Wychwood 🦢

Ascott is a pretty little village in the Cotswolds, which has the advantage of being not quite so pretty as other Cotswold villages such as Burford. This means that all is peaceful and tourists pass us by – no acres of car parks, no 'tea shoppes' or antiques shops.

Stone Age long barrows and an Iron Age camp nearby show that people have lived in the neighbourhood for thousands of years.

Up until about 1874 there was an annual hunt at Whitsuntide in

Wychwood Forest, followed by a week of festivities during which the Ascott Morris men danced in the local villages. With the ending of the hunt, their songs and dances began to be forgotten. Early in the present century, a Mr Reginald Tiddy who lived in Priory Cottage in the High Street collected them and taught them again to the villagers, and the stationmaster's wife made the costumes. In 1912 Mr Tiddy had Tiddy Hall built in Shipton Road for dancing, singing and as a reading room. Sadly, he died in action in France four years later, and is remembered by a stone tablet in the wall.

There are no longer Morris men in Ascott, but a group from Oxford come once a year and dance in Tiddy Hall, and a group in Stony Stratford, Milton Keynes, have a dozen Ascott Morris dances in their repertoire and sometimes perform them on the green.

One of the first Margaret Macmillan Clinics in the country was held regularly in Tiddy Hall, providing free medical treatment for the children. In 1915 the Workers Education Association started one of its earliest rural branches there, which kept going until after the Second World War. Though only a wooden building, it is still in use as a village hall.

On the green there is a tree with a seat round it, planted in memory of the Ascott Martyrs of 1873. The National Agricultural Labourers' Union was attempting to raise labourers' wages to 14 shillings a week, and some men working for Robert Hambridge at Crown Farm, who were only earning eight to ten shillings a week, went on strike. Hambridge brought in two non-Union men from Ramsden, and about 40 local women tried to persuade them not to strike-break. Hambridge took out a summons against some of the women, and they were sentenced to prison with hard labour. Such was the outcry that the women were marched from Chipping Norton to Oxford prison at dead of night, lest the rioters freed them. After questions in the House of Commons they were released. Some say £3 each was collected for them, some say £5, and some say Queen Victoria gave them each a free pardon and a red flannel petticoat. Crown Farm, where the men worked, still belongs to the Crown. A Country Store has opened in one of the barns.

The west end of Ascott is known as Ascott Earl (after an Earl of Worcester) and the east end as Ascott d'Oyley (after Roger d'Oilly who was granted it by William the Conqueror; Roger's brother built Oxford Castle). Each part originally had a fortified castle, with motte and bailey. The one off Shipton Road was probably wooden, and only earth mounds mark the site. The other, off the Chipping Norton road, was built for defence purposes in about 1129, with a stone tower 35 ft square. It was pulled down in 1160 when a garrison was no longer required. The manor house stands within the bailey of this castle, and is partly 12th century. In a dressing-room, people have smelled a sweet perfume as a ghost passes by, and some have seen a lady in blue.

The church of Holy Trinity is mainly 12th century, and quite small and simple. The six bells in the tower are rung regularly for services. At the back of the church are five wooden pews, possibly the oldest in Oxfordshire. These were for the old and sick, whence may have come the saying 'The weakest to the wall' – everybody else had to stand. The series of round depressions near the priest's door is said to have been made by parishioners sharpening their arrow-heads after the service.

Corner House and the village shop used to be the Churchill Arms, where stage coaches from Worcester to London stopped to change horses. When the railway came in the 1860s, a new Churchill Arms – now Wychwood Court – was built near the level crossing. The original signal box is of wood and brick – about the only sign of the brickworks that was once in Ascott. It now has closed circuit television so the signalman can control the level crossing three miles away at Bruern.

The Swan is the only remaining pub. On Monday mornings it doubles as a post office, and you can lounge in comfortable seats while waiting to be served your pension from behind the bar.

The school, on the green, was built in 1873, replacing a building of 1833. In 1989 it became the (private) Windrush Valley School – mysterious, because Ascott lies along the beautiful river Evenlode, not the Windrush.

In the grounds of the Old Rectory up London Lane, there is a pond supplied by a spring which was the source of piped water to the village until 1966.

With converted barns, infill building and council houses, the village has expanded considerably since the Second World War. It now has 501 inhabitants and 198 households. But old inhabitants say the population has remained much the same: where large families with lots of children used to be crammed into small cottages, one or two people live now.

Asthall 🍂

The village of Asthall was originally a Roman settlement, with Akeman Street passing through it. In the Domesday Book it was called 'Esthale' and was 'held of the King by Roger d'Ivery'.

The church of St Nicholas has played a large part in the life of the village and is architecturally of great interest and beauty. It contains a rare medieval stone altar, an early Norman font and many beautiful features. The 14th century tomb of Lady Cornwall, said to be the wife of Edmund Cornwall, grandson of King John, lies under a decorated canopy. In the churchyard a fine wool bale tomb is a reminder of the prosperity that wool brought to this area.

Nearby is the Elizabethan house of Asthall Manor. This was the home of Lord Redesdale and his family ('Uncle Matthew' to all the readers of the Mitford books). The house is approached by a fine avenue of beeches and has a beautiful arch at the entrance.

The Windrush river is a living part of Asthall and a constant source of interest, joy and beauty. A large number of ducks and geese are always to be seen, as well as herons, swans and rare river birds. The blue flash of the kingfisher is always a thrill for those lucky and quiet enough to see him.

Wool and the weaving of it go back to pre-Roman times, continuing through the Middle Ages – the most prosperous times being between 1600 and 1800. The fleeces varied in length and texture according to the breed of sheep. The river was invaluable for washing and cleaning them.

Local industries include farming, and one family has farmed this valley since early in the 20th century. Self-employed industries have been set up by individual people and several country industries – including scaffolding, building, house restoration, dry walling, painting and gardening. The village is very alive now with the comings and goings of these industries and a great feature of it is a feeling of community spirit throughout.

Aston & Cote 🍂

Aston is a village in West Oxfordshire, situated to the north of the upper Thames and four miles to the south of Witney. Cote is a hamlet about one mile to the east of Aston, and nowadays their names are invariably linked together.

The surrounding countryside is very flat with large open fields. Many elm trees died from Dutch elm disease some years ago but plantings of other species have been carried out. Aston is built round the Square, which is in fact a triangle, in the centre of which is the war memorial. Present day Aston and Cote have experienced many reforms during the 20th century. Gas was piped from the diminutive works in Bampton (a mile and a half away) long before electricity arrived but people were still using wells for water until after the Second World War.

In 1890 Kelly's Oxford Directory listed the following occupations that were based in the village – farmers, masons, brickmakers, shoe-makers, blacksmith, wheelwrights, baker, carrier, grocers and general dealers. The farm wagons built by Longs of Aston were considered to be some of the best in the land, and the works were situated behind the post office. Incidentally, the Long family are still active in the village. In Back Lane a laundry was run by destitute young females who were housed by a charity in the present Westfield House, which is now a nursery school. The site of the old laundry is now used for small businesses, which provides some employment but Aston and Cote is mainly a farming area.

Cote consists mainly of farms, most of which have been turned into private dwellings. The Baptist chapel, registered in 1703, stands starkly surrounded by its tomb-filled churchyard – the plain exterior is contrasted by a unique interior of box pews and galleries. Cote House overlooks the fields to the south-west. This stone manor house was built in the reign of James I but incorporates an older wing. One modern addition to the hamlet are the hatcheries where thousands of day-old chicks are raised and exported to all corners of the world.

Lots of changes have occurred in Aston and Cote over the years, with houses and cottages demolished, new estates built, shops closed or changed hands, but the village is still thriving with its two churches – St James' parish church and Cote Baptist church, the school, post office, general stores and lots of organisations from Brownies to a day centre for the elderly.

Although Aston was mentioned in the Giles' *History of Bampton* as 'a humble and primeval looking place with nothing of interest to attract the notice of the traveller', it certainly is not so today. Both Aston and Cote are in the words of the estate agents 'most attractive and desirable places in which to reside'.

Aston Rowant 🪶

Aston Rowant, the Aston meaning 'east tun' and the Rowant after the 14th century Rohant family, is a pretty little brick and flint village lying at the northern foot of the Chiltern Hills. Like all the villages along the foot of the Chilterns it is sited by a stream, the Holbrook, which forms its eastern boundary, the A40 forming its western boundary. To the south of the village the ancient Icknield Way runs below the Chiltern escarpment and to the north the Lower Icknield Way.

The oldest part of the village lies by the 12th century of St Peter and St Paul. In spring the bank of the churchyard is massed with daffodils and blossoming trees. Elizabeth I, when a princess, rode past on her way to imprisonment at Rycote and the bellringers were put in the stocks for ringing in her honour.

The village boasts a privately owned one and a half acre village green with fine trees and daffodils in spring. Around the green is a farmhouse and cottages which were mainly built in the 18th and 19th centuries. To the east a row of neo-Georgian houses was built in the early 1970s.

There has been a manor house at Aston Rowant from 1352. In the 17th century the house was rebuilt in Haseley stone dressed with Bath stone – a fine house with ornamental staircase and picture gallery. Over the years the park and gardens were laid out, together with a two and a half acre lake. 'The manor house with its park and gardens was one of the remarkable seats in the county', as Brewer put it in his guide of 1819. On the death of Edward Dashwood in 1950 the house was sold and used for storage by a grass drying firm – it burned down in 1956. Now 13 ranch-style bungalows have been built in the park and the walled kitchen garden, with its grape, peach and nectarine houses, owned and worked as a nursery until 1986, has been built on.

The village school was built in 1844, much earlier than many in the county. Before that there had been a lace school for girls. Originally pupils spent all their school years in the village, now they leave at nine to go on to Chinnor and Thame. Bucket toilets were only replaced in the late 1960s.

The railway came in 1872. The station was used for the films *My Brother Jonathan* and *The Captive Heart* in the 1950s. Sadly the station closed in 1957 and the site is now used for storage by the County Council.

Up until the 1960s most people worked for the 'big house' or on the local farms. Aston House owned the village, it made its own gas for street lighting, etc, the road through the village was swept daily and woebetide a gardener if a weed could be found!

With the coming of the M40 Aston Rowant has become a commuter village, its inhabitants working in London or the larger towns nearby. Two of the farms have become studs, one stallion being the famous *Daring Do*. The village shop has disappeared but the church and school still thrive. The church has a good team of bellringers and a social committee to organise various social events. Unfortunately a lot of money is needed for its restoration.

There is no public house but there is a thriving cricket club, established in 1881, with a pitch so well cared for that it has been used for Minor County games. Twice the team has got to the semi-finals of the National Village Cricket Knockout.

Aston Tirrold
& Aston Upthorpe

The twin Aston villages merge comfortably at the foot of the Berkshire Downs, in the valley below the A417 Wantage to Reading Road. The parishes stretch from South Moreton to Lowbury Hill and have a population of about 550 people. The Berkshire Ridgeway runs above them to the south. To the west Blewburton Hill, an Iron Age earthwork, has yielded Iron Age, Roman and Saxon relics now in Reading Museum.

Tradition has it that King Ethelred and his younger brother Alfred, later the King, heard Mass together before the first great victory over the Danes at 'Assendune' on the Downs. There is a popular legend that Ethelred, unready as usual, dithered in Aston Upthorpe while Alfred went out and won the battle. The story is erroneous – this was a different Ethelred from the dilatory king known to every schoolchild. Whether the Mass was held in a Saxon church or the royal tent, it is certain that Aston Upthorpe's All Saints' church is built on Saxon foundations, has an 11th century nave, a filled-in Norman door, and a 15th century porch.

St Michael's church in Aston Tirrold dates back to 1080, was re-modelled in the 13th century and a tower and south transept added in the 14th century. Both lovely village churches are well worth a visit. The rectory, next to St Michael's, was sold when a united benefice was formed with the parishes of North and South Moreton. The Astons have a tradition of Presbyterianism, and before the Act of Uniformity in

1662, 'Meetings in the Barns' took place. In 1728 the very interesting Presbyterian chapel was built, making it one of the oldest in England. It is now the United Reformed church.

During the 20th century the Astons have been closely connected with horse racing. At one time there were four trainers in the two villages. Although there is now only one, in Aston Upthorpe, horses can still be seen exercising around the villages. In the early 1960s the stud farm was restocked and subsequently bought by Sheikh Mohammed al Maktoum, who built it up and then gave it to his younger brother Sheikh Ahmed al Maktoum in 1987. Since then new foaling units, stallion boxes and extra paddocks have made this one of the leading stud farms in England.

There are two public houses, one in each village, the Chequers and the Boot Inn. Both serve meals and are places where people can gather, a necessity as over the years the village school, the small well-stocked library and the village shop have all closed. The weekly doctor's surgery in the village hall is also a meeting place to exchange news. There is a large recreation ground where the football and cricket clubs play in season and children have a well-equipped play area enclosed in one corner.

The surrounding land is mostly arable, yielding good crops of wheat and barley. Carrimers Farm and Upthorpe Farms are the two main farms, and the Astons still remain truly rural villages with well preserved old houses and attractive lanes through which to walk from one village to the other.

The Baldons 🎜

> March Baldon, Toot Baldon,
> Baldon in between
> Big Baldon, Little Baldon,
> Baldon on the Green.

In fact there are just two villages with a total population of less than 500 and a large acreage of good agricultural land. Both villages have had a close association with the university as Queen's College has owned much of the land, and in time of plague and when the king occupied Oxford in the Civil War, members of the university retreated to the safety of Toot Baldon.

Toot Baldon is on the top of its hill and the name Toot means a look out. It has attractive houses built mainly of local stone. There is a fine old manor house and just over the road the partly rebuilt old court house. Across the field is the delightful little early 13th century church dedicated to St Lawrence, and a little further down the hill is Baldon Row – once called Baldon St Lawrence – a little group of cottages, again mainly stone built. One pair of cottages has a superb thatched roof, the thatch coming to a few feet from the ground.

Little Baldon is now one farm with noteworthy new houses for the farm workers.

Marsh Baldon, formerly March Baldon, is a 'history book' village, centred around the 24-acre gated village green, as the Saxons built it, just off the Roman road with the manor house and church down the road. There are many interesting houses around the green, but the north side has mainly uniform brick built Victorian cottages. A disastrous fire in September 1866 destroyed the thatched cottages; it had been a very dry summer and the five ponds on the green had dried up. The 17th century Baldon House has been extended over the years.

The present church, dedicated to St Peter, was built by the monks from Dorchester. It has a Saxon Mass Dial, and the east window has some lovely 14th century glass and also the arms of Henry VII when the church was restored. There is also a Jacobean pulpit with sounding board, and a very flowery monument extols the virtues of Ann Pollard who died from smallpox. The tower has an unusual octagonal top.

There is no post office or shop in the village but there is a splendid new village hall for which the small community worked very hard.

Very few people are still engaged in agriculture, most travel to nearby Oxford to work, but there is one employer making use of the fertile soil – in the south west corner of the parish, on an outcrop of greensand, are Mattock's rose gardens. Until recently the farmers used their right to graze their cattle on the village green, now they use it for hay.

These are two delightful villages lying off the main roads, where the singing of Evensong is accompanied by bird song and that real country sound of ball on bat can be heard on the village green.

Bampton

Six miles from Witney, Bampton lies on a gravel terrace, just above the flat Thames valley. It is an attractive Cotswold village, off the usual tourist tracks, but it is so full of charm that its many special features are well worth exploring.

Bampton's history is intriguing. There was a pre- Christian settlement (a Roman altar was recently dug up in a field) and it grew in Saxon and Norman times. It was mentioned in the Domesday survey, when it already possessed a market, and was famous for its wool trade. In the Middle Ages its administrative area was considerable, and included Witney and Burford. The surviving records of the travelling Court of Law (called 'The Oxfordshire Eyre') of 1241 give several details of Bampton incidents. In the 17th century, an important leather trade grew up, and Bampton became famous for its jackets, gloves and breeches.

The chief feature now is the church of St Mary. It is one of the largest in West Oxfordshire. It stands on the site of a former Saxon minster, and is a Norman building, remodelled in the 13th and 14th centuries. It has a noble spire; a recent gale unfortunately blew down one of the flying buttresses and St John, one of the four figures standing at the corners of the tower.

Around the close and green, are four large houses, Georgian in appearance, but of earlier origins. Bampton Castle, previously an imposing and impressive building, now has only the remains of the gatehouse and a stretch of curtain walling, which are incorporated into the farmhouse called Ham Court; however, British Telecom retains the name of Bampton Castle for the telephone exchange. Weald Manor opposite Ham Court, and Bampton Manor to the north, add to the architectural delights; both are set in charming gardens which are open to the public two or three times a year.

The stone cottages, whose roofs were formerly thatched with straw but are now mostly slates or tiles, form terraces leading along three streets to the Market Square, where the town hall and village hall face each other. A corn mill stood at the end of Mill Street, with Mill Green to the south. Old residents remember how the cottages there would be flooded quite regularly, so that the water came up to the third stair indoors; the doctor wore waders, not mere wellington boots, to go through the waters to his patients, who had to remain on the first floor for perhaps three weeks at a time. Now the land has been drained, and the level of the waters controlled by holding ponds at Brize Norton airfield, two miles away.

There are some 2,000 inhabitants, many of whom are concerned at the prospect of further increasing the size of the village. The villagers are a caring group, and are prepared to cherish their inheritance. The traditional Horse Fair may have vanished, but the Bampton Morris dancers flourish; the dancers dress in white, the bells on their leather anklets jingle as they kick and dance to the fiddler's music, and the clown urges them on.

One Bamptonian remembers her father going once a week to wind the clock on the town hall; as a child she had to scrub the upper room for meetings, and all the stone steps that lead up to it. Her family was very grateful to the Countess Münster of Bampton Manor when she organised main drainage, as previously sewage was collected in a tank drawn by a horse and cart on Wednesdays and Saturdays, and taken down the Aston Road, 'and oh, how it smelled!'

On Sundays the baker's oven was much used. At ten o'clock in the morning, the tin with the meat, quite often an H-bone to be roasted with the onions and carrots below the joint, would be carried to the baker, and collected at twelve. 'At four, we'd collect the currant cake he had baked. He charged sixpence for that'.

Today, as well as main drainage, electricity and gas, there are other excellent facilities, such as two banks, eight pubs, five doctors and a dispensary, two garages, seven shops, a post office, two hairdressers, a primary school, public library, fire station, and a daily bus service.

Bampton's inhabitants want to keep their village an inviting one, and are prepared to work to keep it attractive. Two thousand daffodil bulbs planted in open spaces in the autumn of 1989 are now golden proof.

The Bartons 🕊

A long, straggling street with buildings of various styles, periods and materials is the first impression of the Bartons gained by the passing motorist. To the discerning eye, to the explorer of half hidden lanes, and certainly to the inhabitants, there is much more to these communities of about 1,700 people.

There are three villages, Middle and Westcote, virtually joined, and Steeple Barton, quite distinct, approached by country lanes. From Saxon times Steeple Barton supplied the royal manor at Woodstock with food and, later, Osney Abbey. It has a skyline-dominating church and its few houses are pleasingly set in what is now a very small hamlet. The deep-cut narrow road, green lanes and meandering tracks indicate its antiquity. Humps in the fields are remains of a once sizable village, largely abandoned after the ravages of the Black Death. Traces of the old mill and dried up fish ponds tell of a very different past.

Westcote Barton, another old settlement, has an impressive small church and attractive stone cottages, particularly in Fox Lane which leads to a ford on the Dorn. The brook was the main water supply, carried by hand to houses as much as a mile away, until the mid-1930s.

Middle Barton (the name Barton means an outlying farm) was settled by post-plague immigrants from Steeple Barton and those taking advantage of the medieval road from Bicester (now the B4030). A population explosion came in the 18th and 19th centuries when enterprising individuals, lacking opportunity elsewhere or unhappy with squire or parson, moved in, erecting cottages and smallholdings on the road verges of North Street, in no particular style and facing in different directions. There are older, attractive stone cottages from the 16th and 17th centuries in the parallel South Street. Never an estate village, but an open village, it was independent of any squire and people enjoyed the freedom to build and live as they pleased.

In the main road there is a farm and adjoining field with grazing animals, of perennial interest to villagers walking by. Here is a reminder of the agricultural emphasis of the past. There is still a working farrier, though the horses he shoes now are for riding. Few villagers today are farm workers or associated with agriculture and a great variety of professions and occupations is now represented in the population.

Unlike some of its more picturesque neighbours, the Bartons have relatively few weekend-only occupied dwellings and so have retained more of the character of a lively, working community. This is largely due to the development of modern housing estates. Young families have ensured a flourishing primary school, the survival of two shops and a garage.

The Bartons are said to be known for the friendliness and independence of character of the villagers. Until the recent increase in prosperity, life was very hard for many. Even so the Ruridecanel magazine for 1923 describes Steeple Barton as 'the healthiest parish for many a mile'. Today there are energetic nonagenarians taking long walks, tending the garden and recently playing the organ for church services. Independence of spirit was shown by the small Quaker settlement; the graveyard may still be seen. Methodism flourished and the only church in Middle Barton (far the largest of the villages) is the Methodist chapel in South Street, one of the few remaining village chapels in North Oxfordshire.

Barton Abbey, at Steeple Barton, is the 'big house' (it was never an abbey). In part 16th century but substantially Victorian, it was rebuilt (and named) by the Halls, the brewing family. Since 1925 house and estate have been owned by the Flemings, who have continued the tradition of generous support to the villages.

Nearby is St Mary's church with a fine 15th century tower and interesting memorials and carvings. The smaller Westcote Barton church is unusual in its dedication to St Edward the Confessor and entitlement to the wearing of red cassocks by the choir. Much of the building, on the site of a Saxon church, is 15th century.

The Bartons are in gently undulating country, well wooded, with many smallish fields enclosed by hedges, some of which are estimated to be 800 years old. There are numerous field paths, trackways and narrow lanes. Field and other names are of much interest, Purgatory and Hardroad Hill (now Kiddington Road) for example.

Present and past are closely inter-related in the Bartons. Much has been lost but finds are made of medieval pottery and ancient tools in gardens and old out-buildings. Only the old, written records and photographs remain to remind one of the once flourishing Horticultural Shows and Friendly Society activities. Church fetes however are still held in the grounds of Barton Abbey. The strange and ancient mummers' play of Westcote Barton was last performed about a century ago and only a sketchy text survives.

The problems of today are not the isolation and poverty of the past, but such issues as inadequate car parking. Old residents regret some of the changes time has brought but they and newcomers have an interest and pride in the Bartons and regard them with affection as rather special.

Baulking

Baulking, previously in Berkshire, is a relatively tranquil village with about 85 inhabitants, situated in the lovely Vale of the White Horse and bounded on one side by the river Ock, known locally as Rosey Brook. Long ago it was a thriving market town, its market day having been changed by charter in 1219 from Thursday to Tuesday, and has had connections with the ancient abbey of Abingdon and the manor of Kingston Lisle. Parts of the village were in the past owned by the Earls of Spencer and of Craven. Today, although Intercity trains whizz through the cutting (begun in 1839) and under Brunel's bridge, one can neither board a train at Uffington station (which was built in Baulking parish) nor refresh oneself at the Junction Hotel, both now closed.

The main feature of the village is its large goose green around which stand attractive farmhouses, pretty cottages and the remains of the old village pump. This 18 acre green, in former times controlled by two gates, is now necessarily in three separate parts, the natural 'divisions' being the railway and the church, alongside the latter of which there is presently a cattle grid. Certain adjacent land-holders to the green have grazing rights consisting of sheep commons: so many sheep equal one cow, horse, etc, and whereas in olden times flocks of sheep grazed the green and wool was an important industry, today cattle are let loose annually from 13th May to 6th December. It is good to see domestic geese back after a long interval, but guinea fowl and other poultry are no longer around.

The church of St Nicholas was built in this idyllic spot in the 13th century, and has interesting wall paintings which were uncovered and restored in 1988–9. A service is held every Sunday. It is recorded that the present churchyard, for some time previously already fenced with oak, was consecrated and first used as a burial ground in 1849/50. The last vicar of Baulking left in 1951 on becoming Dean of Wells, whereupon the vicarage was sold and the parish linked to that of Uffington and Woolstone.

The spacious village green is a favoured meeting place of the Old Berks Hunt, and records show there was a meet of the Royal Buckhounds on 2nd March 1893 when hundreds of folk turned out and there were waggons, 'musicianers', cock-shies and Aunt Sallies. In the 1920s point-to-points were staged on Baulking Hill. Mention must be made of *Baulking Green*, the horse which put the village on the map in the 1960s, bringing many glittering steeplechase trophies back to this corner of England.

Agriculture is still the predominant industry, though today only two of the eight farms have dairy herds, the lush pasture elsewhere being grazed by store cattle, with in places diversification to arable. In the 1970s open caste mining for high quality fuller's earth and the drying thereof on site began, thus providing an ever changing scene: first the creation of bunds, then excavation to great depths even necessitating the resiting of the road to Stanford-in-the-Vale, and after extraction immediate reclamation field by field.

The village hall, brick kiln, shop, pub, school – and alas the splendid elms – are no more, and inevitably some residents now commute elsewhere. Children are taken to Uffington or Wantage for their schooling, and, although some consumables are delivered to the door, there is a community bus based in Uffington which conveys Baulking people to Faringdon for shopping, while a mobile library attends to the cultural needs of the parish. The village joins forces with Uffington and Woolstone for many activities, including sport, the WI, MU, Scouts and Guides, but it controls its own parochial affairs through its Parish Meeting.

Beckley ❧

'I went to Noke and nobody spoke;
I went to Beckley, they spoke directly'.

This is an old aphorism, quite probably untrue of Noke nowadays, but certainly true of Beckley. It is the friendliest of villages, where passers-by always speak to each other and newcomers are gathered into the fold and made to feel at home.

In spite of Beckley's close proximity to Headington and Oxford, when you cross the B4027 you enter another world. There has been a settlement at Beckley since Roman times; the Roman road from Dorchester to Alcester cuts the village in two. The present village is a survival from the 16th, 17th and 18th centuries with only the original school building and a few nearby cottages representing the Victorian era. Almost every house is in some way associated with Beckley's ancient past, if only because some of its building stone was originally part of the medieval royal palace.

Between the wars many of the tiny stone and thatched farm labourers' cottages became almost derelict as farm work decreased and men took jobs in the Cowley factories. Fortunately their potential for amalgamation and conversion into larger homes appealed to people wishing to move out of Oxford's growing eastern suburbs. Equally fortunately these people wished to retain and even pinpoint the period features of the cottages, so that even when they were practically rebuilt they fitted in with the Beckley landscape. Where two or three cottages were knocked into one larger house, the old door lintels can still be seen through their frame of honeysuckle and roses. One sees with one's physical eyes the pleasing elegance of gracious homes; with one's imagination one sees Beckley's past. Old barns, converted into homes retain their shape and character, and there is still the odd Oxfordshire wagon shed and the old smithy, now a garage. Cripps' cottage, where Cripps the carrier lived, one of the oldest 16th century converted cottages, recalls the time when carriers were Beckley's link with Oxford; Pound cottage recalls the adjacent enclave in which animals illegally grazing on Otmoor were impounded.

Everywhere one walks one touches history and nowhere more so than at Beckley's glorious medieval church standing on its windswept knoll. Each generation, including the present one, has left its loving mark on the church which is a treasury of rare 14th century glass, wall paintings, a beautiful timber roof, a tub font which could be Saxon, a very ancient door, one of the oldest church chests in England, a Jacobean pulpit, and some very fine Victorian glass in the chancel. Mention must also be made of the beautiful moated Beckley Park house and the lovely Georgian Grove House, adding a touch of class to a basically working village. It must not be forgotten how hard Beckley and the Otmoor villagers have had to fight to survive against the monstrous M40.

Sometimes you would be forgiven for thinking the village is dead. Then school erupts, a group of cyclists whizz down the hill, the playgroup fishes for tadpoles in the village pond, riders trot up the high street, the army drives down Otmoor Lane to the rifle range, cars converge on the inn at lunch time, the Hunt canters by, pack-laden walkers pause at the sports field to watch cricket practice, the WI walkers group ventures into pastures old, joggers puff by, and a farm tractor with a trailer of fodder and a joyously barking border collie turns up Roman Way.

At night it is quiet. Two solitary street lamps and the Abingdon Arms light the wayfarer. And over all, signalling to the outside world for many miles, is Beckley's affirmation of 20th century status – the glowing TV mast.

Begbroke

Begbroke was mentioned in the Domesday Book when it was valued at 100 shillings, but the name is much older, a possible joining together of two Anglo-Saxon words 'beck' and 'broc', both meaning a small stream. 'Becca's stream' is another interpretation. Rowel brook which runs from the Spring Hill and flows under the A34 to join the Oxford Canal, is a development of an Old English word 'ra-wella' or 'roe-stream'. Round Castle, a plateau hill fort, is nearby and may date from the Iron Age; while flints, scrapers, arrow-heads, a polished axe-head and a piece of 2nd century pottery indicate early settlement in the area.

For nearly 500 years Begbroke Hill Farm was owned by only two families, the Giffords and the Fitzherberts, the present fine stone house being built by the latter in the early 17th century. This is on the site of a previous medieval building, only the cellar of which remains. It stayed in private hands until the middle of the 20th century. During the Partridge occupancy it was known as 'Brewing' or 'Barley' Farm as George Partridge won international recognition for his barley crops. This enterprising man also introduced steam ploughing to Begbroke and was one of the first farmers to advertise the sale of Christmas turkeys. From 1960 until the mid 1980s the farm was popularly known as 'Weeds' because it was the home of the Weed Research Organisation – continuing this modern development, its new occupants are to be the research scientists of Cooksons industrial group.

St. Michael's Church, Begbroke

The Royal Sun has been a holstelry since the days of Charles II. In 1723 one Hannah Graves, the wife of the landlord, was placed in the stocks for causing a disturbance in the village. Her husband John was ordered not to sell wine, and was fined £40 for being disorderly. Nowadays it is an attractive meeting place for villagers and passing trade alike.

Two of the larger buildings on the west side of the A34, which in effect divides the older part of the village from the newer, are St Philip's Priory and Solid State Logic. The neo-Georgian house occupied by the latter has been used for a variety of purposes – among them a retirement home for elderly clergy, a convent school for 45 years, and a now a centre for sophisticated recording systems. The Priory, home of the Servite Order of Friars since 1896, and given to them by Charles Robertson, was the original manor house dating from 1610. During the Civil War it was occupied by Colonel Butler, one of Cromwell's commanders.

It is unusual to find churches of two religious traditions next to each other in a small village – so near the busy A34 yet they form an oasis of peace in their attractive rural setting. St Michael's retains the simplicity and charm of a small Norman church although it was extensively restored in the 19th century. The third level of the tower with its saddleback roof was added in the 14th century. The arch of the south doorway is in a zig-zag pattern and like the chancel arch it is unusual in being supported by shafts of two different designs. The octagonal font has a 15th century base inset with quatrefoils. Also 15th century is the aumbry in the north wall of the chancel which has the original door, beautifully carved with vine leaves. The more recent stained glass is mainly heraldic in design, but Old and New Testament scenes are depicted in roundels, those of medieval date being Flemish in origin.

There is no school in Begbroke today, most children going to Woodstock, but in the hundred years from 1786 there were several of widely differing types, starting with the 'Begbroke Boarding School for Young Ladies' in what is now St Philip's Priory, which lasted until 1819. By this time there was also a dame school and Sunday school for the poor children, and by 1820 the curate had succeeded in establishing Begbroke Free School. To do this he had to 'persuade' an unwilling Widow Parker to become the schoolmistress under threat of eviction from her home! And while encouraging the teaching of reading (and sewing for girls) he believed it would be fatal to teach writing and arithmetic to the poor as 'these accomplishments would raise them above their station'. The school closed by 1884 after running into debt. The schoolhouse was demolished in the 1960s and the school tablet is now incorporated into the wall of a family house built on the site. The next (and last) time Begbroke had a school in the village was in the Second World War, when St Juliana's Convent was evacuated from Bognor Regis to Begbroke Place, and stayed for 40 years.

The cricket club was established in 1934. They first played in the dairy field opposite Hall Farm and then moved down the lane to the field behind Orchard Cottage. They played mostly against college teams, who would arrive by taxi with crates of beer on the roof. Teas were prepared in the stable block. Present day amenities on the eastern side of the village include a garage, a small, friendly post office/stores, playing field and village hall.

Benson ✇

Benson is a large village beside the Thames, about twelve miles downstream from Oxford, with a population of approximately 6,000.

The first official mention of Benson was in the *Anglo-Saxon Chronicle* of AD 571, where it appears as Bensington. This is still the village's formal name, and is written on the name board which stands outside the parish church of St Helen.

Parts of St Helen's church date back to the 12th century. The interior was completely restored and a nave altar added during the 1970s. This can be removed if the occasion arises, and gives a very open and friendly feel to the church. The work was mainly performed by the members of the church, and other volunteers from the community. The church clock is very interesting, as it is in Roman numerals and contains two XI's and no IX. During the Second World War a radio broadcast was picked up that included the message that the German Luftwaffe were going to bomb the airfield near the village with the church that had two elevens on its clock!

Today Benson is probably best known for its RAF station, which houses the Queen's Flight. It is also the place where the Duchess of York learned to fly. The airfield was built in 1937, and played an important role during the Second World War as home of the Photographic Reconnaissance unit. Many local people work on the station, and the relationship between local residents and service personnel is very good. The annual RAF fete and the flying displays always prove very popular attractions.

The Thames has played an important and on-going part in Benson's history. Fisheries were mentioned here in the Domesday Book of 1086, and today there is still a thriving angling club. Until about 1934 coal was transported from the Midlands through the Coventry and Oxford Canals, and then down the Thames to Benson's wharf. This site now houses the Cruiser Station, where boats can be hired, and a holiday caravan park. This also supplies some seasonal employment.

Another thing unique to Benson is the veteran cycle club. The founder, Mr Ned Passey, has a large collection of over 450 antique bicycles in a museum next to his house, and is pleased to show people around. An annual rally is held on the first Sunday of July, starting from the recreation field and going around the surrounding villages, stopping for a pub lunch on the way. The rally began in 1961 and attracts riders from as far afield as America. Most riders dress up in costumes which reflect the age of their cycles.

The village is on the old coaching route from London to Oxford, and the Crown Inn was built in 1709 for travellers to rest, and to change horses. A mounting stone can still be seen on the corner of the building. In those days many villagers would have earned their living building coaches, and would later have transferred to making railway carriages.

The Mill Stream Day Centre is a new addition to the village, and is used by many elderly people. Lunch is served there three days a week, and on another two days meals on wheels are prepared there. There is also some sheltered housing, with beautiful gardens going down to the stream.

Binfield Heath ✍

Binfield Heath lies in the parish of Shiplake and has no official separate status, but those who live there argue hotly that it is a village in its own right. Certainly there is a strong community spirit and a number of residents have roots there that go back many years. The village has in fact more of a core than nearby Dunsden, as most of the houses are near the two village shops and recreation ground. At the centre of the crossroads, where the road from Dunsden meets the Sonning Common/Shiplake road, stands a fine chestnut tree which is a well known rendezvous. A smithy stood beside this tree, which must have given rise to many references to the old song. The building still stands but caters for motor cars and has not quite the same charm. It is not difficult, however, if you half-close your eyes and pretend the cars are gone, to imagine you can hear the clatter of hooves and the hiss of steam.

The residence of prime importance in the village is Holmwood. For many years this was owned by the Makower family. Their tradition of involvement in local affairs has been carried on by the present owners, Mr and Mrs B. Talfourd-Cook. Many fund-raising events for charity are held at Holmwood and, unlike the case with many 'big houses', nearly every villager has set foot in the grounds at one time or another.

One of the major events of the year is the Binfield Heath and District Flower Show which is open to residents of the parishes of Dunsden, Harpsden and Shiplake. The show celebrated its ruby anniversary in 1988 and is held at Holmwood on the last Saturday in August. Another item in the calendar is the Great Wheelbarrow Race. This was instituted to celebrate the 50th anniversary of the founding of the British Legion but then became an annual summer event. The purpose is to raise funds for the British Legion but enormous fun is had by all.

In olden days there were several ponds in the area, some of which have since been filled in. One was immediately in front of the New Inn, near the blacksmith's, one by the Bottle and Glass, and another by the White Hart. These ponds were essential both to water the farm horses and to provide water for the traction engines which at harvest time used to go from farm to farm, followed by a crowd of children and dogs ready to catch the rats and mice that ran out of the diminishing corn as it was cut. There was also a bakehouse adjacent to the New Inn but this was enclosed and renovated to form a private dwelling.

The brickworks in Kiln Lane provided work for many years and the old road serving the works and some of the houses built for workers are still in use. A few of the houses at the end of Kiln Lane are built of wood and these were donated by Sweden at the end of the Second World War to help the acute housing shortage. These traditional Swedish buildings blend well with the surrounding wooded area.

An unusual covered well stands near Holmwood. Unfortunately the original was completely demolished a few years ago in a motoring accident, but it has been rebuilt exactly as before. In appearance it is a dome on top of a cylinder, built in brick. Various legends surround it, one connected with a ghostly coach and horses which are said to gallop by at dead of night.

It may seem surprising that no church exists at Binfield Heath. Shiplake church is some way distant but that is where parishioners were expected to attend, and a local resident remembers going to church by

34

horse and cart in her childhood. There has been since 1835, however, a Congregational chapel on the corner of Gravel Road and Dunsden Road, a fine site which must have seemed temptingly convenient to local Anglican residents. It is built in an attractive mock-Gothic style and has a pleasantly simple interior.

Very little new building has taken place in recent times, the exception being Heathfield Close, a small development of modern houses opposite the New Inn. Many of the older houses are tucked away and a casual visitor might comment 'There's not much going on in Binfield Heath'. But he would be wrong!

Blewbury ༄

Aldridge, Caudwell, Corderoy, Grace, Street; some family names of Blewbury past which live on in Blewbury today. Justus Corderoy and Zephaniah Grace, were just two stalwart members of the centuries-old farming community that lived in a cluster of dwellings dependent on the line of springs at the foot of the Berkshire Downs.

Agriculture and its ancillary industries supported the inhabitants of Blewbury well into the 20th century. Not only the farmers, but also the wheelwright, blacksmith, maltster, miller, harness maker and of course the farmworkers, who were an integral part of the community. Their tiny cottages roofed with thatch and built of wattle and daub bear witness to their labours. Scattered throughout the village were more substantial farmhouses with their huge barns and pretty orchards. In June, during the Blewbury Festival, some of these houses are open to the public.

The village is intersected by streams and footpaths with lovely wide open spaces at its centre. Thatched cob walls still mark the boundaries of the old farmyards. The cavity of one of these walls is said to be infilled with cattle horns from the village tannery and probably they hide more than one lost treasure. A small gate in the cob wall of Boham's farm, its latch dated 1823, was said to enable the farmer, William Boham, to slip out to the Red Lion unobserved.

For more than a century Blewbury has attracted artists and writers, who found the peace and tranquillity of the downs adequate compensation for cold, damp cottages. Marguerite Steen and William Nicholson endured rats and Tudor drains. A. A. Milne declined to rent Boham's, the home of Kenneth Grahame and his wife Elspeth; perhaps the complaint of a former tenant that the larder was mouse-infested deterred him! G. B.

Cob walls at Blewbury

Stern lived and wrote in a brick-floored cottage on the edge of the Millbrook. Susan Beatrice Pearce, much loved for her 'Ameliaranne' books, lived to reach her 100th birthday in her tiny 'teacosy' cottage. The village still keeps up an enthusiasm for the arts and painting. The Borlase Gallery has regular exhibitions and every August a group of intrepid amateurs sets off with brushes and paints for Venice.

The coming of 'The Atomic' at Harwell changed Blewbury dramatically. It provided employment for villagers and brought in newcomers. New thatch now crowns pristine white cottages and the apple orchards have given way to small housing developments. Community life still centres round the four village pubs and here plans are made for the annual Shakespearean productions which are performed in Blewbury's open-air amphitheatre at Orchard Dene, or for the commissioning of the triennial community opera, or for the summer festival.

The changing structure of society brought new needs, in particular homes for the elderly. One of the very first co-ownership societies providing homes for the over fifty fives was formed here at Dibleys where an estate of well-designed bungalows was built. The accommodation is now leasehold under the management of Dibleys Heritage Ltd.

At one time strings of race horses were a common sight in the village but they have moved onto the downs nearer the gallops. Riders these days are from the busy local riding school, whose comings and goings were viewed from next door by Dick Francis as he wrote his racing thrillers. The former stables of Steve Donoghue have been converted to house a private printing press, The Rocket Press. Stables, barns and outhouses of more than one old farm are now leased to small business enterprises. Where Cavaliers and Roundheads once took shelter and shire horses stamped their feet the only sound is the whirring of computers.

The village today is different but very much alive. The houses are warm, well lit, clean, hygienic and comfortable. If one wants the nostalgia of the past it is here but without the poverty and hardship that once existed. A terraced prehistoric settlement looks down on the village from Blewburton Hill but from its summit only the tower of the church can be glimpsed, half hidden by trees. The charity school and the almshouses beside the church present a view little changed with time. To see Blewbury you must leave the main road and explore its maze of footpaths.

Bloxham

Situated about three miles from the town of Banbury on the A361 route to the heart of the Cotswolds, Bloxham is one of the principal ironstone villages of North Oxfordshire. The main road has not always followed its present route, but formerly passed along Old Bridge Road, where the village war memorial now stands, to the Elephant and Castle public house, where the old coaching arch still forms the entrance to the present day car park.

Since the early 1960s there has been substantial growth to accommodate newcomers who work in Banbury, Oxford and other towns farther afield. However, in times past there were several farms, a brickyard, sawyard and blacksmith's forge to provide local employment. Ironstone was mined by men who were paid 7d per ton and the record is said to stand at 14 tons hewn in four hours. The ore was then pushed in trucks along to the village railway station, once said to be one of the prettiest in

Oxford. In the 1990s the latest company to occupy premises on the A361 alongside the Sor Brook is Jaguar Sport, who will produce the latest 'state of the art' sports car there.

A village with a range of schools, shops and other services vital to modern day living naturally attracts growth. However, the heart of the old village, designated as a conservation area, with picturesque cottages set in narrow lanes, remains unspoilt by the development of new estates on the perimeter. St Mary's church dominates the village and its spire, said to have been commissioned by Cardinal Wolsey, soars to a height of 198 ft.

To the south of the church is a small thatched building known as the Court House. Built in 1689 on the site of the former Town House, it now serves as a village hall. The building is owned by the Bloxham Feoffees who for centuries have been the custodians and administrators of various village charities. In the past this body of men has been responsible for roads, bridges, street lighting, drainage and even the winding of the church clock. The Local Government Act of 1894 saw the creation of the parish council which assumed some of the Feoffees' responsibilities, but they still retain an income to be distributed to those in need. The undercroft of the Court House is home to the Bloxham Village Museum, which is open on Sunday afternoons from April to October.

The village school was formerly housed in what is now part of the Old School and Manor Hotel and one parish councillor can recall when coal fires burned in the school room and Horlicks and milk was served to pupils at break time. Children from the nearby hamlets of Milton and Milcombe walked to school whilst older pupils going to Banbury were provided with bicycles by the education authority – a healthier variation on the modern bus pass. Now a fleet of coaches ferries children daily to the Warriner School from villages in an extensive catchment area.

In the second half of the 20th century rural communities everywhere have faced increasing threats. Small villages witnessing the closure of the school, shop/post office and withdrawal of public transport predict an uncertain future. Such a prospect has never been Bloxham's lot. Most new families experience a warm welcome and that sense of community concern which is more common in rural England than some people imagine. The needs of all are catered for from the baby clinic to the weekly Lunch Club and meals service for the elderly, all run by volunteers and certain indications that Bloxham will thrive as an old village with a modern identity for many years to come.

Bodicote

Journeying north on the A423 from Oxford one could perhaps be forgiven for missing Bodicote village as it is not on the main road. However, why not turn into the village at the first sign and enjoy both the old and new parts. A number of stone cottages and several of the large old mansions still exist (one of the latter now houses part of Cherwell District Council). There is no village green as such but there are lots of green open areas, including a large playing field.

The children are served by the Bishop Loveday school. The church is dedicated to St John the Baptist and each year villagers celebrate the patronal festival. It is a church that is very much a part of the village.

There is a very active WI, Mothers Union, church choir, drama group, Scouts, Guides and Young Wives etc. The senior citizens are not forgotten, bungalows and flats supply good housing and a community centre at Dillon House provides some entertainment on a regular basis. There is also a residential nursing home.

To the south-west of the village the delightful Sorbrook flows, and just above on farmland overlooking Bloxham is an attractive windmill.

Botley

It is difficult today to imagine that Botley was once a peaceful place. Lying between Oxford and Cumnor and roads to the west it seems now to be just a busy highway. But up until the 1920s it was a really pretty village with its rustic look of grey stone walls, thatched cottages and farms, a lovely old bakehouse and corner shop, all surrounded by fields and footpaths and lovely trees. A quiet and serene place it seemed, but all is now lost beneath the encroachment of bricks and concrete, concealing an origin which goes back to the days of the Saxon invaders who gave the place its name.

Botley means 'clearing in a wood'. It was first recorded in 1086, a very wet and watery place with its many streams. The village cannot boast of any grand houses but the mill and Seacourt Farm are both mentioned in the Domesday Book and were very important in their time.

During the Civil War the mill suffered much damage; it is claimed that unknown rebels came from Abingdon and set fire to the mill, destroying it, but tradition has it that Cromwell rebuilt the mill for the use of his men. A sword about a yard long and a cannon ball were fished from the stream years later. Botley Mill has a long history, playing an important part in the lives of the people, as did Seacourt which was also a village in those far-off days with a church and a manor of considerable value.

Botley stayed small and remote until a causeway with bridges over its seven streams was built early in the 16th century, bringing an important road into the hamlet for the first time. Along this stony pathway villagers and travellers had shorter journeys into Oxford and the surrounding areas with views of lush meadows and pastures, when maybe this little rhyme was written:

'Who does not know Botley so small
Where sweet springs expectantly fall
And bridges constructed in line
Span pastures where feed the rich kine.'

It was not until much later that an improvement was made to this road and a toll gate was set up to help pay for repairs. Although this made travelling easier there were other dangers to contend with, as the roads around Oxford became infested with robbers and highwaymen and Botley Road was no exception: it is recorded that one February night in 1784 the Bath coach was held up at the foot of Cumnor Hill and eight passengers lost £28 between them!

As time passed the village of Seacourt was abandoned and by 1722 there was just an old farmhouse with a few cottages and inns – there had been 24 of these at one time! It is likely they were provided to accommodate and refresh the pilgrims and travellers who journeyed to Oxford and to the shrine of St Frideswide at Osney. Botley, it is said, was famous for its beer and was a popular place to stop for a drink.

Sadly, the last two cottages at Seacourt were demolished to make way for redevelopment in 1964. Now Botley is a thriving suburb with its shops, banks and offices, good nursery and primary schools, social clubs and an excellent library, and not forgetting the modern red brick church dedicated to St Peter and St Paul which links with its twin parish of North Hinksey, just a mile away. There the pretty little Norman church of St Lawrence, the thatched cottages, old stone walls and village green remain a place where residents and visitors can wander in peace and tranquillity.

Brightwell-cum-Sotwell 🪶

The main part of the village is bounded in the north by the A4130 Wallingford to Didcot road, and as the name suggests, Brightwell and Sotwell, also Mackney to the south, were once separate settlements. The parishes were not united until 1948, bringing to an end the bizarre situation of the parish clerk of Brightwell writing letters to himself (as parish clerk of Sotwell).

A Roman road ran from north to south from the Sinodun Hills down Mackney Lane (a section of the Alchester to Silchester road), and from east to west a Saxon highway ran from Slade End to Haddon Hill. Village footpaths now follow these routes. A 1st century gold coin (minted in Colchester) was dug up in Mackney Lane in 1873 and is now in the British Museum.

In the older parts of the village, houses are situated along narrow twisting roads, where large trees, high hedgerows and high walls (including a rare thatched cob wall) are characteristic. There are three smallish estates: Greenmere, the council estate, built in 1948 and more recently King's Meadow and Monk's Mead. The recent amount of infilling has reached saturation point and rather altered the landscape.

In 1086 in Brightwell there were 48 families, plus a mill and a church; in Sotwell 22 families and a mill. The 1938 population was 850, a figure now almost doubled to approximately 1,400. There are two shops selling almost anything one requires, one of which is also the post office, and those essentials of modern life, two garages and one pub, the Red Lion, the only one remaining of five in pre-temperance days. Other assets include the village hall and an excellent village magazine. The hall is a handsome brick building with clock tower which, in 1975, was converted from its original use as the 1869 village school after the latter was moved to a newer part of the village in 1961.

Less than a century ago the main work was provided (outdoors) by many small farms, orchards and large gardens and (indoors) by domestic service at the big houses. Here, as elsewhere, the farms now form larger units, with some disappearing entirely. Of the twelve farms identified in 1927, seven remained in 1981 which now form four separate units. The picture of employment has radically changed. The proximity of laboratories such as Harwell, Rutherford-Appleton, JET, Howberry Park and Didcot power station, attracts engineers and scientists, but the range of occupations is as diverse as one could find anywhere.

There is a wealth of old buildings in the village, including many thatched cottages. The most architecturally important house is Smalls in Mackney, built for a burgess of Wallingford of that name in about 1580. It is an unspoiled Tudor house with the unusual distinction of being listed Grade I, a category usually reserved for large stately homes. Other houses dating from the late 16th century include Woodleys, Middle Farm, The Old Priory and Abbot's House, all near St Agatha's church.

Of several moats in the village, the most complete is at Sotwell House, where the stream provides a favourite place for feeding the ducks, and where the lovely garden for many years has hosted the village fete. The moat at Brightwell Manor is partly dry now. This house is not strictly a manor and for part of its life formed part of a group of farms with The Old Priory and Middle Farm. It stands behind St Agatha's church and is chiefly Georgian, but an older part dates from c1605. It is thought to occupy the site of a wooden castle delivered up by King Stephen after the civil war and possibly demolished at that time, c1150.

Dean Inge's tomb, Brightwell-cum-Sotwell

The parish church has the rare dedication to St Agatha; perhaps a relic of this Sicilian martyr was once brought here from Winchester. The oldest parts of the present church are 12th century, possibly on the site of a church mentioned here in Domesday Book. The first entry in the parish register is 1564. The tower dates from 1797, and one of the three 16th century brasses in the church shows an effigy of a priest holding the Host and is the only example in the county. Nearby is the 'old' rectory, now divided into private dwellings. The surrounding high stone wall was badly damaged in the gale of 25th January 1990 by the spectacular fall of a Tree of Heaven (Ailanthus), judged to be near 130 years old.

The smaller church of St James in Sotwell, of ancient origin, had an early history connecting it with churches in Wallingford, but in 1868 it was attached to Brightwell. The 1884 rebuilding in Early English style (celebrated joyfully in 1984) included several features from the old wattle and daub building it replaced. The most impressive of these is a magnificent open roof of oak timbers.

The registers of St James begin in 1684. An entry in 1886 records the first burial of a member of the Free Church, a custom which continued for any dissenter. Brightwell Free Church was founded by Miss Augusta Fairthorne, member of a village family well known for their benefactions. This lady, who disagreed with the High Church attitude of the rector, persuaded her brother to allow services to be conducted in a marquee in his garden at The Red House. A small wooden church was built there in the 1870s and later replaced by the present Free Church building.

Until the advent of the Second World War the children of the village observed the quaint custom of greeting Shrove Tuesday by serenading the gentry with a song begging for pennies to provide the pre-Lenten feast of pancakes: 'Pit pat the pan's hot, And I be come a-shroving'. On May Day they paraded their garlands, and small money prizes were awarded to the most attractive. Christmastide saw the Mummers offering their unique version of St George killing the Turkish infidel.

Brize Norton 🐾

Brize Norton may be a small village but its name is known throughout the world. The RAF base which is called after it and carries servicemen and women to theatres of conflict and overseas postings, was officially opened on 13th August 1937. At that time it was home to No 2 Flying Training School, but with the start of the Second World War it became operational. The Resistance movements in occupied Europe received personnel and supplies through RAF Brize Norton and in June 1944 it was the base for parachute and glider operations over Normandy.

After the war the USAF came in with their B36 and B47 bombers, but in 1965 Brize Norton returned to RAF control and became the Transport Command station which it still is today. RAF Brize Norton is now one of the largest operational stations in the RAF.

The station enjoyed a moment in the national headlines in 1987 when it provided an historic meeting place for Mrs Thatcher and Mr Gorbachev during the first visit to this country by a Soviet leader for 31 years. The red carpet was literally unrolled for the occasion – and a rare policeman was spotted walking the village street to maintain order and prevent sabotage!

This may be the Brize Norton that the world knows. But to those who live here it is their home village, and the glamour of faraway places and international statesmen has little effect on their lives. It is true they hear the planes taking off, but very few service personnel live in the village and local concerns are the same as those of any other community.

Parochial questions have probably concerned the inhabitants of Brize Norton since there was first a settlement here to the north of Bampton, or Nortone, before the Norman Conquest. In the 13th century a Brun or Brown was added to the name and that in turn changed to the Brize of today. The church, dedicated to the unusual St Britius, dates from the 12th century and contains an effigy dated 1346 of Sir John Daubyngy. Another person of note who is buried in the church was Thomas Greenwood, said to be descended from a daughter of Henry VIII's Chancellor, Sir Thomas More. The Greenwoods, who were connected with the Manor of Brize Norton for some 300 years, remained Catholics throughout the 17th century, but one member of the family was nominally Church of England to avoid paying the taxes imposed on Catholics at that time. One wonders what the 'man for all seasons' would have thought of such behaviour.

Most of the inhabitants of the village were not famous and little record remains of individuals. But Brize Norton does have in its past a curious story which centres on an area to the west of the village called Stonelands.

In the 17th century there was a house called 'Sworn Layes Great House' in this area, which through ecclesiastical oversight was not designated as belonging to any particular parish. This meant that people living there could get away with activities that would not have been tolerated by the clergy within a parish. As a consequence, when King Charles I and his court were at Oxford from 1642 to 1646 it appears that Sworn Layes was used by the ladies of the court for the delivery of illegitimate children.

This custom continued certainly into the 18th century when there were references to 'Sworn Lanes, commonly called the Bastard School' and Shilton church records payments to 'poor afflicted lying in women' at Stonelands. The reputation of the place was notorious as late as 1778, for Jackson's *Oxford Journal* in that year reported of one couple that 'the groom eloped shortly after the marriage observing that if his wife had married to obtain a settlement, she was bilked, for he was born at Sworn Lanes near Burford, an extra parochial place where many unmarried ladies resort upon particular occasions'.

By 1801 these matters were obviously more acceptable and could be referred to more directly. An advertisement in the *Journal* reads: 'Private lying in notice is hereby given, that Sworn Lays in the County of Oxford is a house belonging to no parish, well situated to receive lying in women privately, and such may be treated with on reasonable terms by applying to James Hart, at Sworn Lays Great House, near Burford, Oxfordshire'. The children born here were, if lucky, trained for service or labouring but local tradition has it that many were killed in infancy and buried in the grounds. There was reputed to be the ghost of 'a horrible old woman carrying a screaming naked baby'.

Sworn Lays was in the news in the same century when it was also serving as a public house, at that time called the Lamb. The landlord, John Packer, and his wife Ann were committed to Oxford Castle in 1775 accused of murder only to be acquitted when the person who informed on them confessed to the crime.

The lying-in ceased around 1836 as the new Poor Law came into effect and the workhouses began to look after such activities. Sworn Lays, which had also served as a pest house during outbreaks of the plague, lost the advantage that its geographical position had given it and by 1906 it was a ruin. Today no trace of it is left.

Buckland ✥

From the 16th century until the late 20th century nearly all the houses and land in Buckland was in one ownership. Up to the Second World War most people who lived in the village worked on the estate in one way or another. Now that so many houses have passed into other hands, with inhabitants commuting or only there at weekends, village life has changed, but there is still a nucleus of families who were brought up in the village and whose names can be found in the parish records which survive from the late 17th century, eg Goodman, Carter, Shewry, Eyres, Absolem.

The only remaining shop is the post office/general stores, but there used to be another general stores, butcher, bakery and drapers. The drapers, as recently as the 1920s, sold bales of cloth to be made by women into garments for their families, the only made-up goods being men's boots and corduroy trousers. There were also a blacksmith and wheelwright, two shoemakers and a brewery. Buckland still has a Roman Catholic church as well as the parish church, and until recently a Baptist chapel. The village school serves several other villages besides Buckland.

Buckland Manor became known as Dukes' Manor because for a time it was owned by the Dukes of Suffolk. In 1544 the Crown sold it to John Yate of Charney, Merchant of the Staple at Calais. (He also possessed several other neighbouring manors). His son, another John, lived at Buckland and his will, made in 1578, names several of the manor's rooms.

The Yate family remained Roman Catholics after the Reformation. As with most Roman Catholics, the Yates took the King's side in the Civil War and in a survey of 1647 (Sir) Edward Yate was said to be 'beyond the seas and all his estates sequestered'. A stone table in the Old Vicarage garden is inscribed:

> 'Charles Ist, King of Britain spent the night at the house nearby and when he was hungry was entertained by the Vicar of Buckland who brought the King to eat at this table so that the altar and throne might forever be united in friendship.'

When the last male heir died the great-granddaughter of Edward Yate, Mary, inherited Buckland. She married Robert Throckmorton of Coughton Court, Warwickshire.

Buckland House was built in 1757 by Sir Robert. It stands to the west of the old manor house, which was then turned into stables and grooms' quarters. The surrounding grounds were landscaped by Richard Woods and several stone buildings which are still standing were built at this time, including an ice house, still complete, close to the lake which was formed at this time.

In 1811 Sir John Throckmorton wagered 1,000 guineas that it was possible to make a coat from wool off the backs of sheep between sunrise and sunset. On 25th June two sheep belonging to him were sheared by his shepherd, Mr Druett, and the wool given to Mr John Coxeter at Greenham Mills, Newbury who 'spun the yarn, spooled, warped, loomed and wove burred, milled, rowed, dyed, dried, sheared and pressed' – in eleven hours.

The cloth was then given to Mr Isaac White, tailor, who cut the coat out and had it made up within two hours and 20 minutes. Mr John Coxeter, the master manufacturer, presented it to Sir John, who appeared with it on before an assembly of 5,000 spectators who had come from near and far to witness this performance, completed in 13 hours and 20 minutes.

In 1908 the estate was sold to Sir Maurice Fitzgerald who, with his architect Romaine Walker, enlarged the house and built many new buildings in the village. Queen Mary and Sir Winston Churchill were entertained during the Fitzgerald's time. Their grandson, Richard Wellesley inherited the estate from them and to him fell the task of bringing it from near feudal conditions to modern farming methods, and reducing staff almost ten-fold. His son now farms the estate.

Bucknell

Just a short drive from the urban sprawl of Bicester lies the tranquil village of Bucknell. A cluster of beech trees to the west of the village probably gave its original name, which was Buckenelle (Beech Hill). Always predominantly a farming community, Bucknell once boasted a coach house, forge, bakery and village shop. Many of the old thatched cottages remain and the village shop is now situated in what was the old coach house. A large pig farm which produces most of its own feed, the herds of Friesians and Herefords and the surrounding arable land ensure that the village farming traditions carry on.

The history of Bucknell and its church dates back to Saxon times. St Peter's church is unusual in that it has a Norman tower between the chancel and the nave; this formed part of an earlier church. The tower is 12th century with the exception of the crenellated belfry which was added in the 15th century. Behind the church stands the manor house, dating back to the 17th century. It has a chequered past and is supposedly haunted. It was surrounded by a moat and has a ha ha. In 1709 Samuel Trotman took over the estate. He was very eccentric and known locally as 'The Mad Trotman'. At one time Bucknell had no public house because the Trotman family would not allow a licence to be granted in case the poor people of the village spent too much time and money 'tippling'. In more recent times the manor house was used by Oxford County Council as an old people's home but it is now once more privately owned and has been extensively restored.

To the north-west of the village stands the now derelict water tower, built in 1903/4 by Major Hunlocke to supply water to the manor house and some of the farms. The water from a nearby spring was pumped either by windmill or petrol-driven engine. Work has recently begun to develop the site as a nature reserve, providing facilities for visitors from the surrounding areas.

The villagers have always made the most of their leisure moments. The Morris dancing tradition goes back centuries but the all-male team last danced at Queen Victoria's Diamond Jubilee in 1897. The team was revived as a ladies' Morris team in 1979 and they now dance regularly, raising money for charity, their most important date being the 'Day of Dance' in May. A tradition of maypole dancing also dates back at least a hundred years. In those days the maypole arrived on a carrier's cart and the children made garlands and paraded around the village singing songs, led by the King and Queen of the May.

The stone houses opposite the church appear to have changed little over the years, although many alterations have taken place internally. It is here that the blacksmith's shop was situated and is the spot where a Mr Ally killed himself whilst making gunpowder.

There is evidence of two local charities. The Trotman will of 1600 left an amount of money for a 'small portion of meat to be distributed to the poor of the village each December'. Dr Gauntlett's Charity was also distributed in December, one year to ladies, the next to men. The women were given warm woollen cloaks with hoods. After receiving them they were instructed to put the name of the charity on the inside of the collar. The lady of the manor would then check that this had been done. Eight pairs of strong leather shoes were given to the men and the name of the charity was written on the instep of the sole. This would be seen when the men knelt down to pray in church.

The Trigger Pond public house was originally three cottages and then a butcher's shop. In the early 1900s it was owned by a butcher named Golder, a very large man. When he died it was found he was too large to be removed from the shop. A window was taken out and an improvised bier had to be made to carry away the body. The shop later became an off licence. A dartboard was hung on the wall outside and it soon became a meeting place for the locals. At this time it was called the Twigger Pond, the pond being on the opposite side of the road with a well in one corner. The pond is now a very attractive feature of the village. Beautifully landscaped, it contains many plants and fish and is a breeding ground for ducks and moorhens. The Trigger Pond public house has also been extensively restored, retaining many original beams and a straight chimney fireplace.

Burford ✤

In earlier times Burford was a flourishing market town dependent on the sheep of the Cotswolds, the local industries being fulling, tannery, saddlery, glove making, and two bell foundries at different times; all that was necessary could be purchased locally.

In 1990 Burford celebrated the 900th anniversary of its first charter. It may seem strange that a community of barely 1,200 people should have a Mayor and Town Council (the population is probably smaller now than in the 18th century at the height of the coaching era, and much the same as at the end of the Middle Ages). The present arrangement only dates from the reorganisation of local government in 1974, but is a reflection of Burford's earlier history when it was ruled by an Alderman and Burgesses, elected from the Guild Merchants. The Burgesses' roll is to be seen in the local museum at the Tolsey, the 15th century building where the tolls were collected from the traders. It is also still used for the Town Council meetings.

Burford has grown very little because of stringent planning restrictions which ban any expansion outwards, and insist on any new building being done in local materials. This means that the cost of housing in the town is exceptionally high, so that there is very little chance for first time buyers to obtain property.

The two 'big houses' were the Great House, an imposing castellated edifice built in 1685 right on what was once the main road through the town; and the Priory, originally a monastic hospice, which came into private ownership after the Dissolution of the Monasteries, changed ownership several times and has now come back to housing a religious order of nuns. Another striking building is the Methodist chapel, originally built as a private house in the 18th century.

The grammar school was founded by local men of property in 1571 and stayed at the lower end of the town until 1957, when the new comprehensive school was built on the main road above the town. The old buildings have been retained as boarding houses.

When the school celebrated its quatercentenary in 1971, an ancient custom was reintroduced. This is the dragon procession on Midsummer's Eve, said to commemorate the victory of the West Saxons over the Mercians about AD 750. The dragon is a large tent-like structure with an impressive head, carried by some 20 children, whose legs are the only part of the human form to be seen. It goes from the top of the hill to the bottom accompanied by Morris dancers and finishing with dancing on the green in front of the church.

There was another small school run by a couple called Huntley at the top of the hill. Mrs Huntley, as well as her school duties, made biscuits and sold them to coach travellers; eventually one of her sons moved to Reading, went into partnership with a Mr Palmer, and this is the origin of the famous biscuit manufacturers.

The oldest inhabitant recalls the horse omnibus, run by her father, which met every train at Shipton-under-Wychwood and Witney. 'He never missed one'. Between the wars there were frequent buses from Burford to Oxford, Cheltenham, Banbury and Swindon, but now public transport is minimal. Before the Second World War, Burford had three butchers (now one), five grocers (now two), five milkmen delivering (now one), and two baker's shops as well as two who came with vans (now two). There were countless other small shops, and it is only recently that a drapery and the ironmonger have disappeared.

In the distant past Wychwood Forest was only a mile away, and there was a royal hunting lodge on the outskirts. The men of Burford were allowed one deer per annum, but the story goes that this did not satisfy them, and a lot of poaching went on; the carcases would be hidden in one of the 'bale' tombs in the churchyard, and woe betide you if you were found to have one in your larder!

The first private owner of the Priory was Edmond Harman, barber surgeon to Henry VIII. His successor was Sir Lawrence Tanfield who upset the local people by removing (quite legitimately) all the rights and privileges of the Guild Merchants. His wife was even more unpopular and after their demise, they were said to haunt the town, riding in a coach and four over the rooftops. Eventually seven clerics were called upon to exorcise them, which they did by shutting up the spirits in a bottle and dropping it into the river. Rumour had it that if the level of the river dropped below a certain point, they would escape; so, until the 19th century, in time of drought the older inhabitants used to pour water over the bridge to keep the level up!

During the Civil War, a group of soldiers rebelled against Cromwell and were rounded up in Burford. Three hundred were imprisoned in the church as the only building large enough; after three days the three ringleaders were taken out and shot. In the mid 1970s a tablet was erected to them outside the church, and each year since then a great meeting has been held on the church green, followed by a procession round the town.

Burford Community Hospital is the second smallest in the country. There are nine beds, a day centre for the elderly, various clinics and a full-time casualty department. It is a valued part of the community with a flourishing 'Comforts Fund' supported also by the surrounding villages.

Carterton 🦖

Carterton was named after a man called William Carter, who bought up a lot of land locally. He then sold it off in plots, for smallholdings and market gardens. People even came to settle here from London.

The original bungalows were built of wood with outer shells of tin. One family also had a very deep well where they kept their milk and butter in a bucket, dangling on a rope.

Carterton has become best known for the growing of tomatoes, the soil here seems to give them a flavour all of their own. Sadly though, many local nurseries have disappeared over the years, the families not carrying on the business and greenhouses making way for housing development.

Carterton was once part of a parish with Black Bourton, using St Mary's church. A small wooden building, St John's, served as a church until the present day brick-built one in 1965. There are Catholic and Methodist churches for the community here as well.

Royal Air Force Brize Norton came into being in the 1930s. Carterton was to have been the name of the airfield but it was changed to avoid any confusion with Cardington in Bedfordshire. In the 1960s the United States Air Force was stationed here. To take their larger bombers the runway was extended, thus cutting the parish into two, and later Black Bourton became a parish on its own.

There was once a railway station. The line had been there for years from Fairford to Oxford. A platform and buildings were hurriedly built in 1944 during the invasion of Europe to transport troops to the airfield, and it was later used for carrying the tomatoes and mushrooms from a nearby farm. It was then cut off from Carterton when the Black Bourton road was closed with the building of the new runway, although a footpath and cycle way around that side of the airfield is still in use. What a pity that the entire line was eventually closed – it would have helped to ease the present day congestion of getting into Oxford by road!

Over the years a lot of caravan sites were allowed to spring up and Carterton has been called a 'shanty town'. But now only a few remain, being replaced by newer estates and roads. The famous crossroads area has been developed, though not into everyone's ideal centre! The selection of shops and services and the Thursday open air market have helped the surrounding smaller villages to survive.

Cassington

Cassington is a small village of some 800 inhabitants, situated on the gravel strata between the ancient forest of Wychwood and the Thames. Saxon settlers cleared away the woodland which formerly covered this area. Evidence of an earlier Bronze Age settlement was found when excavating for gravel in 1942/3. Cassington is recorded in the Domesday survey of 1086 as Cersetone (ie tun where cress grows), with its hamlets of Worton to the north, and Somerford (now lost) to the south.

For centuries, the village was agricultural, with several farms, large and small, but during the 20th century the emphasis shifted from agriculture; the building of the bypass, the proximity of Oxford with its motor industry and the prospect of better paid jobs, and of course the motor car itself, largely changed the life of the inhabitants. Council houses were built, and later more building took place on the outskirts of the village. However, the centre of the village is still the village green, unchanged through the centuries, with attractive old cottages and the 18th century Red Lion public house, the large former vicarage, now privately owned, the Victorian former primary school, and the beautiful village cross, a memorial to those who gave their lives in two World Wars. It was commissioned in 1919 by the then vicar, who lost three sons in the first war, and was designed by Mr F. D. Howard of Oxford. The two figures, of Christ and the Madonna, were sculpted by Mr Alex Miller of Chipping Campden.

The most interesting building is undoubtedly the ancient Norman church of St Peter, built as a private chapel by Geoffrey de Clinton, Chamberlain and Treasurer to King Henry I. The Cartulary of Eynsham Abbey records that the church was consecrated by Bishop Bloet in 1123. Four of the original consecration crosses are still visible. The magnificent Norman arches remain, unchanged, a tribute to the dedication and skill of the men who built them centuries ago. Recently, the remains of a Doom painting over the chancel arch were uncovered, showing evidence of the exceptional quality of the paint used, now, alas, faded. The church retains many of the original bench pews, 15th century, said to be among the oldest in the country.

Cassington village green with war memorial

53

There are several old houses in the village, the largest being the farmhouse which stands on the site of the manor house of the de Clintons, still retaining its moat and a rectangular dove house. It is known as Reynolds Farm, after the family who owned property in Cassington and Eynsham in the 15th and 16th centuries. They were Roman Catholics, and during the religious troubles of the 16th century Cassington became a refuge for recusants from neighbouring Oxford. Later, during the Civil War, men who had been deprived of their posts because of their royalist sympathies gathered at Cassington. Antony Wood, the diarist, came in 1653 to 'shake off a fit of the ague in the pure country air'! He also learned to ring on the peal of six bells then newly installed.

Bell ringing has always been one of Cassington's activities. Until recent years it had a team of bellringers well known throughout the diocese, members of the Diocesan Guild; unfortunately, enthusiasm has declined somewhat during the past few years.

Cassington Mill on the Evenlode, mentioned in the Domesday Book, continued to grind corn into this century. The last miller lives in the village. The buildings still stand, and in the surrounding field is a flourishing caravan site, bringing many visitors during the summer season.

The village is justly proud of its modern primary school, situated in a large playing field, where conservation work has been carried out to preserve a pond, and encourage its wild life.

Not all is progress, however! The bus service has deteriorated during the past few years, and the post office now opens only three mornings a week. The one remaining shop is a lifeline for elderly residents.

Chadlington 🌿

Chadlington was first mentioned in the Domesday Book in 1086 as Cedelintone. It is said to have been named after St Chad, who came from Northumberland and lived in the area for a while.

Chadlington is reputed to have two ghosts. College Farm was once farmed by Mr Gardner, whose ghost is said to have walked the passages carrying a red handkerchief. The other ghost is an old gentleman wearing carpet slippers who walks across the upstairs hall of Langston House.

There is another story relating to College Farm. Many years ago the farmhouse was broken into and a robbery took place. The robber escaped with his booty, but because he was disturbed dropped his hat. This clue was used in quite an original way and resulted in his eventual capture – a man could be recognised by his hat in the 18th century! The Chadlington robber's hat was taken to a fair at Chipping Norton and put on top of a stick. When someone from Duns Tew came along and said without thinking 'That is so and so's hat from our place', the game was up and the robber caught and dealt with.

Langston House, a large imposing house in the east end of Chadlington, was originally built by Squire Langston MP as a rectory for the Rev Carpenter, who paid a nominal sum of £1 per annum rent. About 50 years ago it was occupied by Colonel and Mrs Schofield. Mrs Schofield used to ride around the village on a large tricycle with her two pug dogs in a basket on the back. She would also try to keep the verges clean and picked up any rubbish, only to throw it over the wall into the nearest garden she was passing!

Sir Henry Rawlinson, the diplomat and expert on Assyria, was born in the manor house in 1810 and was the owner of the horse *Coronation*, which was trained in Chadlington and won the Derby in 1841. One villager's grandmother in her young days was a 'stillroom' maid at the house and used to tell how she sometimes went to Chipping Norton on a donkey led by one of the stable lads. The roads were made of white stone and were very dusty. The manor house is now a country hotel.

Squire Langston also built the reading room, which was used originally as a school. In addition, from 1840–50 there was a private school at the Baptist chapel. Children used to enjoy the annual village fair on Easter Monday when processions of horse-drawn vehicles came to the village with their roundabouts, swinging boats, coconut shies etc. The procession, led by the village drum and fife band, went first to a service in the parish church, and this was followed by a dinner in the Malt Shovel for the band.

Many of the family names in Chadlington go back through many generations and one story is told that you can always tell a real 'Townsend' because they always bat or bowl with their left hand!

It is also said of one of the former butchers in the village that when his mother died the undertaker asked if he would like her buried in a double grave with his father. After a little thought the butcher said, 'Well, they never got on well in life so they're not likely to now. Maybe we'd better have separate graves!'

Chalgrove 🌿

Although not a large stream, Chalgrove Brook was once powerful enough to turn five mills, as is revealed in the Domesday Book. Meandering across the fields to the south of the village, it flows on through Stadhampton and then to Chislehampton where it joins the river Thame, a tributary of the Thames. During the 19th century a sluice gate was constructed at the eastern end of the village and from the original stream (the back brook) water was diverted to run alongside what is now the High Street. This artificially created loop (the front brook) has become an attractive feature in Chalgrove.

Flooding was apparently a regular occurrence and is strong in the memories of Chalgrove folk. Written accounts, dating from the late 19th and early 20th centuries, indicate that stilts were popular among the young as a means of getting about in such conditions. However, even stilts were rendered useless when, in January 1881, the temperature dropped sharply overnight and the floodwater turned into a thick sheet of ice.

The effects of flooding were exacerbated by the fact that Chalgrove village is situated in a dip. A former occupier of Cromwell Cottage recalls melting snow water running off Belson's meadow into her garden and under the back door. It was then necessary to open the front door to let the water run out, which it did, into Chapel Lane and down to the flooded High Street. The damage to property and attendant disruption of family life are of course most unpleasant aspects of natural disasters. A Chalgrove farmer's note book records that in 1879 22 houses were seriously flooded in the lower part of the village.

If excessive amounts of water could play havoc with everyday life then so could an extreme lack of it. In 1921 a severe drought reduced the stream to a trickle and for a long time the mill wheel never turned. As an emergency measure a steam threshing engine, borrowed from a local farmer, was connected to machinery inside the mill in order to grind the corn. More recently, in 1976, another drought left the stream bed dry in places and surrounding land became hard, cracked and almost impossible to cultivate. An interesting by-product of the last mentioned drought was the discovery, by aerial reconnaissance, of filled-in moats and earthworks next to the back brook. Apparently such features are more easily identified in hot, dry conditions. Subsequent archaeological excavation at this location revealed the remains of an impressive medieval moated manor.

The brook is also a source of entertainment. Generations of boys have learned their fishing skills here and, even now with a greatly reduced flow, it is possible for a lad to surprise Mum and Dad with a lively trout. In the early 1970s an enjoyable, but sadly short lived, custom known as the Chalgrove Brook Race was an annual event. The race was contested by several teams over a three quarter mile course from the top arch to the Lamb public house. Teams ran in relays carrying a ball and had to scramble under or over each of the 40 or so bridges.

The importance of the brook to Chalgrove should not be underestimated. Its presence was undoubtedly the reason for early, possibly pre-Roman settlement here. The stream provided water, motive power for mills and probably a good number of fish. Even today the intrusion of massive housing development cannot take away the pleasing aspect of the High Street and its brookside cottages. Yes, the brook has shaped Chalgrove's character and, as the old saying goes, 'You don't belong to Chalgrove until you have fallen in it!'

Charlbury ✍

The name Charlbury is of Anglo-Saxon origin, from the old English 'burgh', a fortified place or earthwork, belonging to 'Ceorl', possibly a personal name but more likely meaning that it was inhabited by freemen.

In the 8th century it belonged to the Mercian kings and in 1094 it was given by the Norman Bishop of Lincoln to Eynsham Abbey. When the abbey was dissolved by Henry VIII, there were two claimants to the manor of Charlbury. One was Sir Henry Lee of Ditchley, who had installed his mistress, Ann Vavasour at Lee's Rest, the other Sir Thomas White, who founded St John's College, Oxford in 1555. Eventually the courts found in favour of the President and Scholars of St John's, who leased Charlbury to Sir Henry Lee and his descendants for the term of three lives. In 1857, by exchange, the property passed to the owner of Cornbury Park. St John's College still appoints the vicars of Charlbury.

Cornbury Park was an important part of the history of Charlbury. An Elizabethan hunting lodge, the gift of Queen Elizabeth I to the Earl of Leicester, it was demolished and a beautiful house built in its stead by Lord Clarendon in the reign of Charles I.

Spinning and weaving went on in many homes, and in the early 1800s the gloving industry was revived by leading Quakers to help alleviate the poverty resulting from the Napoleonic Wars. Gloving continued as a cottage industry and then in small factories until the early 1960s and the glove-makers Fownes, whose crest was a falcon, built Falcon Villas in Hundley Way for their employees. Charlbury was mainly a self sufficient agricultural community, served by its own craftsmen and shopkeepers, its own corn mill (pulled down in 1935), several malt-houses, inns and many beer-houses, its own water supply and gasworks, until after the Second World War.

In 1853 the Oxford, Worcester and Wolverhampton Railway was opened. In 1977 heavy lorries were banned from the town centre, a one-way scheme was devised and a ring-route for through traffic designated.

Charlton ✣

Until the middle of the 20th century this small settlement had existed as a separate entity from the market town of Wantage, a mile away, since at least the 11th century, when it was mentioned in the Domesday Book. An 18th century map shows the land divided into strips giving each family a share of the arable and grazing lands. The whereabouts of a mill mentioned in Domesday is now not certain.

Since the Second World War Charlton has been almost swallowed up by housing estates and is now firmly joined to Wantage. The 'Atomics' came first and built their well-landscaped estate along the Humber Ditch on part of the old Charlton House estate. Palmers Farmhouse still stands in the middle of a cul-de-sac and Truelocks and Barnards Farms have become Charlton Heights estate, although the farmhouses are still there. Sadly, Truelocks Farm lost its old barn in a spectacular blaze one Friday afternoon in 1989.

The Victorian church of Holy Trinity, which was built as a chapel of ease, stands near the old stone school house with its rolls of honour of prize winners proudly displayed on one wall. Many families bearing these names are still to be found nearby.

The new Charlton primary school and adult training centre are across the road and Maude House for the elderly now stands on the site of Chestnuts Farm – or Pococks – where Charles I is reputed to have had 'supper and bed' with Sir George Wilmot in 1643 and again in 1644. This farmhouse and several thatched cottages disappeared as recently as the late 1960s and a well-loved pony – *Smokey* – almost came to grief in the old well soon afterwards.

The town pound is only remembered by house names in the locality but a number of old houses still stand. The fifth generation of Castles are at Home Farm where they have provided a field centre for schools in one of their barns. The old farmhouse has recently been sold as a private residence. Parsonage Farm – scarcely visible from the village street – is also a working farm and further on, past the eyesore of the scrapyard, Gypsy Lane leads across the fields, over the canal, to Grove.

Charlton is still a community, somewhat larger than the 40–50 households of years gone by, and hopefully the remnants of the original village will survive for many years to come.

Charlton-on-Otmoor

A sleepy village in the heart of the country, Charlton is one of the seven towns of Otmoor, where the village folk know the main priority is a pair of wellington boots! The wetlands of the moor attract all kinds of wildlife. On a winter evening flocks of geese and swans are seen travelling from some unfortunate farmer's field back to the moor.

This is a place where villagers in the past have fought for their rights to graze livestock and enclose their strips of land. Today visitors come to see the wildlife, enjoy the quietness or walk the Roman road where Joseph's Stone can still be found. Some say this is a Roman milestone but others think it is more likely to be a horseman's mounting stone. Fog and storms still engulf the moor. Years ago a curfew bell would be tolled at 8.00 pm to guide the traveller back home. It was this bell which was heard by Thomas Tryte when he lost his way crossing the moor to Bicester. There is a poem written about his famous walk and Tryte's distressing time while lost on the moor.

This bell has long since ceased but the bells of St Mary's, known locally as the heavy five, still ring out. Many generations have rung the Charlton bells. The Hayneses, the Millers and the Maycocks are all familiar names in Charlton tower. Quite a character was Old Tom, one of the Maycock brothers, known so well for their thatching skills in the county but otherwise working a smallholding in the village. Old Tom was rarely seen without his bike, which he rode mainly in the middle of the road. With his shock of white hair, two or three days' stubble on his chin and the inevitable pipe, Tom was known to everyone in the village. Besides ringing one of the bells his strong baritone voice led the church choir and

59

for a funeral he donned pin stripes and bowler to act as bearer, that was after giving a hand to dig the grave. His greeting in the street would almost certainly be 'Ello Gel', so long as you were of that sex. Tom now lies in St Mary's churchyard and Charlton has lost a real character.

The farms which provide much of the work in the village are fast disappearing. Farm barns are being converted to houses. However, there are some farms left. One farmer still draws water from a black water well. The black water spring runs right through the village and in olden days farmers used the water to treat sick cattle. Village folk used it for eczema. That same farmer also uses a fresh water well to water his stock. The wells are beautifully built, mainly of stone and some are bell shaped. One well, obviously designed to serve two households, is built under a dividing wall and pumps are set up each side of the wall. Most of the old cottages are built from the lovely mellow stone, some of which was dug locally. A few thatched roofs remain and many of these old houses have cellars, in some cases still in use but when the water level rises some are known to flood.

May Day celebrations are still held in Charlton. Many years ago the villagers used to carry their May garland across the moor to Horton-cum-Studley. Now the school children process from the school to the church, each carrying a floral cross. A long rope garland is at the head of the procession, colourfully decorated with flowers and ribbons. The children make several stops to sing the May Carol:

> Good Morning ladies and gentlemen
> We wish you a happy May
> We've come to show our May garland
> Because it's the 1st of May
> A May garland we have brought you
> Before your door we stand
> It is but a bit but it smells very sweet
> And it comes from the Lord's right hand.

A service in church follows and every year the cross on the rood screen is redressed in box for the occasion. Afterwards the children give a display of country and maypole dancing in the Main Street. This happens on 1st May every year no matter what day it falls on.

Charlton does not have a country mansion or a famous person within the parish but it still boasts a village pub, its very own bus service and a community spirit next to none.

Charney Bassett 🦢

Roughly in the centre of the triangle formed by Abingdon, Faringdon and Wantage, lies the village of Charney Bassett, nestling on the north bank of the river Ock. It is believed that the river, in Celtic times, was called the Charn, from which the name Charney is derived, and Bassett from Ralph Bassett who held land hereabout and died in 1127.

A small compact village, its dwellings number just about 100, the only large house being the manor, which since 1947 has belonged to the Society of Friends and is used by them as a Meeting House, and also a guest house and conference centre. In the Middle Ages the manor, or Grange as it was then called, belonged to the Benedictine Abbey of Abingdon and it contains some fine examples of medieval building, still in constant use. Village organisations are encouraged to use the manor, and such events as the harvest supper and biennial church fete, to name just two, are always held there.

Hard by the manor stands the church of St Peter, plain and simple, built mainly in Norman times but probably on the foundations of an earlier Saxon place of worship. Its main attraction is a very fine example of a Norman carved tympanum, re-set in the north wall of the chancel above the entrance to a squint passage; there are only a very few of such examples to be found in the country. Another original Norman carved archway is over the main doorway. The unusual bellcote houses two bells which are uninscribed but believed to be medieval.

Close by the manor and the church is a water mill and records show a mill was here when the monks occupied the manor. Obviously rebuilt over the centuries, the present day structure was in constant use for grinding corn until the First World War, when the miller's son, James Douglas, went off to war and his father eventually had to cease milling. The building stood almost intact until visited by a local industrial archaeological group in the 1970s, who were so fascinated by their find, they have toiled to restore it to working condition and open it to the public.

On the village green, which is opposite the Chequers Inn, stands another medieval relic — a stone shaft on three steps. It is thought this may have been a market cross, where goods could be offered for sale at certain times of the year. A sundial was added to the top later and this would have been used as the village time-piece. After the First World War the centre step was replaced with a dressed stone as a memorial to those whose names are carved thereon.

One mile to the north of the village, but still in the civil parish of Charney is Cherbury Camp, believed to have been built about the beginning of the 1st century AD. It is similar to the better known Uffington Castle on top of White Horse Hill, although slightly larger, but unfortunately is not protected so well, and consequently is being quite considerably eroded. There is a legend that the tribe or army camped in Uffington Castle moved out towards Cherbury to do battle, but a shepherd boy lying out in the fields saw them coming and sounded his horn, so warning the Cherbury occupants, who were then able to go out and meet their enemy and win the battle. Hence it is said the area around the crossroads midway between Charney and Buckland is where they 'gained the field' and it became known as Gainfield. The shepherd boy was supposedly given all the land within the sound of his horn for his part in this, and this eventually became the Pusey estate.

True or legend, there is a Pusey Horn in the British Museum, and another inn in the village, which was closed during the Second World War, was known as the Horn Inn. Cherbury Camp and other land to the north-west of the parish is still the property of Pusey estate, but in 1908 a large portion of the houses and many hundreds of acres east, south and west of Charney were sold to Berkshire County Council, who divided it into many smallholdings, of about 40 acres, which were worked by tenants. Today the ownership has passed to Oxfordshire County Council, who have sold off a majority of the dwellings, and the dozen or so smallholdings in Charney parish have been converted into just three large farms.

The village school, which closed in the early 1980s, was always known as the Bouverie Pusey School. It was built in 1871 by the Pusey family of Pusey House, probably at the same time as the New Road was made and the six pairs of houses were built on the east side of the road. These houses are of a most unusual design with stone mullioned and arched windows and high pitched roofs, often described as similar to small churches. The only other houses similar to these are to be found at Black Bourton on the road from Faringdon to Burford, probably by the same architect.

Many more dwellings have been built in the last 40 years or so, just about doubling the number which existed at the turn of the century, but it is fair to say the character of the village has not altered unduly; it remains very compact still within its original confines, with a close-knit, caring and friendly community.

Checkendon ✤

Checkendon is a rambling unspoilt village 600 ft above sea level, eight miles north from Reading. Entering the village from Reading you pass the Four Horse Shoes, the old village inn, the older portion thatched as it has been through the years.

The fine old Norman church of St Peter and St Paul stands in the centre of the village. There are two Norman arches in the chancel. On the wall of the apse are fresco paintings of the 13th or 14th century, which have been painstakingly restored. The brasses on the sanctuary floor are of interest, the larger of John Rede being early 15th century. The many monuments are worth a study, and say much of Checkendon's notable forebears.

The drive to Checkendon Court runs by the church. This estate dates from 1030. Beside the church is its own primary school. In front is the village green on which the children have their maypole dance. The old village forge still stands but is no longer used as a smithy. At the rear is a flourishing agricultural supply company. A group of interesting houses and cottages nestle around the village green. The village hall was built in 1913; there the children have school meals. The play group and all the village events are held here. The main development has been one road, and here is the post office and stores.

The village is surrounded by beech woods, with bluebells in the spring, and the rich colour of the autumn leaves. There are a few public footpaths in the woods. Farming goes on around the village and the fields reflect the passing seasons.

Chilton ✤

Chilton has been in existence since before the Domesday survey and its present church since a few years after that time. Over the centuries many changes have taken place.

The duck pond on the upper green is gone. Instead there is the drainage pond for the noisome A34. But the Aylesburys have been replaced by wild mallard which home in at night to rest safely in the middle of the fenced-about water, and wait each morning for the kindly lady who saves her crusts for them.

Church Farm, the pride and success of old Jo Church back in the 1800s, is now an estate of desirable residences. Likewise, Lime Tree Farm

Lime Tree Stables, Chilton

no longer feels the warm breath of calves on a frosty morn, but the rattle of 'Clean-Your-Own-Seeds' machinery setting out on its perambulations. The old, red-brick barns of Manor Farm, once the first welcome to the village, have long since given place to chalet-type houses.

By the side of the Bargeway, there used to be famous orchid nurseries which despatched their patiently-cultivated treasures as far off as Japan. The nursery site, too, is a new housing estate, commemorating its famous origins only in its name. The National Garden Centre's headquarters is over by the A34.

There were once two racehorse training establishments. Wide-eyed yearlings still ballet-dance down Main Street on the long rein learning about life; and the elegant three year olds lift the heart with their beauty as they pace on air up South Row from the Lower Road stables. Children's ponies whinny greetings over the fence of every available few yards of pasture – including what was once the pig-farm, Place Farm, which even had pigs recorded in the Domesday Book.

From time beyond memory the unofficial emblem of Chilton has been the rook, perhaps stemming from the ring of 'immemorial' elms round the churchyard, which are now, alas, no more. But Chilton's rooks are faithful and there stands now on Harwell airfield's old bomb-dump a grove of sycamores with one of the largest colonies of rooks in South Oxfordshire. And they, and all wildlife, have fair fling on the beautiful country park which was, until 1990, the prefabricated estate, for workers at AERE.

The tiny Methodist chapel in South Row (surely one of the smallest in the country with a capacity of 25) would have been crowded out 50 or so years ago, when the 12th century parish church had fallen into disrepute under an unpopular rector. Now the chapel languishes almost invisible in a losing battle against the elements and a large holly tree.

Chilton appears regularly in the media as the home of the Rutherford Appleton Laboratory, whose scientists gather information on outer space with their spectacular microwave dish which forms a landmark, purely white by day and eerily green by night, at the foot of the downs. They have collaborated with France in the *Ariane* rocket explorations and in NASA's *Ampte* project, increasing our knowledge of the formation of stars and galaxies. The laboratory supports university research in physics and is Britain's centre for academic computing since its merger with Atlas.

Hard by the runway from which the RAF glider-spearhead took off for Normandy on D-Day (which event is commemorated by a plaque and granite plinth near the A4185) is the National Radiological Protection Board, recently selected to lead European research into all aspects of radiation.

Chinnor ❧

Chinnor is situated at the base of the Chiltern Hills, 18 miles east of Oxford and just five miles from the M40. There has probably been a settlement here for many centuries because of the proximity of the ancient Icknield Way running from Lincolnshire down to Wiltshire, which is thought to be pre-Roman and was certainly used during the Middle Ages for driving cattle and sheep.

Still standing in the village today is the mostly 14th century church of St Andrew, although parts of it go back to the 12th and 13th centuries. The wooden screen is reputed to be the sixth oldest in England and a splendid collection of wall-mounted brasses include a foliated cross from about 1338. The stained glass windows date from 1350 through to modern. The bells link the Elizabethan reigns, the tenor having been cast during Elizabeth I's time and the sanctus in 1965. The church is undergoing much needed restoration.

There is also a Congregational church built of brick and flint, the local building material, opened in 1805, the year of the battle of Trafalgar. The Methodist church is the most recent of the three places of worship, having been rebuilt in 1873 after blowing down the previous year two months after opening.

Because of Chinnor's position near Oxford a certain amount of Civil War activity took place in the vicinity. Oral tradition maintains that Prince Rupert was involved in a skirmish in the High Street before the battle of Chalgrove Field in 1643.

Industries based in and around Chinnor included lacemaking, chairmaking and agriculture. There were four lace schools in Chinnor in the early 19th century. Among the 268 lacemakers there were many children working to supplement the very low agricultural wages. Timber for chairmaking was known to be stored in the barn at Chairmakers, a 16th century property in the High Street. 'Bodgers' were the men working the beech woods in the surrounding hills.

In more recent times the cement works opened in 1908 which brought facilities to the village earlier than in surrounding areas. The village is the centre today for several small industries including a sawmill and a funeral director. In *The Parish Pump*, the monthly village newspaper, there are many advertisements for professional people working locally.

The Reading Rooms in the High Street were originally built in 1878 as an alternative centre for the men of the parish to read or play billiards. In the 1920s it was changed to a public hall and women were at last allowed to use it.

Nowadays Chinnor, with its population of approximately 8,000, serves as a base for people working virtually anywhere in the Central Midlands/South corridor. With the opening of the M40 extension towards Birmingham there will probably be people in the future based here with an eye to the North Midlands.

Expansion in Chinnor began with new housing estates being built around the village from the 1960s onwards and it now supports various playgroups and two primary schools, one of which has a special unit for autistic children. There is a village dentist, an optician and two doctor's surgeries, one of which won a design award in 1967. There is sheltered housing for the elderly in Leverkus House and a private nursing home at Hempton Field.

Culturally there is a branch of the county library next to St Andrew's School, a thriving evening class programme, a cricket field, football pitches and playgrounds in the the village centre and Mill Lane. For entertainment there are many societies locally, including the Chinnor Players and Chinnor Operatic.

Chipping Norton 🦢

Chipping Norton is a small, hilltop market town as compact as a village; everybody meets in the High Street. It is built mostly of hard, grey limestone, has no urban sprawl and is picturesque enough to be under several conservation orders. It is still a working agricultural community with whiffs of pig manure and bedding straw. Even the dozen antiques shops don't affect its everyday rural busyness.

Approach roads are lined with trees, and the High Street manages to be both cosy and spacious; cosy because it is completely enclosed by 18th century stone frontages, spacious enough to hold the September Mop Fair with its swings, roundabouts and flying boats.

It has nurtured only two nationally famous figures, and is rather shy about both of them. One was Charles Stewart Parnell, the Irish politician who came unstuck politically over his relationship with Mrs O'Shea. He went to the vicar's school down Church Street. The other was Charlie Hind, as notorious a highwayman as Dick Turpin. After his hanging, his head was stuck on the Bridge Gate in Worcester. He was a High Street butcher's boy. Another poor boy, Henry Parish, found himself pressed into the Oxfordshire Militia during the Napoleonic wars. He was shot on Brighton downs for stealing flour, which he wanted to eat and the army wanted to use to whiten his pigtails. The scandal led to army dress reform.

Few national figures, then, but plenty of local characters. Reg Johnston, for instance, used to support Hospital Saturday by stalking through the town on stilts. He kept a leather shop, now the Indian restaurant, and one morning a lady asked if he had any good plastic handbags. 'There ain't any good plastic handbags', said Reg very loudly, 'Next customer'.

Some of the clergy were as forthright as the townfolk. One was sentenced to be hanged from the church tower for refusing to use Cranmer's new prayer book. A cherished item in the town's museum, run by members of the Local History Society, is a school register of the 19th century. Against one of the names the headmaster has written 'kidnapped by the curate', an echo of the friction between the Church and National schools. The National school, at the top of New Street, is now a recording studio.

Travellers westward along the Worcester road never fail to notice in the valley the palatial stone building with its great Tuscan-style chimney piece. It is Bliss Mill, where at one time hundreds of Chippy people worked producing its famous tough tweeds. It is now being converted into luxury flats with views over the old weaving shed. Not everyone who once worked there was sorry at its demise. There was often 'trouble at t'mill' and during the great strike of 1913 there was a huge gathering on the town hall steps addressed by students from Oxford and much ill feeling about 'scabs' who had to be escorted home by the police.

Chippy claims fame for the discovery of aspirin as a pain killer. In the middle of the 19th century a clergyman living in the town, Rev Edward Stone, followed up a local story that the bark of the willow trees which line the banks of the Common brook yielded a juice that eased rheumatics and fevers. He tested it and confirmed the countrymen's remedy. Much later pharmaceutical chemists followed up the clues and in 1899 marketed aspirin to their great profit.

While not particularly wealthy, Chipping Norton people are well provided for from the cradle to the grave. The War memorial hospital and maternity unit are cherished institutions. The two medical practices are models of friendliness and efficiency. There are four churches and the public library maintains a list of more than 50 recreational organisations. What annoys some of the older native inhabitants is that Chipping Norton seems to get no credit for the startling claim that, after the First World War, it ran three baseball teams and introduced the game to the United States!

Cholsey

The prehistoric road, the Icknield Way, crosses the river Thames here at Cholsey. The people who settled and farmed in the village, well after earlier Roman occupation, must have found Cholsey attractive with its mixture of arable land, pasture, marsh and woodlands. By the 7th century the people had been brought to Christianity by Birinus, the Abbot of nearby Dorchester.

The pride of the village is the church of St Mary, founded in AD 986 on monastic land donated by Ethelred the Unready. The present attractive building of stone and flint was erected in the early half of the 12th century and has a fine dog-toothed Norman doorway and a sanctus bell cast in London between 1290 and 1310. Henry I gave the church lands to the Abbots of Reading, who also owned a summer residence at Cholsey. A walk around the churchyard reveals a wealth of wild flowers, especially in the spring. Buried in the north-west corner is Agatha Christie, author of over 100 crime novels and stories.

Cholsey's focal point is the village green, long known as 'The Forty'. Dominated by magnificent horse-chestnut trees, it has been the centre of Cholsey since the Middle Ages. There are several local traditions about the origin of the name, but the most likely explanation is that it is Saxon in derivation, meaning 'island in the marshland'. An estate map of 1695 clearly shows water around 'The Island'.

Take a walk round the village to see the many interesting properties; attractive flint and brick houses, thatched cottages and barns. Follow the footpath from Cholsey to Aston Tirrold to see Lollingham House, built in 1516 and the former home of John Masefield, the Poet Laureate. There are many fine walks around Cholsey, with a bird sanctuary between Bow Bridge and the river Thames. The handsome Cholsey Viaduct, designed by the 'little giant' Isambard Kingdom Brunel, forms a distinctive feature in the landscape.

Cholsey now has a population of around 4,000 and has over 35 organisations in the village. It has a thriving community organisation, the 1000 Plus. This arose from the millennium celebrations in 1986 when the whole village celebrated in a series of events from March to October. These included a gymkhana, exhibitions, the Big Day Fete, a procession, community hymn singing on 'The Forty' and a Saxon feast in the large barn.

As with other communities in the country, Cholsey is concerned with provision for the elderly and is now working towards providing a day centre, to be situated in the old village school.

Churchill ✒

Leaving Chipping Norton, along the Churchill Road, the magnificent tower of All Saints' church soon comes into view. This is a replica of Magdalen, Oxford and is a much loved local landmark in the area surrounding Churchill.

The village itself is not so picturesque as many nearby beauty spots, so the casual visitor may be inclined to drive straight through. However, there is impressive history here. For instance, Warren Hastings was born here in 1732. At the age of 17 he sailed for India. During a colourful and, at times, tempestuous career there, he became the first Governor-General of India in 1773. After several more years he returned to England and finished his days at nearby Daylesford, where he died in 1818. There is a commemorative plaque on the wall of his birthplace in Hastings Hill.

William Smith, 'Father of British Geology', was born here in 1769. One of his many achievements in an illustrious career was the publication of the first geological map of the whole country. He had constructed this entirely without assistance and it is still used today. The Smith Memorial, donated by Earl Ducie, stands centrally in the village.

The handsome fountain is in memory of Squire Langston who died in 1863. He was a great influence in the life of Churchill, responsible for building the church and school. Through him farmhouses, barns and cottages were built or renovated. Neglected land was taken over and cultivated. Evidence of the involvement of the Langston family extends beyond Churchill. Close by is Langston Priory, now a residential home for the elderly. This was formerly the Langston Arms Hotel and its position near to the railway station was a great asset.

The remains of the original church stand at the foot of Hastings Hill. In recent years much work has been done to preserve the building. Though not now in use, it is an important link with the past.

The Methodist chapel in Kingham Road, completed in 1927, is on land given by Mrs Crudge. The chapel has been refurbished in recent years, with general amenities greatly improved. There is a very good relationship between church and chapel and joint services are always well attended.

Inevitably there have been changes in the village. Reduced roll numbers at the school led to its closure in 1981. However, its conversion to five houses has been attractively achieved. Elsewhere in the village, small developments and conversions have blended well with existing buildings.

For many years, the Chequers Inn was the venue of an annual Horn Blowing Contest. Many notable personalities came to judge the event and a good time was had by all. Funds raised on the occasion were given to a worthy charity.

One event which has become a tradition is the lighting of a Christmas Tree. This is installed on the village green and there is always a good turn-out for carol singing around the tree. A collection is taken and the proceeds sent to a charity. Then all adjourn to the village hall for hot soup, rolls and mince pies!

Clanfield ❧

The village of Clanfield lies on the flat expanses of the Upper Thames Valley, not far from Radcot Bridge. Clanfield was mentioned in Domesday Book as having 14 villagers, 13 smallholders and four slaves. There is a much ploughed-over barrow on the outskirts, which must mark the grave of one of its earlier inhabitants. Perhaps the most interesting approach is from the south over Radcot Bridge. Here in the meadows on your right you will see Friars Court, built on the site of a previous building that belonged to the Knights Hospitallers. Part of the moat and fragments of early masonry remain. Here lives a farmer who is also a pioneer conservationist. He and his wife have planted trees and shrubs, created a lake for wild fowl and a farm trail for visitors.

The church is dedicated to St Stephen and on its 14th century tower is a statue of the saint, holding in his hands the stones of his martyrdom. Above the Norman doorway is an early mass dial. Near to the church stands Chestlyon Farm, where once lived a wealthy family of that name. The present house dates from the 16th century, but it has at one corner what could have been a small Norman chapel.

The village has a Methodist chapel, still in use. Methodism once flourished in Clanfield. Camp meetings were held on the green, where the preacher would address the crowd from an old farm wagon. These early evangelists were often pelted with rotten eggs. There is a story of one such preacher, a Clanfield man, who while marching at the head of the procession towards the chapel, was jeered at by the local lads. 'Thee bist afraid to preach now' they yelled, whereupon the old man stopped in his tracks, carefully removed a clean red spotted handkerchief from his top pocket, laid it on the ground (to save his Sunday corduroys) and knelt down and prayed for their conversion!

A stream runs through the village towards the Thames, its banks in spring bright with daffodils. This stream is crossed in several places by perfect little stone arched bridges, which cannot be properly appreciated unless you walk along 'the causeway' under the weeping willows. This path may be part of the ancient trackway that led from Clanfield to Radcot. It would have been above the flood plain, very necessary when in the old days the Thames frequently flooded in winter. The old records tell us that it had to be kept clear, which was something not always adhered to, as more than once a local scallywag was fined for dumping a load of manure on it!

There are two village greens, and 'the causeway' links them. One is overlooked by the Plough and the Tavern, the two village inns, and also by a group of attractive cottages. Here too, the village cross once stood.

In 1758, when the inhabitants were 'all husbandmen and labourers' and the number of houses around 40, a report went to the Diocese of Oxford that 'there are too many who absent themselves from publick worship on the Lord's Day, and those, chiefly servants employing themselves in Fishing and Fowling, and such like exercises . . .'. In 1826 there were 102 houses and the inhabitants numbered 490. Today the population stands at around 800.

Clanfield is a friendly village and its residents are drawn from all walks of life. There are retired folk and there are young families, fortunate in having a fine post office and two very useful shops, one a newsagent's. There is an agricultural engineering repair shop, and on the site of what was once 'Knapps' is an agricultural engineering implement agency. 'Knapps' was an old Clanfield firm: L. R. Knapp and Co Ltd, established in 1745, 'Makers of Drills, Distributors and Hayloaders'. They employed as many as 40 Clanfield men at one time. Today agriculture employs about 20 and that includes the four farmers.

Ghosts? Well at one time there was talk of a 'white lady', sometimes seen in Mill Lane. Wending his way home one dark night, the miller's son heard a groan and looking anxiously in the direction from whence it came, saw a white form. He took to his heels and ran. However, common sense or sheer pluck made him return, and he discovered that his 'white lady' was a white cow with a bad cough.

Cleeve

Being considered part of Goring Village, the identity of Cleeve appears to become lost in the activities of Goring. However, Cleeve has a number of buildings and amenities in its own right.

The name of the hamlet of Cleeve refers to a cliff or clift, ie the cutting of a channel by the force of the stream. Cleeve clusters round the crossroads, half hidden in the hollow.

Goring Fire Station is, in fact, in Cleeve. The Volunteer Fire Brigade was formed in 1990 and in April 1976 a new fire station was opened in Icknield Road.

In Elvendon Road is Elvendon Priory, the present home of Sir David and Lady Black. It is a beautiful and interesting house and is reputed to date as far back as the 12th century. It most certainly has a colourful past. There was also a Goring Priory and an underground tunnel is said still to exist between both priories.

Cleeve Mill was built mostly of wood in the late 16th or early 17th centuries. No corn has been ground at the mill since 1888 and it is now residential properties.

Cleeve Lock was built of timber in 1797 and rebuilt in stone in 1874. In the long ago days of Goring Regatta, Cleeve Lock presented a busy and colourful scene.

Clifton Hampden

This attractive village sits astride the A415 almost equidistant from Abingdon and Dorchester on Thames. The church, restored in the 19th century by G. G. Scott, stands on a cliff above the river and faces the school with its gabled clock tower and mullioned windows. On one side of the village is the thatched Plough Inn and after crossing to the other side of the main road, past several old cottages, all with traditional 'cottage gardens', the bridge, also rebuilt by Giles Gilbert Scott, is the focal point of the village.

The Barley Mow – the other village pub – is popular with locals, visitors and those who sail on the river Thames which washes, and sometimes covers, the bankside garden. Jerome K. Jerome, who is buried in nearby Ewelme, ensured that the Barley Mow remains in one's mind. He wrote about staying here in his book *Three Men in a Boat* and should you wish to stay in the inn then you may just be given the Jerome Room.

Walks may be taken along the towpath to Abingdon or Dorchester, to Day's Lock at Little Wittenham or to the nearby Wittenham Clumps.

The home of the late John Masefield in the adjacent village of Burcot is now a 'Cheshire Home'. Opened in the 1970s with the help and inspiration of local people – the grounds may be seen from the river.

Combe

Combe is an unspoiled village on the fringe of the Cotswolds, centred around a delightful village green, which has a public house on one side and a church on the other. In spring daffodils grow all around the green; these were planted by the WI on their 50th anniversary.

The 13th century Anglican church of St Laurence is reputed to have been moved by the monks of Eynsham Abbey from the old village, which was down in the valley – near the site of Combe Mill. One of the main features of the church is the Doom painting above the chancel arch. There are also several other wall paintings, a lovely stone font and pulpit and some old stained glass.

Across the playing field is the Methodist church which has been recently renovated. A fitted kitchen has been added and the school room is used by the village playgroup.

The playing field, which was opened by the Duke of Edinburgh in 1949, has a children's playground. In summer it is used by the local cricket club; sadly there is no longer a football club in the village. The field is very well kept and the views across the Evenlode valley are marvellous.

Combe Feast is one of the main social events of the year. A fair is held on the village green, an open air service takes place on the Sunday evening, cricket matches are played on the two following days and there is general fun and games at the fair.

May Day is celebrated by the school children who parade around the village carrying flowers and singing May songs. The children congregate at school for tea. After tea everyone gathers on the green for the crowning of the May Queen and maypole dancing. School records show that this tradition has been carried out in Combe since 1870.

Although the village remains unspoilt, there has been careful development and this has helped to keep the community 'alive' by ensuring that there is a good mixture of age groups. There is a good local bus service and a railway halt just outside the village on the Cotswold Line (Oxford – Worcester). The village has one shop/sub post office.

Combe Mill, which is situated between Combe and Long Hanborough, as well as being a commercial saw mill for Blenheim estate, houses a Cornish beam engine which is 'in steam' on special week-ends. There is a museum in the same building.

The village has retained much of its truly rural character, although gone are the days when cows wandered through the village at milking times; there used to be five farms in Combe, but now there is only one, which is highly mechanised.

Cropredy

The village is situated at a crossroads in a valley through which meander the river Cherwell and the Oxford Canal. Cropredy became famous during the Civil War when King Charles' army was travelling north from Oxford. Parliamentary troops under General Waller intercepted the Royalists by the river and a battle took place. Charles won the day and was able to cross Cropredy Bridge. Some of the soldiers who were killed in the battle were buried in the churchyard. There are, to this day, bloodstains on the vestry floor, where a young messenger was killed. The lectern was thrown into the river for safekeeping and was not recovered for some 30 years after the battle. A foot in the form of a lion was missing and this was replaced in bronze, but when the lectern was cleaned it was found to be made of brass. The lectern to this day has one bronze and two brass feet. Armour from the battle was left on display in the church. School children would polish the armour and learn all about the battle, up until the mid 1980s when the armour was stolen.

Many years ago a gentleman was walking home across the fields when a fog came down and he was lost, then he heard Cropredy church curfew bell and realised where he was. So thankful was he that he gave the land now known as Bell Land so that the rent from it could pay the Cropredy bell ringer. The curfew bell was always rung at 6 am to awaken workers, at 12 noon calling the workers in from the fields for dinner and at 8 pm. One story tells how the poor ringer on a very frosty, slippery morning crawled to the church with the aid of sacks tied around his legs only to find he had left the key behind. Cropredy is one of the very few places in England where the curfew is still rung regularly. This is on Tuesday, Thursday and Saturday evenings.

The canal opened in 1790 when barges carried coal, corn, stone, bricks and other items. There were two wharfs. Today the canal has a new

Cropredy Lock

leisure use for numerous pleasure boats, a canoe club and, of course, fishermen. Competitions take place and children still get much pleasure from fishing in both the river and canal. When winters were colder and the canal used to freeze, many workers and school children would skate on the canal to Banbury. The last time when the ice was thick enough for this was in the winter of 1963/4.

A highlight of those far off days was Banbury Fair, when children had two days holiday from school. Children were also allowed out of school when the hounds started off from the village green. It was exciting to see ladies riding side-saddle and gentlemen in red coats and top hats. The children would follow as far as they dare but had to be back in school by 1.30 pm or the cane might be administered!

The village has two village greens. The main one at one time stretched

76

down to the river and was surrounded by a manor house and thatched cottages. A red horse-chestnut tree stands in the centre and this was planted to commemorate Queen Victoria's Diamond Jubilee. The village stores on the green recently closed and is now an antiques shop, and there is also a craft shop and blacksmith on the site of the old smithy and wheelwright's premises. There are two inns, the Brasenose and Red Lion, and a village stores on the banks of the canal. Adjoining the second village green is the Methodist chapel built over 100 years ago by Thomas Cherry, whose descendants still have a builder's yard and offices in the village.

The beautiful church of St Mary the Virgin, parts of which date back to the 11th century, was known as the Mother Church for Wardington, Great and Little Bourton, Mollington and Claydon until the 1860s. Next to it stood a large 17th century vicarage with many stables and outbuildings. Unfortunately this lovely building was sold in 1964 and in its place two blocks of bed-sitter flats were built. Eleven modern houses and bungalows were built on the rest of the gardens.

Several roads have quaint names, such as 'Round Bottom' and 'the Jetty', where bargemen used to lead their horses for stabling at night after a hard day of pulling coal-laden barges. 'Backside', newcomers know as the Claydon Road, but older residents still use the original name. 'Cup and Saucer' is believed to be the remains of an old stone preaching cross, withered away and now shaped like a cup and saucer with a spoon. 'Creampot Lane' is another old lane, leading to a farm which is now a private dwelling house.

Crowell ✥

Crowell parish covers some 996 acres extending from the Lower Icknield Way approximately three and a half miles in a south-easterly direction up onto the Chiltern ridge, reaching a height of 800 ft at one point. Nowhere is the parish more than half a mile wide. Crowell Hill is covered in the main with beech wood and lower chalk slopes. The lowland is mainly arable. It is thought that the name Crowell comes from crow's well, spring or stream as the village grew up at the source of the Pleck, a tributary of the river Thame.

Ellwood House is the only remaining farmhouse north of the B4009, of which there were four in 1839. The house dates from the 16th century, the front of which is of timber-frame construction concealed by chequer brick. There still remains a raised granary to the rear of the house. In the late 19th century the house and land was bought by Joseph Hill of Kingston Blount and the house restored as a farmhouse. It still remains in the Hill family today.

Ellwood House was named after Thomas Ellwood, a Quaker and friend of John Milton. Thomas Ellwood was born in Crowell in 1639 and attended the grammar school in Thame for a short time. He became a Quaker in 1659, probably as a result of several visits to Isaac Pennington at Chalfont St Giles. Because of his beliefs he was imprisoned for a short while in Oxford Castle. He finally left Crowell in 1665, the year in which he read Milton's manuscript of *Paradise Lost* and asked him what he had to say about Paradise Found. This is said to have prompted Milton to write *Paradise Regained*.

The village used to be larger than it is today and according to the 1851 census there were 16 lacemakers, three chairmakers, a chair bottomer, a wheelwright, a carpenter, a victualler and a number of farm labourers. Today although there are a couple of houses in the village housing farm workers and a farm at the top of the hill, the majority of people work either in Oxford or towards London. One of the longer established village families runs a funeral service business, the mortuary and chapel of rest being situated close to the church and village pub.

The Catherine Wheel public house was used by drovers in the last century herding their cattle from the west country to the eastern counties. There was a lean-to shelter with an earth floor to the rear of the pub where they slept. This area now forms part of the bar. In 1859 a great part of the village was destroyed by fire including the pub, which was one of the first buildings to be rebuilt.

John Bunyan is said to have stayed at the Catherine Wheel between his spells in gaol. He entertained the locals on his flute and there was until recently a copy of the chair that he used in prison in which one of the back struts was in fact his flute. Rumour has it that the prison officers never discovered the hiding place and so he was able to play his flute when alone in his prison cell.

The parish church of St Mary the Virgin serves Kingston Blount as well as Crowell. There is evidence to suggest that the church existed in the 12th century though the first documents only date back to 1231. The church was almost totally rebuilt in the 1870s, using as many of the original materials as possible so as to keep its 14th century appearance. The lychgate was added in 1879. In 1895 the west window was filled with stained glass in memory of the rector at that time.

There is no longer a school in Crowell though records show that there was a writing master here in 1713. During the 1830s there was a day school teaching 30 boys and girls, supported by the rector and payments from the children's parents. By 1854 the older children were going to school in Chinnor at the rector's expense and by 1878 the school in Crowell had closed, the children attending school in Aston Rowant or Chinnor as they do today.

Crowmarsh Gifford ✐

This village, which now includes Newnham Murren, lies on the eastern bank of the river Thames, across the bridge from Wallingford. The name Crowmarsh can be taken literally and the Gifford part comes from Walter Giffard who was given this land by William the Conqueror. Walter had been Standard Bearer to William in Normandy.

Many of the houses straddle the busy main road to Henley. There are pleasant rows of old cottages as well as small estates of more modern houses. The wide street in the centre of the village for centuries held an annual fair. It was said in the Middle Ages to be the most considerable in Oxfordshire. The horse fair, as it later became, died out about the end of the 19th century.

Much of the village's history is linked to that of nearby Wallingford. For instance, during the 12th century King Stephen constructed a series of wooden forts close by the bridge, opposite Wallingford castle where he was laying siege to Empress Matilda who contended the throne. No traces of these buildings remain today, unfortunately. The parish church of St Mary Magdalene was apparently used during the siege as a fortified post, and desecrated. Later, during the Civil War of the 17th century, some of King Charles' troops sought refuge in the church when Cromwell's men marched on Wallingford from Henley; the vestry door, which was formerly the west door of this Norman church, has supposed bullet holes in it. A leper hospital, with its own chapel, was established in Crowmarsh by the burgesses of Wallingford in the 12th century and was closely associated with the hospital of St John the Baptist on the southern side of Wallingford. But in times of plague Wallingford tried to keep Crowmarsh people out of the town by posting wardens on the bridge.

A foundry was set up in the village about 1865 by one of the local Wilder family. Walter Wilder's made castings, mainly for agricultural machinery but also for, amongst others, street lamps and drain covers. Have a look for them as you go around South Oxfordshire!

Some of the old farmhouses have gone now. One row of cottages next to the foundry was once part of Howbery Farm which at the beginning of the 18th century was tenanted by a farmer of national repute – Jethro Tull; he was a pioneer of mechanized agriculture, producing the first seed-drill that really worked.

A hundred years ago the village had more small shops than it has today, and included a baker and butcher, as well as two grocers and a post office. There is still a post office and general stores but the other present businesses are mainly concerned with the building trade. There used to be two beerhouses in addition to the two public houses that are still open, the Queen's Head and the Bell. The Queen's Head is the oldest secular building in the village. It was originally a 14th century aisled hall of a kind which was usually the dwelling of a man of considerable status. The elaborate design is still evident in its timber frame. The Bell has been much altered as well as enlarged over the years, but has been an inn since at least the mid 18th century.

Crowmarsh Gifford has a modern primary school which also takes in children from Mongewell and North Stoke, having outgrown two former school buildings that have since become private houses. One cottage, next to the Bell, and some land, was left to the village under a charity set up by one William Emery. There is a tradition that Emery had a lot of money because he had found a buried hoard on a plot where he farmed in nearby Ipsden. The cottage became known as the Poor's Cottage and the land is now used for allotments.

South of the village are meadows and farmland, while on the north side the 18th century Howbery Park now houses Hydraulics Research Limited, the Institute of Hydrology and headquarters offices of the District Council. Visitors to Crowmarsh may choose to stay at the Bridge Villa camp site which is close to the river south-east of Wallingford bridge. Watery Lane, the bridleway which runs alongside it, sometimes lives up to its name!

Like so many villages Crowmarsh suffers from too much through-traffic, but a north–south bypass was built in 1987, and the proposed bypass for Wallingford with a new bridge over the Thames should help to restore some of the village's lost tranquillity.

Cuddesdon & Denton ✺

Cuddesdon is a small village of 126 dwellings. It used to be known as the 'Holy Village' and differs from other villages because it has an Anglican theological training college and also used to be the official home of the Bishops of Oxford at the Old Palace.

The college was founded over a century ago. During the Second World War it was taken over by the government as a hostel for Irish girls who worked in the Cowley factories. One amusing story comes to mind: an altar cloth was missing. The special constables were called in to investigate – they learnt that the girls were having sewing classes so decided to play a waiting game. The following Sunday one girl turned up in church wearing a beautiful skirt (made from the altar cloth) to confess her sins! The principal of the college is also vicar of the parish and over the years practically all who have held this post have become bishops – notably the Archbishop of Canterbury, Dr Runcie, who held the post between 1960/69.

The Old Palace as it was known, opposite the college, stood in twelve acres of trees. Over the centuries it has a history of fires, the last being four decades ago when it was burned to the ground. In the 1960s part of the woodland ground was sold for executive-type houses – in the kitchen garden four staff bungalows were built and a modern palace/house for the Bishop was also built. The Bishops have since preferred to live elsewhere and the house is now a Toc H conference centre.

The village has a hamlet known as Denton on the south-west side which has 27 houses. The big house has windows built in its surrounding garden wall which were purported to have come from Brasenose College, Oxford, in days gone by. There are two picturesque timber-framed black and white thatched cottages, and a small brook running through.

Denton has a large spring which in years gone by supplied the hamlet with its water. Because of its quality the water was collected by the then Oxford Eye Hospital and used for eye treatments. Now of course it is all mains water.

Like other villages most people go outside to work – the only employment now being three farms, the college, one small garage, a public house and a small post office shop. Public transport is a thing of the past. The Parish Council and the County Council devised a car transport service which is known as CADETS (Cuddesdon and Denton Extra Transport Service). About six to ten car owners driving their own cars at certain laid down timetables pick up passengers to meet buses at Wheatley and Garsington and also for shopping in Wheatley and attending the doctor's surgery once a week, plus hospital journeys on request. A set fee is paid by the passenger – car owners are reimbursed for petrol on a mileage basis, and the scheme is subsidised by the Oxforshire County Council.

There is still a village hall and a recreation ground, but no sports club which was flourishing years ago. The only real event in the year is the annual church fete which involves the college, church and village all getting together.

Cumnor 🌿

Cumnor is an extensive parish three miles to the south-west of Oxford. The village itself is situated on high ground, rising in Cumnor Hurst to 825 ft. The name signifies 'Cuma's hill-slope', Cuma being an 8th century abbot of Abingdon. Housing connects it with the former hamlet of Chawley and in the valley are two other rapidly growing settlements, Farmoor and Dean Court. The name Cumnor is first found in a medieval copy of an Anglo-Saxon charter of AD 982 granting land to Abingdon Abbey, and it was mentioned in the Domesday Book.

Until recently agriculture was the main occupation. Today Cumnor is almost a suburb of Oxford, but still maintains a village atmosphere. The village has a church which is well worth a visit, St Michael's, with an interesting graveyard. Visitors should see the tomb of William Godrey, who fought with Charles I in the Civil War, and notice a slab marking the grave of Dr Benjamin Buckler, vicar from 1755–1780. Among the many features of interest inside the church are a chained Bible, a statue of Queen Elizabeth I and a memorial to the Forster family. The church bells were first rung in the 17th century. In July 1989 these bells were rehung and six old bells and the sanctus bell were rededicated; in addition two new bells and the frame were dedicated.

The field beyond the church was for many centuries part of the park belonging to Cumnor Place. The remains of Cumnor Place have long gone, apart from a small wall beside some steps and what was probably once a hearth for a fire. The house was made famous by the mysterious death of Amy Dudley, wife of Robert, Earl of Leicester, better known as Amy Robsart; she is buried in Oxford. In September 1560 the whole household went to Abingdon Fair, leaving Amy behind. When they returned they found her lying dead at the bottom of the stairs in the hall. This story was used by Sir Walter Scott in his novel *Kenilworth*.

A hill leading out of the village towards Farmoor is called Tumble-down Hill. The story is told, and as far as residents know it is only a story, of Dick Cromwell, son of Oliver, riding back after a battle – or was he returning from hunting? – and falling off his horse on Tumbledown Hill. He was known as Tumbledown Dick.

Near the Post Office is a 16th century farmhouse with a knot garden.

A tradition in the village is Pumpkin Night (Halloween), arranged now by the Bear and Ragged Staff, a public house in the Appleton Road, for the best and heaviest pumpkin from the villages of Cumnor, Standlake and Bampton. The proceeds of the party go to charity. According to stories it is also the night when the Mayor of Cumnor gets ducked in the village pond nearby. The Bear and Ragged Staff is a very old building – about 400 years old, and was for several centuries an old farmhouse.

There is a physic well off the footpath through the fields on the way to Bablock Hythe: difficult to spot now as it is overgrown, though it can be found if you know where to look. It is said to have healing properties for eye ailments.

Near the thatched cottages in the centre of the village is the war memorial, a tithe barn now converted into a home and, close by, the small area used for many centuries as the cattle pound for the village. Daffodils have recently been planted round the war memorial by the WI.

Deddington

> Aynho on the hill,
> Clifton in the Clay,
> Dirty drunken Deddington
> And Hempton high way.

Deddington is an old village sitting on top of a ridge overlooking the Cherwell valley between Oxford and Banbury. Here the wind comes straight from Siberia, say the old residents. Part of the church and some of the houses date back to the 13th century.

In its time the village was an important stage between its neighbouring towns and had a flourishing trade in cattle, sheep and horses. Old records show that at the November 'Pudding and Pie' fair as many as 600 or 700 horses changed hands. The old street-names like Bull Ring and Horse Fair are still in use. The fair marked an important day in the village in the 18th and 19th centuries. It offered villagers a fine day out with a band playing, and a chance for them to buy clothing, linen and household goods. After the Second World War it turned into a fun fair. Otherwise Deddington was self-sufficient and supported the usual trades like glove-making, a forge, candlemaking and clock making. The old industries included a paper mill and a beaver hat factory at Clifton. It was also known for good malt, hence the third line of the rhyme.

Today, Deddington is still a beautiful village of some 2,000 inhabitants. The older houses are built of golden Hornton stone and some of them are of considerable architectural and historical interest. Many are built right on to the streets, which makes for the surprise and pleasure of finding large gardens behind them. A number of these are beautiful enough to be on show in the summer for the Open Gardens Scheme.

The village is big enough to offer all sorts of amenities and small enough to be a sociable community where people know and trust each other. There are plenty of shops and one of the pleasures of living in Deddington is to go shopping on a Saturday morning. It takes ages. Friends meet and chat at the butcher's and at the grocer's, and more often than not there is a market stall in progress, fund-raising in aid of one of the many clubs.

The village has a new hall on the Hempton road, the Windmill Centre. Scouts and Guides use it as a venue, and major events and big meetings are staged here. There are adult education classes and the grounds of the centre have tennis courts, football and cricket fields.

The village has three churches, the old handsome parish church of St Peter and St Paul, the Congregational church and the Wesleyan chapel. And how many villages still have a real live set of bells? Deddington does, and the residents are lucky to be able to hear the chimes on practice evening and the ringing for Sunday services and weddings. On special occasions the Tower Captain opens up the bell tower and visitors are allowed to climb up and up, gasping as they reach the top, and are given an interesting insight into the art of bell ringing and a breathtaking view over miles of Oxfordshire.

Deddington also has an elusive ancient monument. In recent years English Heritage have put up a sign directing tourists to Deddington Castle. Alas, a moat and a couple of stones are all that represent what was once a castle.

Dorchester on Thames 🦢

Travellers north on the busy A423 from Shillingford can see across the vast ploughed field to the sturdy crenellated tower of Dorchester Abbey; they leave the new bypass and enter the village over the long curved bridge spanning the willow-lined river Thame as it winds its mile long way down to join the Thames.

The river and the abbey have been the main influences in the history of this beautiful village.

In AD 635 the king was baptised in Dorchester. The Christian King Oswald of Northumbria wished to marry the daughter of the king of the West Saxons, King Cynegils. Cynegils became a Christian having been converted by Birinus, the 'Apostle of Wessex'. The two kings gave Birinus land on which he built his first church, probably this first Dorchester Cathedral was timber-built. (Soon after he dedicated a church in Winchester which later became Winchester Cathedral). In the abbey is a reconstruction of the original shrine to St Birinus, a stone from which was placed in a silver processional cross, carried on a recent pilgrimage to Winchester and presented to the bishop.

Following the Danish Invasion, the Dorchester diocese stretched from the Thames to the Humber. After the Norman Conquest, Dorchester's importance decreased. Remegius, the new Norman bishop had his seat transferred to Lincoln. Later a house of Augustinian canons was set up and during the next three centuries they built the magnificent abbey. At this time Wallingford, Oxford and Abingdon were the flourishing market towns, and Dorchester, apart from the abbey, was just a village.

There are no traces of the monastery buildings destroyed on the orders of Henry VIII, only the Guest House survived to become the grammar school in 1652.

There have been many restorations of the abbey over the years (early last century much of it was ruinous). The last major effort was in 1970 when there was another 'royal occasion' when the rededication was attended by the Queen Mother.

The main road through the village, called the High Street, has many interesting houses, some dating back to the early 15th century, but over the years they have been repaired, refronted, or reroofed making their study fascinating. Cruck construction, thatched cob walls, Elizabethan jettied houses, herringbone noggins and many other architectural features can be found.

Near the bridge, built in 1815, is the little toll house, for this road through the village became one of the first turnpike roads in Oxfordshire and two of the 15th century coaching inns still remain, the George with its gallery and external staircase and the White Hart which had its coaching yard at the back.

A hundred years ago the population was just under a thousand. Many of the men were agricultural workers and the village had many small shops and ten public houses; there were butchers, millers, carpenters, a tailor, baker, blacksmith, wheelwright, undertaker, grocers, carriers and coal merchant – a typical self sufficient village. There was one unusual employer, a Missionary College where young clergy were trained for work overseas.

Twenty men were killed in the First World War. After the war the first council houses were built, rehousing some of the families living in primitive one up, two down cottages. Dorchester was not affected by the Depression, for there was plenty of work in the new Morris Motors and Pressed Steel factories at Cowley, and also at the Ordnance Depot at Didcot. Some men cycled and some even had cars to get to work. There were frequent buses, to Cowley for work and to Oxford, Reading and London. New houses were built on the Abingdon and Oxford roads. There was a flourishing school which included one of the new senior schools. It took children aged from eleven to fourteen from the surrounding villages, those travelling less than three miles were provided with bicycles, others were brought in by bus. School dinners were ten pence a week. It was a lively friendly community. The cows walked up the street for milking as two small farms remained.

September 1939 brought the evacuees to Dorchester; this so-called safe village (surrounded by airfields!) was bulging. Part of the old Missionary College became a school, the primary school worked a shift system, and the biggest room in the senior school had a class of 70 pupils! Most of the mothers did not stay long, they did not like the lack of running water and indoor sanitation of most of the cottages. The children settled in and enjoyed the countryside, although there was a gradual drift back to London.

After the war the character of the village changed completely. Mains water and drainage were laid on and then any spare bit of land was built upon including the two small farms; small cottages were bought and improved and it became a much sought after village. (The population is still just about a thousand.) Luckily young people came in as well, so there is still a flourishing primary school; the senior school became a comprehensive moving to a larger site in the new, mainly council built, development on the disused airfield in the north of the parish now named Berinsfield after our first bishop, St Birinus.

Today, it is still a lively friendly village with clubs or societies catering for all ages and for all tastes. The lakes of the old gravel pits support sailing clubs and are a paradise for birdwatchers with their enormous flocks of winter migrants. Throngs of visitors come to enjoy the river and to be uplifted by the splendour of the abbey. The old grammar school is still a place of learning as a small museum and weary travellers can be refreshed in the tearooms in the old Guest House of the abbey.

Drayton 🌿

Drayton is two miles from Abingdon on the old A34, once in Berkshire, now in Oxfordshire. It is the centre of an agricultural area, and was once famous for its walnuts. On the village green stands a stone cross in commemoration of Queen Victoria's Golden Jubilee.

Drayton has several fine houses, including Lime Close, parts of which are Elizabethan, which was visited by the diarist James Woodforde in 1763. Other houses of note are the Grange, Sutton Wick House, Gothic House and the Manor, opposite which is a cruck cottage.

Gothic House has a mural on the gable-end of St George killing the Dragon painted by Charles Sykes in 1949, the design taken from the original, smaller mural inside the house. Drayton people used to perform a mummer's play of St George and the Dragon annually at one time. Charles was an artist and sculptor, and in 1911 he designed the 'Spirit of Ecstasy' for the Rolls Royce motor company.

St Peter's church contains some fine carving done by Rev F. E. Robinson, who worked on it each day from 5.30 am until his parochial duties took over. He was also a renowned campanologist, and was the first Master of the Oxford Diocesan Guild of Bellringers, and claimed to have rung in every belfry in England. A brass plaque above the pulpit states 'In every work that he began, he did it with all his heart'.

In 1959 the church roof was badly damaged by fire, but a village wedding went ahead as planned, after willing helpers had cleaned up and decorated the church with flowers and branches, after which it was closed for repairs for a while.

In 1780 the casual act of throwing away hot ashes started 'The Great Fire of Drayton' which wiped out half the village and caused a national appeal to be launched. Drayton bricks made of Kimmeridge clay, dug, shaped and fired behind the Wheatsheaf, were used to rebuild the village.

In 1957 a Beverley aircraft came down near the village with some loss of life. More recently in 1989 a Tornado jet crashed on the outskirts of the village after flying into a flock of starlings.

There is reputed to be a ghost of a white lady on horseback, riding down Gypsy Lane, but she has not been seen recently!

One well known village lady was Mrs Marion Caudwell. Mrs Caudwell died in 1987 at the age of 93, after a lifetime of community work as area organiser of the WRVS, 25 years on the Abingdon RDC and eight years as a County Councillor. She gave a piece of land and raised money for housing and a day centre for the elderly which bear her name, and opened her garden each year for the church fete, an idyllic setting.

The busy Abingdon–Steventon road passing the green follows the line of the old toll road through Drayton used by the Oxford–Southampton stage coach in the 18th century. Whatever transport you use, Drayton is worth a visit!

Ducklington 🦢

Ducklington is situated one and a half miles to the south of Witney, close to the river Windrush. It is on the A415 road to Abingdon, but the village is fortunate in having a bypass which relieves it of much traffic.

St Bartholomew's church, commenced in Norman times, was once plundered by Cromwell's men and some of the damage can still be seen. They cut the heads off eight statues, only those that stood in the shadows escaped. Present day parishioners have embarked on mammoth fundraising to rehang the bells which now ring out over the village.

In a nearby field grows a rare plant, the Snakeshead Fritillary. These are depicted in a stained glass window and on the altar cloth, and their flowering is celebrated each year on 'Fritillary Sunday', usually the first Sunday in May. The church is open to visitors with many interesting things to see and refreshments are available in the nearby village hall. An elderly villager relates that, as a lad he and his friends were paid to gather these beautiful flowers and send them to market at Covent Garden. They are now protected and must not be picked.

The village hall was once the church tithe barn. It was used for many years as a meeting place and was known as the 'Parish Room'. In 1974 the room was purchased by the village, and much fund-raising and hard work resulted in a 'new' hall with modern facilities. It is now in great demand by all organisations, from playgroup to pensioners.

A small book titled *Living and Lifestyle in Ducklington 1640 to 1740* was published by the village History Group who studied records from the period, giving new insight into life at that time. The majority of 140 or so villagers worked on the land but there were a few craftsmen who plied their trade such as weavers, tanners and blacksmiths. It is very different today with only one working farm in the village and a population of over 1,000. Most people go much further afield to work, and all trades and professions are represented.

When the post office and shop recently closed, the building was converted into a bungalow. An enterprising villager seized the opportunity and has reversed the process, converting his bungalow into a post office and shop! This is the fourth or fifth location of this business in living memory. This, together with a ladies' hairdresser, a garage and two congenial public houses are the only traders in the village.

There has been little crime in the village, although one notable exception was the theft of the post office safe. It was wheeled away in the early hours on a trolley. Several people were awoken by the noise as it was trundled down the road but although they saw two men pushing some-

St Bartholomew's church, Ducklington

thing, they did not seem to think it unusual and went back to bed. The booty was later recovered from a ditch and except for a broken handle was none the worse for its outing.

Author and broadcaster Mollie Harris spent her childhood in Ducklington, her book *A Kind of Magic* depicts life in the village in the 1920s. Many of the places she mentions have changed little since that time. The footpaths, streams and rivers are a constant source of pleasure to us, as they were to her then.

A short walk from the village leads to a lake, left in the mid 1970s from the construction of the Witney bypass. It is inhabited by a wide variety of wild fowl. Swans, grebe, Canada geese and ducks can frequently be seen. Early morning visitors may catch a glimpse of a heron fishing.

Dunsden 🦢

Like many areas near the Thames, Dunsden has poorly defined boundaries. Situated on the uplands rising from the river between Caversham and Shiplake, the area was apparently used from early times as a passageway between the low lying, often flooded river valley at Sonning and the higher ground at Sonning Common where safe grazing could be found.

The name appears in Domesday Book as Dunesden. Much of the land was wild heathland and belonged to the Bishops of Sarum, whose influence was considerable as they owned the manor of Sonning and huge tracts of land in Berkshire. Bishopsland Farmhouse still stands at the northern end of the parish, commemorating the connection.

For many hundreds of years farming has been the main activity. The names of more than ten farms are commemorated by farmhouses which are now in private hands. The lands have been amalgamated and form part of Phillimore Farms operated by the Phillimore Settled Estates. The Phillimore family have been benevolent and conscientious landowners for over 150 years. Members of the family still live at Coppid Hall and are much respected; it is largely due to their careful husbandry that Dunsden remains a rural sanctuary even though only a few miles from the town of Reading.

Although not strictly in Dunsden, the brickworks in Kiln Lane at Binfield Heath must have provided local employment. A resident remembers the explosion when the works were blown up and demolished in around 1932. Ancient bricks can still be found and many people have used them to build garden walls or incorporated them in their houses.

Chalk quarrying was another activity, and a small quarry is still in use near Playhatch.

Playhatch House is a fine old building and one of the most gracious houses in the parish. Several houses and two pubs make up the hamlet of Playhatch around the foot of the steep hill that leads to Dunsden from the main Reading to Henley road. This hill road is of comparatively recent origin. The original road, known as Foxhill Lane, still exists, as does the old drovers' road from the Flowing Spring public house, going up the hillside and coming out at the George and Dragon pub, now a private dwelling. There are probably more footpaths and old roads in the area than macadamised roads and walkers are well rewarded by peaceful scenery and spectacular views. Another pub now turned into a house is the Old Black Boy at Dunsden Green. This was also a post office but now customers must travel to Binfield Heath for their stamps and pensions.

An old covered well stands at a fork in the road near the top of the hill by the village green. This was opened for use in June 1878 and is 150 ft deep but has been closed off for safety. It was provided by Miss Susanna Palmer and Mrs Isabella Crawshay. The Crawshays were ironfounders from Wales who owned Caversham Park, then the local 'stately home', and the Palmers were part of the famous Reading biscuit family. The two families also founded the village school in 1846 which was described at the time as 'superior to anything hitherto seen in that rather wild and inaccessible country'. The school closed at Christmas 1973, the remaining children being transferred to Shiplake Church of England primary school, and the building fast fell into disrepair. Eventually the descendants of the owners were traced, the building was renovated and it has now become a village hall of considerable character, retaining its raftered ceiling and high windows, no doubt designed to prevent idle pupils being able to stare out at the view of the valley spread out below.

The church was built in 1842, the architect being John Turner who also designed Rugby school. The land was given by the Crawshay and Palmer families and lies a mile away from the village green further to the north. It is a fine example of Victorian simplicity, built of grey and pink brick with a slate roof. Inside is a memorial plaque commemorating the First World War poet Wilfred Owen who lived for a time at Dunsden vicarage as assistant to the vicar. The graves of his parents and sister can be seen in the churchyard. After Wilfred's death they came to live in nearby Emmer green.

An interesting feature of the area is the incidence of swallow holes or 'swillies' as they are known locally. These are apparently bottomless ponds and streams that surface only intermittently and then are 'swallowed up'. An impressive example of this occurred in 1955 when a pond formed in old clay workings collapsed into a pit 100–150 ft deep, taking four mature trees with it. During heavy rain, water will collect for a time in certain areas and then disappear suddenly overnight.

Dunsden has its own ghost. The legend is that a girl from Coppid Hall used to travel regularly to Caversham to visit her lover. When her husband discovered the liaison he went to Caversham, found her and murdered her. Her ghost is now said to haunt the road that leads to Caversham past the Coach and Horses.

Duns Tew

A name like 'Duns Tew' cannot fail to excite curiosity and its origin is the subject of considerable speculation. It is thought that Tew means 'ridge', and the village does lie on the North Aston fault, separating limestone and sands in the south from the clay of the north, but there is not a ridge in the usual sense of the word. Duns might come from an Anglo-Saxon called Dunn, perhaps a landowner, and possibly living after the Conquest, as the full name does not appear until the 13th century. Perhaps there is some connection with the names of the other 'Tews', Great and Little Tew, but these villages are some four and five miles distant.

Duns Tew is a very attractive little village with its stone cottages and winding roads. It is well-loved and well-cared for, as is demonstrated by the fact that it has several times won the Best Kept Village competition, including the Best of the Winners category.

The church of St Mary Magdalene is an important centre in Duns Tew. Set in its beautifully cared-for churchyard this medieval church has a healthy congregation of all ages and has a thriving Sunday school. An army of flower arrangers, cleaners and gardeners ensures the church itself is looked after. In 1985 an appeal was launched to raise funds to restore the church roof, and characteristically the whole village played a part. Favourite recipes were collected for a village recipe book, one man ran in the London Marathon in 1987 in aid of the roof, the annual church fetes added funds and together with personal donations, the village raised the total of £30,000.

Farming plays an important role in village life today, and there are now six working farms, four of which are based on farmhouses in the village. Ivy Miall remembers arriving at Lower Farm in 1929 when there was grass growing in the middle of the road into the village. The farm did not have electricity until 1965, so they had to rely on big oil lamps with glass shades which were 'devils to clean', although Ivy was proud to have a maid to help her, even though Lady Dashwood (then lady of the manor) did not. She tells how she had to wash four sets of hunting clothes sometimes three times a week for her husband and sons in a copper boiler with a fire underneath. She used to dress her own poultry and pigs, making her own chitterlings until just a few years ago. She used to gather mushrooms out of the fields and sell them for 4d a pound, and she would use her 'mushroom money' to buy new willow pattern crockery to replace pieces that had got broken during the year.

The closure of Duns Tew village shop was a great loss, particularly to people without transport, and also because another meeting place has disappeared. People shop in Banbury or Deddington or from the various mobile shops that come to the village, which is in stark contrast to how things were in 1841 when there were a family of stonemasons, five carpenters, five wheelwrights, four shoemakers, four tailors, three blacksmiths, two slaters, two grocers, two bakers, one butcher and one joiner – all in Duns Tew! Fortunately the pub still survives, so all is not yet lost. But this survey does underline how occupations have altered. Although the village does have two building firms, Goundrey's Nurseries, a kitchen joinery firm and a children's clothing company, most people do not work in Duns Tew, but commute to another nearby town, or even to London.

There are no good ghost stories relating to Duns Tew, but this is more than compensated for by the fascinating story of Ann Green, a maid-servant at Duns Tew Manor. In December 1650 this young woman was committed to the sessions after her dead baby had been discovered at the Manor, and she was found guilty of murder. The father of the baby was the son of Sir Thomas Read, the then lord of the manor; Ann had apparently resisted the young man's advances for some time. After protesting her innocence, declaring the baby had been still-born, she was hanged in Oxford Castle Yard. To accelerate her death some of her friends and relations swung on her legs, and after half an hour, Ann was taken down. However, when she was being prepared for dissection by Dr William Petty, the anatomy professor, they saw signs of life, and on helping her recovery, by the second day after the hanging, she started to talk a little. Five days later she could walk with help. Not surprisingly,

Ann Green became a celebrity and people flocked to see her. She was later pardoned, the legal fees being paid for out of donations from the public. Afterwards she went to stay with friends in Steeple Barton (some two miles from Duns Tew) where she married and had three children. She died aged 31.

East Challow

The village lies at the foot of the Downs, about five and a half miles from the famous White Horse Hill. It has expanded over the last few years, growing from a village, which consisted of houses dotted either side of the main Faringdon Road, west of the nearest town of Wantage, to a fairly large area populated by about 1,500 people.

Not many of the buildings are of a great age, except a farm called Woodhill, whose deeds date back to the 1400s, and one or two old cottages situated alongside the village green, where the now defunct water pump still stands.

Opposite the green stands the church, which has had restoration work done to the exterior over the years and has some interesting features inside, such as a Norman font, 13th century arches and a window which dates from 1100. The chancel screen was erected in memory of four villagers who drowned in the North Sea in 1905.

Originally the main industries were farming and foundry work, which took place in what was an old coaching inn before being altered by Nalder and Nalder to house the equipment for making coffee grinding machines. These were exported all over the world.

This building was on the banks of the old Berks and Wilts canal which thrived by means of shipping coal, hay, coffee machines and other goods throughout its length. A former village resident, a Mr Hiskins, used to ply his coal barges from Wantage Wharf past Challow and on to Swindon and beyond.

Now with the closure of the foundry, smaller industrial units are housed on the site, making various components for use in other products.

The old school, which was designed by C. E. Street, has been converted into a residential home without losing its original charm of grey stone. Villagers have a choice of social activities. There is a thriving cricket club and British Legion, both of which are situated up the hill, the village hall, and at the lower end of the village is a newly built country club with a sports complex.

There are two public houses which offer food and drink to locals and

94

travellers. One of these, the Goodlake, so named after a benefactor who lived in nearby Letcombe, was run by members of the Lovegrove family for 130 years until the death of the last member of the family in the 1970s.

East Hendred ✎

East Hendred is a lovely old village lying at the foot of the Berkshire Downs, surrounded by farms and orchards. It is four miles from Wantage and to the south of the A417 trunk road. Its name is derived from the Anglo-Saxon 'Hennerithe' or 'rill of the waterhens'.

Like many another English village its roots go deep into the past, to Saxon times and beyond. After the Norman Conquest, Norman knights and abbots were given land in Hendred. The village was divided into five manors and names like King's Manor, Abbey Manor and Framptons are reminders of those feudal days. King's Manor still retains a Crown Stewardship last exercised in 1901.

The manor of Arches or Hendred House has been occupied by the Eystons since 1453 and this gracious house is a focal point in the village. Incorporated into the house is the little Saxon chapel of St Amand. In 1688, when William of Orange was marching to Oxford, some of his soldiers desecrated the chapel. The Eyston family were related by marriage to Sir Thomas More, Chancellor to Henry VIII. They have two precious relics; the drinking cup of Sir Thomas More and the staff used by the aged John Fisher, Bishop of Rochester, as he climbed to the scaffold at Tyburn to be executed with More.

The chapel of Jesus of Bethlehem stands on what would have been the centre of the medieval village. With its priest's cottage attached, it was built in an unusual design by the Carthusian monks of Sheen in the 15th century. It now houses a small museum, open on Sunday afternoons, showing different aspects of village life. The Parish Council also meets there.

There are Anglican and Roman Catholic churches in East Hendred with a good record of ecumenism over the past years. The ancient parish church of St Augustine stands on a slight rise. Its architecture is Early English and it has a fine peal of bells. The faceless clock, with its wooden workings still intact, plays 'The Angels' Hymn' every three hours. Inside the church there is the 13th century nave and a Crusader lectern thought to be unique. The Victorian-Gothic Roman Catholic church was built by the Eyston family in 1858.

It is not difficult to imagine the bustle around the core of the village during its hey-day in the 14th and 15th centuries as an important centre of the wool trade which filled the coffers of king, monastery and merchant. Many of the old cruck cottages belong to this period and the house which is now shop and post office and probably belonged to a wool merchant, is considered to be one of the finest examples of early Tudor architecture.

'Pit pat, pan's hot,
Here we come a'shroving
With a batcher up my back
A halfpenny is better than nothing.'

This is the jingle sung by the children as they converge on Hendred House at midday on Shrove Tuesday accompanied by parents and teachers for the traditional bun and a halfpenny ceremony. The centuries-old custom is enjoyed by the children, each of whom, after chanting the song, is given a bun and (today) a penny by the Squire, Mr Eyston.

Another custom which still prevails is the distribution of flour to 24 old people on St Thomas' Eve. In the old days this was given as corn which was then taken to the mill in Mill Lane to be ground.

For many years East Hendred has been associated with racing stables and a common sight is that of a string of fine racehorses going to and from the gallops on the downs. A Grand National winner came from the Turnell stable.

Most age groups are catered for in the village. Football, cricket and tennis are played on a fine sports field used by young and not so young. Although the forge is no longer in use, other crafts are practised here, from pottery to hand-carved furniture. There is also a small vineyard where the MacKinnon family grow, press, ferment and bottle their grape harvest.

The village is especially fortunate in having two schools, three pubs, a shop and post office and an hourly bus service to Wantage and Didcot.

Originally an agricultural community, mechanisation has meant the loss of many jobs on the farms. Fortunately the siting of the Atomic Energy Research Establishment, the Esso Research Centre and the JET Project, in the neighbourhood, has meant an influx of people into the villages around, including East Hendred, whose numbers have swelled to 1,300 with the arrival of scientists, engineers and other staff.

Ewelme 🌿

The school is reputed to be the oldest building in the county to be used as a primary school, with about 40 children attending now. The roof in the upper class room is of the same style as the roof in Westminster Hall in London. The church draws many visitors. John Mortimer's book *Paradise Postponed* was filmed mostly in Ewelme, featuring the church, school and old rectory and many villagers.

The church, dating from 1436 bears many resemblances to those in East Anglia, built in flint, stone and brick. It was built by William and Alice de la Pole, Countess of Suffolk and said to be modelled on Wingfield Church in Suffolk. There are still families in the village by the name of 'Winfield'.

There have been about 30 new houses in Ewelme in the post war period and many of the older ones have been modernised. Luckily there is still a shop-cum-post office and a bus service runs to Wallingford 3 times a day. A car service is run to Benson Surgery 2 days a week and people with cars kindly transport those without. This service is much appreciated by the Doctors and patients.

The Almshouses built in 1437, were modernised a few years ago, and in order to do so the 13 had to be reduced to 8. Alice, Duchess of Suffolk, ordained that that there should be 13 Almshouses and a Master's house so, now the odd 5 have been built in the main street. The Master is the Regius Professor of Medicine at Oxford and he and his family can use the 'lodgings' whenever they wish and many of them make full use of them. The snag to the almshouses for the elderly is that whichever way they are approached there is a slight hill or steps to get up. Not very thoughtful of Alice?

There is a manor and a common, known as the Cow Common. This was taken over during the Second World War by the Government and cultivated to help produce food, and after the war it was handed over to the Parish Council and an auction is held every year for the rights to graze for a year, and the rent is used to fence it in and general upkeep. Previously it was common land for anyone. It was also used as a 9 hole golf course, with the 9th hole at the far end on the other side of the road.

Sadly the famous watercress beds are in limbo, which is sad after being a well-known feature throughout the years. Ewelme watercress was highly sought after in London and Birmingham.

There was a honey factory in the village for 40/50 years which has caused many traffic jams, when big lorries arrived from all over Europe.

This has now been moved to Wallingford which has meant some local people have lost their jobs. But at least there are no more lorries up and down the main street.

You are not considered a true Ewelmeite unless you have fallen in the brook which runs all down the street and through the watercress beds on its way to Benson and the river Thames. Otters have been seen at the Benson end, and kingfishers are often seen near the bridge at Ewelme, plus many other water birds.

Eynsham

Over the centuries the name of the village has changed no less than 13 times. The 'old 'uns' used to refer to it as Ensam, spelt Ensham, its last spelling before the present one which has been in use for most of the 20th century and is not likely to be changed again.

A Benedictine abbey was founded here in 1005 and became very wealthy, owning land throughout Oxfordshire. The abbey was surrendered to Henry VIII in 1539. The ruins stood for a couple of centuries and then, as they began to deteriorate, the land became a quarry. The only remains now are carved pieces of stone built into many of the cottages and garden walls. Perhaps the villagers were encouraged to cart it away and build their own dwellings, some which still remain today.

The abbey also owned the flour and corn mill, the yearly rent payable by the miller being ten shillings and 450 eels. Many years later it became a paper mill supplying fine paper for the bible presses, and it was there that experiments were carried out to make paper from grass. During the early part of the 20th century it became a glue, rag and flock mill. Rags were turned into cheap flock mattresses. This all came to an end in the late 1920s, but the old mill buildings had a further use. The rubble from them was used as ballast when the nearby A40 was built in 1935. The lovely mill house still remains.

One fly in the ointment for the people of Eynsham, and of course further afield, is the toll bridge at Swinford, which has been here since the 18th century. Apparently one day King George III was travelling through to Burford, but at that time there was nothing but a ford across the Thames. The river was high, and the King's coach and horses almost foundered in the river. It was because of this that the owner Lord Abingdon was granted, by Act of Parliament, the right to build a bridge and charge a toll on everything that passed over, the takings to be tax free for ever. This of course still holds today. But the owners have to keep both the bridge and roadway over it in good repair. Now only mechanical vehicles are charged to drive over.

Eynsham villagers were, and still are, proud of their Morris dancers. There has been a side here on and off for 125 years. They are known as The Eynsham Morris, their dances differ from any other group and are renowned for their speed and vigour. Before the First World War the dancers used to perform at all the big houses at Christmas time, including Blenheim Palace. One of the members of the Eynsham Morris was called 'Feathers' Russell, because he always wore pheasants' feathers in his hat. He was a tall and very good looking man. He must have impressed the Duke of Marlborough, because he commissioned a painter, William Nicholson, to paint a portrait of Feathers in his Morris dancing outfit. The portrait called 'Chairing the Dancer' now hangs in Cecil Sharpe House in London.

War broke up the Morris men, but in 1980 Keith Green, a member of an old Eynsham family, formed a new group. Now they dance all over Great Britain and are often invited abroad to dance at big festivals. A delightful song called The Eynsham Poaching Song is often sung at their gatherings.

Eynsham has, like many other places, changed dramatically over the years. Once an agricultural village, now there are only a couple of farms here. At one time many of the menfolk went off to work in the car factories at Cowley, now there are several new factories on the outskirts of Eynsham, employing both local men and women.

Fernham ✎

Fernham is a cluster of houses, two farms and a pub, clinging onto a bend in the B4508 road. It was frequently used as a short cut by Oxford/ Swindon traffic. Now Faringdon has a bypass the road is slightly more peaceful.

The village presently consists of 67 homes. At one time mainly agricultural, it is now very varied with most people working out of the village and a high proportion of retired people. The part time post office and stores housed in an old stable at the Woodman Inn was closed by the Post Office without warning a while ago. Thankfully for a country village, there is still a bus service. The village hall and youth club is no more, the old chapel is now a house and the parish business is conducted in St

John's church. The church, consecrated in 1861, was built at the instigation of Rev John Hughes, vicar of Longcot with Fernham, and still serves the faithful with at least one service almost every Sunday.

The village green is just a name only since the council laid a tarmac road across it as access to the sewerage pumps. Left with two wide grass verges, no longer do the villagers congregate at the village pump on the green to gossip or play at tossing horse shoes at an iron pin. The pump cover erected over the well has recently been restored but the pump is a symbol only, although the old eight ft deep stone-lined bottle well is still intact underneath, safely capped off. The bakehouse behind the original manor house, which was justly famous for its bread and cakes, is gone, the site cleared and three large houses erected on it.

At one time Fernham could boast three general stores, one with a post office, a shoemaker's shop, a coal, oil and candle merchant, a smithy, a hurdle maker, a small market garden, a wagon builder and undertaker, and the obligatory pub. Before that there were two pubs; the house now known as Forge House and previously as The Red House, is thought to have been the Black Horse pub. It's the only house in the village with a cellar! There could also have been a rope maker, with his premises in Baganetts Alley perhaps? Sad to relate now, all that is left is a pub, the Woodman Inn, a free house dating from the early 1700s and a very popular haunt summer and winter.

Fernham residents could look forward to an annual flower show, harvest suppers, a Christmas party for the children and old people at Ringdale Manor and the summer spent cheering on the village cricket team. There was a dame school by the church, the children paying 1d on a Monday for a week's tuition – no penny no admittance! Now the only organisation is the Women's Institute, supported by the neighbouring village of Shellingford. The social highlight of the year is the village walk in June, started a few years ago to keep the local footpaths open and finishing up with a tea at the Woodman barn.

Fernham has some outlying guardians at 'Nightingale' along the Longcot road, the community of Benedictine nuns at the priory. At one time this was the original Ringdale manor house, but it is now over-looked by the later Ringdale manor, built on the edge of an ancient British camp similar to the one on White Horse Hill. From Ringdale Hill there are some wonderful views of White Horse Hill and the vale directly below, and long may the county planners let this remain so.

Filkins, Broughton Poggs Langford & Kencott 🌿

Filkins, Broughton Poggs, Langford and Kencott are all small villages built in the local stone, bound together by a twisty ribbon of lane, and if you walk across the fields by the old paths none is more than 15 minutes apart.

Each village has a very definite character of its own. Kencott is so quiet and tidy, the grass so green, the flowers so brilliant. It is no surprise that over and over again it wins the 'Best Kept Village' award. Look a little closer and find a more mysterious side: the dog sees a friendly ghost walk to and fro through a door that was blocked up in 1690; the church was dedicated in the 12th century to St George and on the tympanum and the village sign are figures that most take for St George slaying the dragon – not so, it is Sagittarius the Archer shooting into the mouth of the hound of hell. Hens still wander in the road and the whole street comes alive when the gardens are open in the summer. Then you can wander from cottage to cottage, from stall to stall and buy best home-made produce.

At Broughton Poggs, aeroplanes may roar overhead but inside the thick stone walls is the sweet music of bell ringing. The Old Rectory is said by some to have inspired Trollope to write the *Small House at Allingham*. Queen Anne Boleyn may glide down the Ladies' Walk – who are we to argue? It is certainly a creepy spot – much more pleasant to sit on a sun-warmed tombstone by the small Norman church, remembering the monks who looked after the fishponds, and puzzle over the bumps on the field, which are all that remain of the old village.

Langford is the lucky village with a thriving primary school and an enthusiastic cricket club. The highlight of the year is the dance held in a large modern barn, when the caller gets young and old on their toes to the country and square-dance music. All the money goes to charity. Perhaps this energetic out-going life really is good for the health; certainly the oldest inhabitant, Elizabeth Jones, is now 101 years old and still enjoys an afternoon out at the Happy Circle Club. She is the centre of a caring circle that shows village life at its best.

Filkins has a quarry that produces stone slates, and Saxons Close has been listed by the Dept of Environment because they were the first houses to be built by the district council using vernacular materials and traditional skills. It was argued at the time that the small extra initial cost would be outweighed by low maintenance costs, and so it has proved. Next door is the Centre: the doctor's surgery, the community post office (once the village hot baths), the swimming pool and the bowling green. In August the Bowls Club organise the annual flower show in the Carter Institute with skittling on the paddock opposite. Step inside and admire the Edwardian portrait of Mrs Amelia Carter draped in a fur stole. She funded the hall as a reading room for young men – to keep them out of the pubs! – from the profits made in the development of Carterton. No alcohol was allowed but there were two big open fires and a fine billiard table. At the top of the village the Crosstrees farmyard has been redeveloped. Woollen cloth, smocks and shrugs, pictures, furniture, green rushes and stone trefoils have replaced sheep, calves, hens and bulls.

Finmere & Mixbury 🦚

Finmere and Mixbury are located on the borders of Oxfordshire, Buckinghamshire and Northamptonshire, rich in history and spectacular scenery of outstanding beauty.

According to old documents the name Finmere means 'pool frequented by woodpeckers'. At the present time several woodpeckers are reported to have been seen in the vicinity.

There has been a church on the hill at Finmere since 1287. The present St Michael's, built in the 14th century, is well worth a visit. The carvings on the pulpit, pew ends and reredos were done by Rev Seymour Ashwell (1866–1902) who also farmed the Glebe himself; he must have been a very busy man!

In the lane just below the church gates is the old village school built by the Duke of Buckingham in 1824, closed in 1948 but recently tastefully restored to serve as a storeroom.

The old rectory, built in 1867, replaced the original which was destroyed partly by a violent storm, then three years later by fire. The beautiful gardens were laid out, or rather improved by 'Capability' Brown when he was working on the grounds of Stowe, just a few miles over the Buckinghamshire border.

Finmere House was granted by Henry VIII to four of his Queens in turn. Guess which one with 'her head tucked underneath her arm' is reputed to have been seen in the past drifting through the gardens at night. Some villagers can remember the late King George VI and Edward, Prince of Wales using the Finmere House stables for the hunting season in the 1920s.

The former manor house or court house, now called Bacons House, was owned by the Duke of Buckingham, lord of the manor. Standing on the bank of the Ouse it had a watermill but the Duke destroyed this, pulling down part of the house at the same time and reducing it to its present size. In 1858 all of the land north of the parish church was sold to Merton College, Oxford.

In the mid 19th century there were two blacksmiths, several butchers, a baker, carpenters, shoemakers, a cattle dealer, cooper, a brickmaker employing three labourers, an innkeeper-brewer, and 98 women and 48 girls above the age of ten made lace. How different now when there is just one shop at the Yew Tree Garage and the King's Head public house, with hardly anyone working on the land.

During the Second World War there was an aerodrome at Finmere, now this has become the site for what is said to be the largest Sunday market in the country. There is a recently built village hall on the northern outskirts of the village, abutting on the playing field.

Mixbury is a small quiet village now, but you can walk through to the old jousting ground and visualize the Knights of Old fighting for the honour of their chosen damsels. Many ancient relics have been excavated on the site of the old castle.

There is an ancient 11th century church and an old school building (now the village hall). It has been said that at dusk on summer nights children can be heard singing, though it has not been used as a school since the 1950s.

Monk's House Farm is also reputed to be haunted. This contains a bricked-up room and at one time a tunnel led to the church.

Like Finmere, this village has changed considerably. In the 19th century there were five farms (these remain), two carpenters, a mason, a baker, a tailor, a blacksmith and a shopkeeper. Now a number of new houses and bungalows have been built, inhabitants working further afield.

Horse riding is popular in both of these villages and the disused railway provides an interesting nature reserve.

A tributary of the river Ouse runs through the adjoining hamlet of Fulwell which links the two villages.

Finstock 🌿

Finstock is the sort of place you've been to without noticing. People in cars on the B4022, along the ridge of high ground between Witney and Charlbury, may be briefly aware of a road sign and a scatter of houses as they race past, without realising that they are missing Finstock itself which straggles down the eastward-facing slopes of the ridge, overlooking the Evenlode valley. Turn off at the crossroads at the top of the High Street and you will probably pause a moment to admire the view over rooftops and rolling fields into such a far blue distance that at least one awestruck visitor has been known to suggest that you must be able to see to Moscow. You can certainly see the John Radcliffe Hospital and the Beckley Mast. As you follow the bends of the High Street downwards, you will look in vain for any signs of commercial splendour which the name might suggest and it was presumably so called simply because it was higher than the rest of the village. There is a certain dogged obviousness about Finstock street names. High Street, therefore, leads, inevitably, down to The Bottom from where the road curves up again to flatten out into School Road.

Apart from a school, Finstock also boasts a post office, which used to be in someone's garden shed but is now incorporated into the shop, a recreation ground, a village hall, two pubs, a Methodist chapel, a church, marooned by itself on the main road, a railway halt and a bus service, of sorts. The village hall, which started life as a gloving factory, is the meeting place for various village organisations and with the seasonal round of parties, summer fetes and bazaars one always has the impression of something happening in Finstock.

In days gone by, as 19th century census returns show, the inhabitants of Finstock would have earned their living entirely in or around the village, the men mostly as labourers on the farms of the large estates of Cornbury, Blenheim and Wilcote, which surround it, and the women engaged in gloving to eke out the family income. Probably many people would hardly have left the boundaries of the village in a lifetime. Today, however, only a handful of villagers work locally on the land and most commute by car or train to Witney, Oxford, or even further afield to London.

The churchyard, which is carpeted with primroses, violets and lesser celandine in the spring, is a sunny place to sit and contemplate the view over the village, but although Finstock, with the smoke curling lazily upwards from its chimney pots, may appear tranquil enough now, many a lurid tale tells of a more violent and boisterous past. In fact, at one time Finstock must have resembled a frontier town of the American West as it was on the route of the drovers' road from Wales and the West Country to the London markets and at regular times of the year was invaded by gangs of strange men with their bellowing, trampling herds of cattle, looking for a watering-place.

Today, the great forest of Wychwood only marches up to the line of the B4022 but centuries ago Finstock was still within its borders and the forest was a dangerous place. Footpads, vagabonds and highwaymen haunted its coppices and thickets and any well-to-do farmer unwise enough to set off for Charlbury with his pockets stuffed with money was liable to end up thrown in a ditch with his throat cut. The Crown public house, which dates from the 14th century, seems to have been particularly notorious as a rendezvous for thieves, who frequently had to make hasty exits from upper windows, one step ahead of the law. Apart from the incidence of serious crime, there seems to have been a great deal of unruly behaviour in the form of drunken brawls and gang fights between rival villages. Even within living memory, as older inhabitants will tell you with relish, Finstock had a reputation for being both tough and rough and an elderly lady in an adjoining village still recounts with a rueful smile how in her childhood a walk through Finstock often meant risking a hail of stones from hostile urchins.

Until earlier this century, anyone walking about in Finstock must also have been aware of the constant sound of running water as several streams, fed by springs high up on the hillside, cascaded down the valley. At least one ran down beside the High Street cottages, which had little bridges across to their garden gates. It must have been a picturesque scene worthy to rival the well-known Cotswold tourist traps of today. In 1928, however, the streams were enclosed in pipes and covered over and like them Finstock seems to have been gradually quietened and tamed.

If you are interested in astronomy, Finstock is a good place to live as there is no street lighting to dim the starlight. From its valley slopes you not only have a panoramic view of the countryside by day but a sweeping skyscape above you by night.

Forest Hill 🪶

With a current population of about 650, Forest Hill (technically part of Forest Hill with Shotover) lies on a hillside just to the east of Oxford. A cluster of stone houses, two pubs and a Norman church form a central conservation area while Shotover House and its surrounding park lie to the south, separated by the main A40 road.

The road system, which still exists, was fundamental to the primitive hamlet of Forst Hyll (Old English meaning 'hill ridge'). At the bottom of the hill ran a road to Oxford, to the west went the Roman road from Dorchester to Alchester, and a Saxon track ran to Brill. But the most important of these routes was the one to Islip (birthplace of Edward the Confessor) and now the B4027. This ran on to Woodstock, with its royal palace, and in stagecoach days was part of the turnpike to Worcester and Holyhead.

The village appears in Domesday Book as the manor of Fostel. It passed to those great Oxford landlords, Oseney Abbey and the monastery of St Frideswide, while the adjoining manor, held by the prioress of Littlemore, is still remembered in the modern Minchincourt Farm. The parish church, originally a chapel of the church at Stanton St John, was dedicated to St Nicholas the Confessor.

The best known of the tenants of Manor Farm was Richard Powell, a spendthrift Royalist who had borrowed £500 from a John Milton of Stanton St John. Interest on the loan went to Milton's son John, the great Puritan poet and pamphleteer. While in pursuit of his money the poet met and in 1642, to general astonishment, married Powell's daughter Mary, then aged 16. It was an unhappy alliance and Mary soon returned from London to a happier life in Forest Hill. She bore Milton four children, but died in 1652 aged 25. This sad episode forms the core of Robert Graves' *Wife to Mr Milton*.

In the late 18th century Manor Farm again had literary associations when William Julius Mickle lived there and translated the Portuguese epic, the *Luciads*. Mickle was a considerable poet, a friend of Boswell and Johnson; he was buried in the village churchyard. But perhaps the most colourful individual of this period was the Reverend John Mavor who in the 1820s ran into debt over the building of a new vicarage. He spent some time in Oxford gaol, from where he managed to fulfil many of his parish duties, even apparently being let out on Sundays to conduct services.

Later in the 19th century, the village changed rapidly. Manor Farm was demolished and rebuilt in 1854 by Lincoln College, red-brick houses were built and, important to daily life, a post office opened in 1882. Standpipes in the streets supplied water from the village well. An austere Methodist chapel was built at the end of the century and facing it an equally austere village hall. Most villagers were still employed on the land while the local woods enabled hurdle makers to follow their craft.

The First World War changed all this. Sixteen men did not return, a large number for a small village. New agricultural techniques meant fewer men were needed on the land, but above all the motor works at Cowley became the main employer. The first council houses were built, the telephone was available for the prosperous, and electricity and street lighting arrived in the 1930s. Transport was much improved – buses made the shops and cinemas of Headington and Oxford accessible and the vigorous social life of the pre-war village was to some extent replaced by more urban pleasures.

Since the Second World War many new houses have been built and the village remembers its brushes with literary history in Milton Crescent, Powell Close and Mickle Way. Apart from members of the families, employment on the two highly mechanised farms has almost disappeared. Work in the motor industry has waxed and waned with the fortunes of Cowley. The almost universal ownership of cars has made the large supermarkets around Oxford available and there are no shops, not even a post office, left in the village. Deep drainage has made even the oldest houses more pleasant and recently mains gas has become available.

Many of the villagers are now newcomers, finding Forest Hill pleasant and convenient. The Methodist chapel has been converted into a private house but the village hall is still put to good use. The church is now combined with those at Wheatley and Stanton St John but still attracts a significant congregation.

Freeland

Freeland is a village not on the way to anywhere. It straggles along a road between the Oxford–Witney and Witney–Woodstock roads. On approaching the green, splendid with daffodils in spring, the cluster of cottages and pond with ducks make a typical village picture, and on going past the pond to take in the view towards Oxford, one can sometimes find a shoot of bracken – a defiant relic of the old heathland.

Freeland began as a squatter settlement on the outer reaches of Eynsham as early as 1650, and after the enclosures of the 18th century the settlement grew. Squatter cottages were built with the narrow wall by the road, thereby using the minimum frontage.

One of these cottages in the centre of the village is now the Oxfordshire Yeoman pub. In 1973 the brewers, Morrells, wanted to rename one of their public houses after the old county regiment. As the site of the New Inn, Freeland was acquired in 1842 by one William Merry, yeoman, it was the one chosen. At the other end of the village, on the Witney–Woodstock road is another public house with a long history. Although not quite in the Cotswolds the area provided grazing for sheep. By the drove road was an inn providing all the shepherds needed, and it became known as the Shepherds All. In later years, someone who evidently thought the locals were unable to speak properly added an 'H' and Shepherds Hall it remains to this day.

Back on the main road through the village is a cottage which can answer a common question asked by strangers about the unusual name of the road – Wroslyn. This ivy-covered cottage was once an inn (suitably far from the centre of the village) where wrestling bouts were held. In this part of Oxfordshire wrestling was pronounced 'wrosling' so when road names were requested the Parish Council preserved this little part of our history. The cottage is called Wrestlers and the bungalow built on the field where the bouts took place, Wrestlers Mead.

Although it was in the parish of Eynsham, Freeland is nearer to the Hanboroughs, and before the church was built villagers would walk to Church Hanborough for services. Not many people, however, liked to walk alone after dusk down what is now called Pigeon House Lane in case they should meet the ghost of Mother Skolpepper (ie Mrs Culpepper). Children dared each other to go down, and at least one father offered his children a shilling to 'Pop down to Hanborough in the evening', knowing his money was safe! A less fraught way to Long Hanborough was across the fields, and early this century Sarah Merry would go this way to shop and visit her brother and sister with her pet pig trotting dog-like beside her.

The little stone Methodist chapel was built in 1805, to the 'greatest mortification' of Thomas Symonds, then curate, later vicar at Eynsham. It is the earliest of such buildings in the Witney–Faringdon Circuit. Through the members' long friendship with New Zealand hymn writer Colin Gibson, there is now a hymn tune called *Freeland*.

With the completion of the building of the church in 1869 Freeland became a separate parish. Since the population of the hamlet was only about 200 at that time, it is perhaps an unexpected place to find a 'gem' of a small church designed by one of the greatest Victorian church architects, John Loughborough Pearson. This virtually unchanged Tractarian church was built thanks to the generosity of the Taunton family and other benefactors from the Oxford Movement. The stained glass and interior decoration are by another leading Victorian firm of Clayton and Bell. The chancel is decorated with 13th century-style wall paintings which are echoed on the pulpit and font. Pearson later added a carved alabaster reredos. The parsonage and a school were designed and built as one group of buildings with the church.

At the end of the 19th century there were some brick kilns which used clay from North Leigh common, and the row of houses at the north end of the village known as Red City are made of these local bricks. A number of villagers were employed as out-workers by the Woodstock glove factories. Now, in common with many Oxfordshire villages Freeland has a 'light industrial complex'.

Fritwell

Fritwell in the Elms the old books say, though alas most of the elms have gone now. It is L-shaped, divided into two parts by the brook, the source of the Little Ouse. The east–west road now runs to Somerton and crosses one of the few stretches of the Portway that remains north of the Thames. A number of the stone-built houses date back to 1636.

The church, situated by the village green at the northern end of the village, is 11th century, dedicated to St Olaf. It has many interesting features including a fine tympanum with ball and chevron over the south door. Over the north door is cable moulding ending in grotesque animal heads. There are traces of a small monastery nearby.

The school opened in 1872 is still thriving and now serves five villages. May Day used to be a big day in the school calendar. A king and queen elected by the children paraded round the village, followed by the scholars singing traditional songs and carrying a garland of spring flowers. After a scrumptious tea, the day ended with dancing round the maypole. This event is still held each year, but takes place at the school, as the village has become too big for the children to visit each house.

The playing field was established in 1973. This is used mainly by the local football team and has facilities for children. To get the field in good condition a sponsored stone pick was organised.

After the Queen's Silver Jubilee celebrations in 1977 when the whole village united for a carnival day, it was decided to carry on the fun and have an annual carnival, all organisations in the village participating.

In 1908 *Rubio*, owned by Mr Bletsoe of Dove House Farm and trained by Mr Withington, won the Grand National horse race. Prior to the race, it was shod by local blacksmith Mr Gibbs. The forge has now been replaced by a road of houses called Forge Place.

Each end of the village had its own manor house. The older one at the southern end is now Lodge Farm. The Elizabethan manor at the northern end dates from 1596 and is reputedly haunted. Sir John Simons (Chancellor of the Exchequer) lived in this one during the 1930s. During the time he lived there, a magnificent stone water tower was built which is still used, also a substantial villa in the gardens along with a recreation hall.

Transport has changed, not for the better. In the 1930s buses ran from the village garage to Banbury and Oxford very frequently and a good train service existed from Fritwell and Somerton station. The carrier's cart went to Banbury several times a week and the driver would make purchases and deliver them for a small fee. Now buses run to Banbury and Bicester two days a week — very infrequently, and the station is closed.

Two public houses survive, two shops and a post office. Dew's stores opened in 1885 and in its heyday almost anything could be bought there. People were employed there and at the butcher's and slaughterer's, garage, post office, blacksmith, bakery, farm, railway and laundry. The blacksmith, bakery and laundry have gone but the others still serve the community well. Individual craftsmen covering a wide range of skills offer employment.

Fritwell, on the edge of the Cotswolds, is still unspoilt. It is easy to take a walk in solitude with views of idyllic countryside, or if you favour progress watch the M40 slowly carving a swathe across the Cherwell valley.

Garsington 🌿

About five miles east of Oxford lies the village of Garsington. It is mentioned in the Domesday Book but its origins date back well before that time.

The lovely parish church of St Mary, situated on a hill top, is visible for many miles around. The site commands magnificent views. The Norman tower of the church is the oldest part dating back to 1160, the nave and chancel having been added later in the 13th century.

Garsington boasts many splendid houses of historic value. Although dating back to the early 16th century many appear little changed from the time of construction. The most famous of these is the manor house built about 1625. Prior to that time, however, it is said that such a house was built on the site as early as the 13th century.

The present manor is thought to be one of the most beautiful of the smaller period houses throughout Oxfordshire, set in superb grounds which are open to the public two or three times a year. The garden incorporates two yew hedges which are said to be the highest in England.

During the First World War when Philip Morrell, who was the MP for Oxfordshire South, and Lady Ottoline took up residence, the manor became much celebrated. Firstly for its use as a refuge for conscientious objectors and later because of the many famous people entertained there, among them Bertrand Russell, Aldous Huxley, D. H. Lawrence and Virginia Woolf. A small two-storey cottage contained within the manor grounds, known as the Bakehouse or Monastery Cottage, was used by artist friends.

Another prominent building, a Tudor Gothic-style school house was opened to its first pupils in 1840 and was used until a modern primary school was built nearby in 1982. The old school house still stands resplendent in the centre of the village and in spite of being converted and modernised for dwelling purposes, the exterior is little changed.

Near the end of the old school wall stands a medieval village cross, recorded in 1240. A new head and shaft was needed but the base has survived the passage of time. This cross held pride of place on the village green many years ago, but the green is now sadly depleted.

The Gizzle, meaning a field or spring-fed pond, should surely be mentioned. Until modern pumping equipment was installed, many people from the village drew water from the Gizzle in buckets, using wooden yokes to carry it home. Recently cared for by the Garsington Scout troop, it is a pleasant corner to rest awhile, if rather tucked away. It can be approached via a footpath from the church or by road passing the manor.

With regard to footpaths, it is said that Garsington has probably more than any other Oxfordshire village. The fields are criss-crossed with them, probably due to the fact that during the 19th century many of the villagers earned their living on the land with so many farms and market gardens nearby. Some of the old stones, placed upright as stiles, can still be seen.

The major landowner in the village is still the University of Oxford.

Whilst farming dominated, a flourishing brick works at Kiln Farm was started about the middle of the 19th century. This provided alternative employment for the villagers and as well as being used locally, the bricks were transported to other nearby villages.

The population could not have been large at the time of the 18th century, nonetheless six victuallers were then licensed. Today the number has been reduced to three.

The close proximity of the motor industry starting up in the 1920s, and the ease of travel, has made Garsington a popular village in which to live. Many modern houses have been built, and the population has almost doubled in recent years, numbering 2,000 or more.

A wide and varied programme of traditional activities is enjoyed, incorporating the church, village hall, public houses etc. Splendidly situated in a field on the outskirts of the village is a sports club much used for sporting and social events.

Goosey

The manor of Goosey was given to the monks of Abingdon Abbey and a cell was established here in the 12th century. Abbey Farm still serves as a reminder of the monastic connection, and legend tells of an underground passage used by the monks leading from the farm to the church, but it has never been found. The monks wore long black serge robes and are remembered today, with their geese, on the altar cloth in the tiny 13th century church which stands at the south-east corner of the spacious and open green.

The Pound village inn stands at the western entrance and was the setting for music and dancing at the Goosey Feast held every November in the 18th and 19th centuries. This Feast has been revived and still takes

Church Farm, Goosey, dated 1670

place on the village green each year, but at the beginning of September and in a rather different form.

Five beautiful old farmhouses and the village school, now a private residence, surround the green. Goosey mere stands in the south-west corner and is now somewhat overgrown but was once used as a skating rink by the villagers and also supplied the water for their domestic chores.

Geese no longer graze on the green as they did in the monks' time, but villagers still retain grazing rights and its character has remained unchanged over the centuries.

Goring 🦢

Goring has developed as a rural community on the east bank of the river Thames in the Goring Gap. It lies in one of the most attractive reaches where the river flows through an area of outstanding beauty.

Here, long ago, the Icknield Way, one of the great early highways, crossed the river by means of a ford and joined up with the great Berkshire Ridgeway. Today these two ancient ways form the basis of the modern Ridgeway Path running from Ivinghoe Beacon in Buckinghamshire to Overton Hill near Marlborough.

The two highways were used extensively for driving sheep from East

Anglia to the great fairs in the west. This unfortunately attracted the attention of sheep rustlers which proved difficult to contain.

From Saxon times Goring had a corn mill which was of great benefit. From Norman times until the 15th century it was owned by the prestigious Abbey of Bec in Normandy. Later, the mill provided electricity for the village but it is now a residence.

The church of St Thomas of Canterbury is late 11th century and was probably built by Robert D'Oyley, the first Norman lord of Goring. In the 12th century a small group of Augustinian nuns founded a priory adjoining the church, which building they shared with the parishioners. Later, the nuns built their own church to the east of the parish church, separated from it by an interior wall.

The parish church has an interesting brass of Hugh Whistler and his family. Hugh's age at his death appears to have been '216' years according to the inscription. This is probably a careless engraving of the more likely '46', too great a flourish being provided to the first downward stroke of the '4'.

The church also has one of the oldest bells in the country, cast about 1290 by Richard de Wymbis. It hangs on a bracket in the church but is no longer rung.

In 1303 Isabella of Kent, a very wealthy woman staying at the priory, attracted the unwelcome attention of William of Huntersull. Isabella had to take to the tower of the church when William with some 21 men rode to the priory and then through the church to the High Altar. The chaplain of Goring and a lay brother were attacked as they sought to protect Isabella, who was seized by the men and carried away. The men were subsequently excommunicated and Isabella brought a civil action against them. The priory was eventually dissolved in the 16th century at the Reformation.

One of the greatest disasters in the village's history was the tragedy in July 1674 when a boat returning to Streatley after the Goring Fair and containing 50–60 persons, passed too close to the weir and overturned. All but 14 persons were drowned, together with one horse. This was before the first pound lock at Goring was built in 1787.

The earliest recorded bridge over the Thames at Goring was erected upstream of the old ferry in 1837. It was a toll bridge and the various charges created some rather absurd situations. A person crossing by foot was required to pay 1d, but if he drove a calf or pig over he paid only ½d. It is said one Goring man always took his pig with him when he crossed the bridge to save himself a little money. The bridge was rebuilt in 1923 and all tolls abolished.

The oldest lay buildings in the village are reputed to be a 15th century barn belonging to the Old Farm House in Station Road and parts of the Old Vicarage which may be 16th century.

A number of large houses were demolished in the 20th century and small housing estates developed on the sites. The demand for more housing accommodation indicates how Goring has changed in recent times.

The oldest inn is the Catherine Wheel in Station Road, which was the main street at one time; the inn may date back to Elizabethan times. The largest inn is the Miller of Mansfield, a name taken from an old legend concerning a miller who entertained King Henry II with a pie made from poached royal deer.

Goring lies in fine farming country providing a source of employment, particularly in the past. Notable industries no longer existing include the boat building firm of Samuel Saunders, who took over Goring wharf and built the Springfield Works near South Stoke. Later the firm developed successful speed boats and steam launches and then moved to Cowes. In 1929 it operated under the name of Saunders-Roe of flying boat fame.

The village also had a brewery, established in the 19th century, which later became Gundry and Co. The business declined and was sold in 1940.

Today, despite a certain reputation for becoming a commuters' dormitory due to the convenient train service to London, there are numerous organisations, most of which are thriving. Various river sports have their own clubs but sadly, the Goring and Streatley Regatta, one of the most important on the river in its heyday, failed to survive the First World War.

Great Coxwell 🦎

Great Coxwell lies two miles south-west of Faringdon, and before the boundary reorganisation in 1974 was in the county of Berkshire.

Evidence of Mesolithic, Neolithic, Iron Age and Romano-British occupation has been found in the form of flints and pottery sherds (broken pieces) scattered in and around the village.

Most of the surrounding farm land is owned by the National Trust, as are the Great Barn and Court House, which are also maintained by the Trust.

A Neolithic site was recently found near the Iron Age hill fort of Badbury Hill, part of which is planted by the Forestry Commission. There are lovely walks around it, and a new route encompasses the Great Barn, Court House and thence the village.

The Great Barn and parts of the Court House are all that remain of the 13th century Grange, once part of Beaulieu Abbey. The Great Barn, built about 1250, is 152 ft long, 44 ft wide and 48 ft high, and is described in a leaflet available on site. It is an impressive building and is open to the public at all times, although the nearby Court House is not. A sit-down lunch for over 250 people was held in the barn in celebration of the Queen's Silver Jubilee in 1977.

The main village, most of it a conservation area, stretches to the south of the barn for about one mile down the main street, once called Horsleaze Lane.

The older properties are built mainly of corallian limestone rubble (the local stone, quarried from behind the village) and there are some 19th century brick-built cottages. The original roofing was of Cotswold tiles or thatch, in later years replaced by slate, corrugated iron or modern clay tiles. The majority of new building is post-1960.

Little more than 50 years ago the village had a church, chapel, school, public house, reading room, shops, a butcher, a seamstress, farmers and a laundress. Now only the church, parish reading room (opened 12th December 1901) and a small part-time sub-post office remain. The school closed in 1965, the Royal Oak public house in the early 1960s and the last shop in 1987.

The small 12th century church of St Giles, with a 14th century tower, is plain and simple inside but has atmosphere and feels well cared for. Note the brasses of the Mores (Morys) family, circa 1509 and the kneelers, all worked by village ladies in the early 1970s. The church registers from 1557 are now in the county archives at Reading but copies remain with the vicar. The churchyard is not now used for burials and a survey during the summer of 1989 identified over 75 different species of wild flowers and grasses. If seen in June or July it gives the impression of a pre-war meadow. From the south side of the churchyard there is a distant view of the Uffington White Horse.

Great Haseley 🦢

This lovely little village with its thatched cottages and many listed buildings, is situated south of the A329 which runs between Thame and Stadhampton. It nestles to the south of the ridge and is thus to some extent sheltered from the north winds. Houses on the south side of the village enjoy views of the Chilterns stretching from Chinnor to the Wittenham Clumps.

Roman coins have been dug up in the churchyard and it is thought that there was a settlement here from very early times. A document, now in the Bodleian Library, Oxford, shows that by AD 800 there was a church here, dedicated to St Peter, as it still is. Part of the font is thought to be Saxon. The village is mentioned in the Domesday Book and at that time belonged to Milo Crispin, who held it as a reward for his services to William the Conqueror.

At the Restoration of the Monarchy in 1660 there were two rectors living here, one of whom had retired in Cromwell's time because of disagreements over the services. In Charles II's reign he reappeared and tried to turn out the rector who had replaced him. At one service both rectors tried to preach at the same time; the congregation took sides and there was a great furore, hats and other objects being hurled about and fighting going on.

In the 1700s considerable building work took place in Haseley. Among the houses built were Highway Cottage, Long Row (the whole row cost £173 to build), Sundial House, Church Farm (note the windows blocked up when a window tax was imposed to help pay for the Napoleonic wars), the Crown Inn, now a private house, the Windmill and the middle part of Haseley Court.

During the 19th century the church fell into decay, but an appeal was launched to put it in order. None of the 180 different coats of arms were replaced but the Muirhead family, who lived at the Court, and who traced their ancestry back to Roger le Bigod, had their coat of arms (with Norman ships and shells) placed in a window of the south aisle. The Muirheads took their responsibilities as squires of the village very seriously and were liberal benefactors to the church.

In 1885 there was a disastrous fire in Haseley, when the village laundry at the bottom of Church Hill was destroyed. A spark from the chimney set fire to the thatched roof. Flames driven by a high wind set fire to the thatched roofs across the way and six cottages were soon alight. Some-

Haseley Windmill

one on horseback galloped the six miles to Thame to call the volunteer fire brigade. By the time the horse-drawn fire engine arrived and got water from a quarter of a mile away, all the cottages had been burned to the ground.

During the 19th century a carrier service was begun. On Wednesdays and Saturdays the carrier went to Oxford, departing at 9 am and reaching Oxford at midday, having stopped on the way to deliver and pick up parcels. He started back at 4 pm reaching Haseley between 8 and 9 pm. Transport consisted of a covered van with two horses, benches ran along the sides of the van and straw lay on the floor. Rugs were provided to cover the legs of passengers in cold weather. Candles were set in storm lanterns.

On Tuesdays there was a carrier service to Thame market town. Passengers had to endure an open cart with seats back to back along the middle. A large umbrella was provided for the passengers in wet weather.

Canon Ellison, the rector of Haseley, listed 19 activities going on in the village in 1883, including a drum and fife band, a night school, for which 2d a week was charged and a lending library.

Now, more than a hundred years later there is still an active village life, with a cricket team, football team, a mobile lending library and an active village hall committee which ensures that there is a varied programme of events, particularly during the winter months.

In 1988 and 1989 the village was united against a proposed new town to be called Stone Bassett. This would have been situated near the recreation ground. Together with the support of surrounding villages, and many from farther afield, fund raising events took place, and the planning application was finally rejected after a public enquiry.

There have been few changes in Great Haseley over the years as much of it is within a conservation area. There are many well sign-posted public footpaths and ramblers regularly walk the old footpaths to keep them open for future generations; the scenery and views of the Chilterns are breathtaking.

Great Tew

Visually the setting of Great Tew is its greatest asset – who could go wrong with such a sweep of hills and fold of valley? Loudon, who made the planting design, had an eye for a well placed tree and there is no doubt that the trees are the crowning glory. Such a range of species, shapes and colours to clothe the hills and soften the outlines, to settle in clumps and woodland, must have been giving pleasure for many years.

Our history is covered for about the last 900 years by the church; our wall paintings, tombstones and monuments are our link with past residents of the parish. The gardens round our church, along with the pub, remind us daily of our most famous resident and lord of the manor, Lord Falkland. He walked and talked here with his Oxford friends before being killed in the Civil War, torn between his duty to his king and an understanding of the rights of the citizen expressed by Parliament. A civilised man.

The children of our village learn in school what it was like to live in this village in the past – as a Roman farmer at the villa at Beaconsfield farm, as an Anglo-Saxon eating pigeon stew cooked over a fire in the study area, at a medieval banquet, a Tudor court, or seated in a hard wooden desk with a 'Victorian' teacher fixing you with a gimlet eye

119

telling you to be silent and speak only when you are spoken to!

We are always told not to live in the past – far too limiting – look always to the future, but how much easier to understand and appreciate the present and plan the future when we know what happened in the past. Experience is a great teacher.

Here in Great Tew we try to plan for the future. We are encouraging more children to come to our school, adults to study in our evening classes and to use our village shops. We invite visitors to explore the village – please use our new car park, it reduces the congestion – to come to our church and share our worship in such a beautiful place. Then, perhaps, enjoy the convivial atmosphere in our village pub named after our 'great man' and welcoming so many customers with good cheer.

Grove

Grove today is the largest village in the Vale of the White Horse, its vast sprawl of housing estates seemingly never-ending. From the sparsely populated hamlet shown on an early map in the 1700s it now looks set to burst its boundaries in the 2000s.

The village is recorded as far back as 1142 when King Stephen granted a manor here to the Abbot of Bermondsey, and two local watermills are recorded as early as 1622. During the 1770s the turnpike road (now the A338) was built as a more direct route between Wantage and Oxford, and this remains as Grove's eastern boundary.

At the beginning of the 1800s the Wilts and Berks Canal cut through the village bringing with it all the colourful characters associated with the canal trade. The Great Western Railway opened Wantage Road station in 1840, two miles from Wantage on the northern boundary of Grove. To connect this with the town, the Wantage Tramway Company in 1875 laid a single track alongside the turnpike road and provided England's first steam-powered passenger and goods service. This was hauled by a succession of engines, attaining fame through an ignoble defeat in a race through Grove between the tram and the local sweep's donkey cart, and notoriety through frequent and inconvenient derailments. On one occasion a spark from a passing engine set fire to the thatched roof of a cottage.

With the outbreak of the Second World War an airfield was built over the agricultural acres to the west of the village. In August 1944 a sextet from the Glenn Miller Band came to play at a dance in the camp ballroom.

By the beginning of the 1960s the airfield was no longer used. The canal had long fallen into disuse and the three mills on the Letcombe brook suffered the same fate. Buses and lorries now provided passenger and goods transport so the tramway rails were taken up and the road widened. Dr Beeching short-sightedly closed Wantage Road station, and many older houses were demolished to make way for the new; small farmers gave up farming and sold their land to builders – the age of the housing estates had begun!

Yet Grove tries to preserve its history. Visitors come and see where the airfield once was. Although it is now almost entirely covered with housing and a new business park, it is perpetuated in many local road names. And one may stand on the road bridge and look down at what was Wantage Road station, or go to Didcot and see *Shannon*, the last of the tramway engines which is displayed in the railway museum there. Walking through the fields it is possible to trace the line of the canal, and a small stretch of it is now being restored by local enthusiasts. Although a few houses from the 16th and 17th centuries remain, sadly there is now no evidence left of Grove's clockmaker, or wheelwright, or sawmill, forge and blacksmith, nor of the bakery or bacon factory, though one mill still stands and traces of the other two can be found.

Grove now has a modern parish church; three others on the same site fell down over the centuries. There is a Methodist chapel built in 1890 which now has extensions on either side of the original building, and a much older Strict Baptist chapel was completely rebuilt in the 1980s.

There are two village halls. The 1950s one became inadequate, and the 1980s one is of unusual but practical design – a good conversational gambit for those using it! Also in duplicate are the shopping centres, schools, doctors, dentists and sheltered accommodation for the elderly. Soon there will be two graveyards, the one at the church now being full up, future customers will have to be buried half a mile away. There also used to be two ghosts, but it would seem they have moved on due to lack of interest in them and pressures of everyday living – or haunting!

Traditions too have died. The famous Duck Races, part of the ancient village feast, were stopped in the 1950s by the RSPCA as a protest against cruelty to ducks. The May Day celebrations, revived after the Second World War, in which the whole village took part, are now observed only by schoolchildren as part of the school fete. The annual summer Horticultural Show survives with the scent of the summer produce tent intact, though its venue has changed from the common to the recreation ground: but lost are the nationwide Tug-of-War Teams Competition and the AA races. However, members of societies, sports clubs, church leaders, educationalists, and even the Parish Council, manage to preserve a community spirit among this huge and changing population.

Hailey 🌿

Standing as it does on the south-eastern edge of the old Wychwood Forest, the village of Hailey has always had strong connections with Witney, even sharing in medieval times the spoils of the annual Whitsuntide hunt. Like Caesar's Gaul, the village is divided into three parts: Delly End, Middletown and Poffley End. Delly End was once a wooded area with thickets. Poffley End, more quaintly, takes its name from 'poffle', a word in use in the 14th century to denote a small parcel of land, probably tapering to a point. Middletown links the two hamlets and all three lie in a clearing in the forest where hay was grown – a 'hay-lea' in fact.

Although of no historical importance, Hailey has lived on the edge of history: the reverberations of the Civil War must have shaken the village when several hundred Roundheads were imprisoned a mile away in Witney church.   Later John Wesley made frequent visits to the district and it is believed that Priest Hill Lane was named in his honour.

Some of the old Hailey houses have been restored. The manor house in Poffley End was built in the 15th century and has connections with the ancestors of the famous naturalist, Gilbert White of Selborne. Swanhall Farm dates in part from the 14th century and the old School House in Middletown had the date 1649 on one of its chimneys.

However, until comparatively recently life in an Oxfordshire village was neither easy nor affluent. People depended on local charities for winter blankets and extra rations. In despair, the vicar at the turn of the 20th century opened a reading room for men which he 'confidently expected' they would prefer to the tap-room. To judge by statistics in Kelly's Directory for 1907 he may well have been disappointed: the number of Hailey businesses then included three public houses and three beer retailers – all for a population of less than 1,000!

In those days villagers made their own entertainment. An annual fair was held and Club Day was a very special date with two brass bands, morning service and a splendid dinner in the loft of the Lamb and Flag.

122

Ascension Day was a red letter one and a school holiday. The children had sticks specially prepared, to which were tied bunches of flowers. In their best clothes and hats they gathered at Hailey manor to play games, run races and dance. After a picnic tea and armed with flowers and banners, the young people processed to church for the service. The next day all the flowers were taken to Oxford to the patients in the Radcliffe Infirmary.

What of today? Two world wars and improved communications have brought changes in their wake, mostly for the better. Instead of rising at 6 am and walking to work in the blanket mills, the people at Hailey had a wider choice of jobs and went out into the world. The 'hay-lea' is now a very pleasant mixed village, newer homes mingling with the old. There are all the ingredients which make a complete village – church, school, post office, public house and three shops. Best of all, there is enough council housing for young people to be able to stay in their own village and, eventually, to buy their own homes. Newcomers are made welcome and most of them enter happily into local affairs. The older activities have now ceased but an annual Peace Service still takes place round the memorial on Delly Green – erected after the First World War by Mrs Phipps, then living at Hailey manor.

The Hanneys 🦋

The Hanneys (East and West) are two of the 'island' villages of the Vale of the White Horse. One reminder of the fact that the Hanneys were once an island is that the footpath that connects the two villages is a raised causeway, because until recent years the road soon flooded in the winter months.

The parish church of St James the Great stands in West Hanney on an ancient Saxon site. The church contains two stone Saxon coffins. The present building dates back to Norman times (1160), and over the years there have been many additions and alterations. On the north wall of the church, near the font, is a commemorative tablet to Elizabeth Bowles, said to have died in 1718 at the age of 124 (the longest recorded life span of an Englishwoman). There is a collection of brasses, commemorating 30 people altogether. One of the brasses commemorates the Ayshcombe family, who had ten sons and four daughters.

In East Hanney is Hanney Mission, an evangelical chapel dating back to 1862, when it was erected by the 'Frilford and Longworth Home

Mission'. The Mission closed down for a time between the wars and was almost sold to the British Legion as a clubhouse. The price was agreed, the plans for alteration were drawn up, but the sale did not go through. The Mission was reopened as a place of worship about 1943.

Letcombe brook meanders through East and West Hanney, providing the power for two (now unused) mills, locally known as the 'Upper' and the 'Lower' mills. Earlier in the 20th century, the Upper Mill (correctly known as Dandridge's Mill) supplied flour to Boffin's Bakery in Headington. The horses left Hanney at 8.30 am, and did not return until 7.00 pm. The flour milling died out in 1920. At the 'Lower' mill, near Philberd's Manor, prisoners of the Napoleonic wars carried out silk weaving. There is a public footpath along the brook here, and in the spring it is particularly beautiful, with daffodils growing by the mill.

At the turn of the 20th century there were a number of shops and farms in the two villages. There were carpenters, blacksmiths, thatchers, a midwife, a harness maker, a baker, a coal merchant, a wheelwright, two carriers and an undertaker. The post office in East Hanney was kept by two sisters, one of whom delivered letters up the street and the other down! Hanney even boasted a rat catcher, whose sister-in-law was the village midwife who delivered babies for a fee of 7s 6d.

The last village shop in East and West Hanney closed a few years ago, but on a site next to the village hall is a thriving community shop and post office. The community shop is run completely by volunteers and is open every day, except Sunday. It carries a variety of goods including delicious pork supplied by a village pig farmer, and bread from a local bakery.

In 1916, there was a Missionary Pageant five miles away at Betterton, near Ardington. Children from local village schools were invited to attend and asked to wear costumes from other lands. Mr Edwards, the well-respected headmaster of the Hanney school, hired some Red Indian head-dresses and leggings and purchased some greasepaint. The children were taken to Betterton in a flour waggon from Dandridge's Mill, pulled by two horses. The children enjoyed the pageant and at the end of the event, they sang 'God is working His purpose out', and then piled into the waggon for the return journey. On the way home a storm broke, the greasepaint smeared, and the dye from the leggings ran down the children's legs. There must have been some hard scrubbing in Hanney that night as apparently the dye was very difficult to remove.

There is an excellent village hall, which has recently been extended. Many people in East and West Hanney have worked hard over the years to raise funds and care for the hall, which is the home of many clubs and societies.

Most of the organisations using the village hall are prefixed by the name 'Hanney', showing a unity between the two villages, which has not always been there. There used to be, on occasion, some intense rivalry between the children of the two villages. One year, the single field that separates East and West Hanney was planted with turnips, and after school (and after some arguing) the older schoolboys got into the turnip field, uprooted a lot and threw them at each other. In the morning there were turnips all over the road. The police were called but, of course, nobody had seen anything. Today, the two villages live in harmony with each other, and there have been no turnips thrown in anger for many a year!

Harwell ❧

It is impossible in Harwell to ignore its historic beginnings. The old Cherry Barn with its thatched garden wall was, in 1200, part of Middle Farm, known then as Bayllol's Manor. Walk down Townsend and on your right is Bishop's Manor – once the grange of the Bishop of Winchester, with records dating back to 1209. Again, go down King's Lane bearing right at the bottom. Head for the tower of the 13th century church of St Matthew and on your left is Prince's Manor, awarded by William the Conqueror to Robert D'Oily – renamed Prince's Manor by the Black Prince.

Down the High Street is Adnams Farmhouse, which survived the Great Fire of 1852. In its farmyard, it is believed, a discharged labourer set fire to a hay rick, and left most of the houses down as far as the Crown public house and Allen's Farm in smoking ruins.

On the next street corner is Jennings Lane – he was a successful yeoman and is commemorated with his wife and their twelve children by a brass memorial in the church. Across the High Street from this corner is Gaveston Road, named after Piers of that name, Duke of Cornwall, and lord of the Upper Manor (Prince's) 1308–12. His coat of arms can be seen in the church's east window. He was executed by the barons during their disputes with King John prior to the signing of the Magna Carta.

Walking up Gaveston Road, first on your right is Loder Road. Robert Loder was tenant at Prince's Manor, paying rent to Queen Mary Tudor. He was able to purchase the property, leaving it to his son, Robert. Loder

Road now gives access to a modern housing estate, tucked away and discreetly infilling the land behind the houses and the back of the Crown pub. The developer planned to build houses right down to the A34 but Harwell voted unanimously against that threat to its ancient boundaries.

In 1985, at a Millennium Pageant, various village groups 'put on' the different historical events of 1,000 years: Ethelred the Unready's signing of the Royal Charter, the ten freemen, the Bishop of Winchester's Feast still commemorated each year, the levy of archers for the Black Prince's French Wars, the wedding of a yeoman's son to a daughter of the manor, a 17th century horse fair, the Cherry Teas of the 1760s and the Great Fire of 1852, with Harwell's entry into the 20th century providing a climax.

What a climax! A march past represented two world wars with a boy bugler on the church tower playing the Last Post, while others in white coats ushered in the atomic age of Harwell's Atomic Energy Research Establishment and the Rutherford Laboratory, and the nearby JET Project at Culham.

That Millennium Pageant not only brought all groups together, the old timers and the newcomers, the scientific establishments, the fruitgrowers, the farmers, the retired, the workers and the schoolchildren, but demonstrated how Harwell village and its people had developed from that historical foundation.

Stand on high ground and you can see all of Harwell lying below you, the curve of the orchards stretching down and past the A34, nearly all under Grove Farm management now. Some of the famous cherry trees still belong to the Lay family of Bishop's Manor. The 'Golden Mile' of the ancient highway, so named because so many important personages travelled past the village along old travel routes such as Icknield Way, Portway, or the Ridgeway Path, is now only a collection of names on the ramblers' maps. There is a new kind of Golden Mile now and Harwell's scientific research centres attract experts from all over the world.

Hatford ❧

Hatford is a small parish of some 1,000 acres lying within the Vale of the White Horse. It was formerly part of Berkshire before the reorganisation of the county boundaries in 1974.

Its history goes back long before the Norman period. The earliest evidence of occupation so far is a bronze spearhead found near the river Hat, dating back to the Bronze Age. Signs of an early Iron Age settlement

126

have also been found and there is thought to have been at least one Roman villa in the fields adjoining the present village. The manor of Hatford has changed hands many times since 1086, when the Domesday survey recorded that it was held by Payn under Gilbert de Bretevile.

Hatford was in the public eye in 1628, when the second recorded meteor to fall in the country landed in the vicinity at Bawlkin Green. It also featured in the Civil War, when the church register records the burials in 1634 of two soldiers killed in action. Hatford has also appeared in literature, since the Wiltshire thresher turned poet, Stephen Duck, who worked here in the early 19th century, commemorated life on a Hatford farm in one of his last poems.

Perhaps the most striking feature of Hatford is that it has two churches, although one is now a private residence. St George's stands on the site of the Saxon church mentioned in Domesday. It is basically Early English with a Norman south doorway to nave and chancel arch and a Norman font and one Saxon window still visible. There is a sundial carved in the stone near the doorway. One tomb in the church is believed by some to be that of Sir Robert de Hatford, reputed founder of the church and lord of the manor in the reign of Henry III, while others think it is that of Thomas Chaucer, son of Geoffrey, the author of the *Canterbury Tales*. Thomas held the manor in the later 14th century and became Speaker of the House of Commons in 1414. But whose body actually lies inside the tomb still remains a mystery.

The church also houses a mausoleum containing the remains of Rev Samuel Paynter, a former rector of the parish, and his wife and daughter. When St George's fell into disrepair, it was Samuel Paynter who had Hatford's second church, Holy Trinity, erected in 1873–4 at a cost of around £4,000. It was built in the Early English style and is particularly notable for some fine, random-coursed stonework. After serving the village for almost a century. Holy Trinity itself became dilapidated and was finally sold in 1972 for use as a private dwelling. St George's was reopened in the same year, reroofed in 1973 and reglazed in 1974 to once again assume its role as the place of worship for the village.

Apart from the two churches, there are some interesting secular buildings. Hatford manor house, adjacent to St George's church, has an 18th century frontage, but parts of the house are much older, dating from the 15th century and possibly even earlier. It stands in a commanding position at the approach to the village and enjoys an uninterrupted view of the distant Berkshire Downs and the famous White Horse. On the other side of St George's stands the rectory. The present building was put up in 1869, slightly behind the site where the previous 300 year old rectory stood. Next to the rectory and fronting the road through the village is Hatford Cottage, which was converted into a delightful single dwelling from a row of very early cottages, originally occupied by the workmen involved in building the manor house. The little green in front of the entrance to the church was where Hatford Feast used to be held until well on into the 20th century. This always took place on the Monday following the 13th of August and several old photographs show the villagers enjoying the roundabouts, swingboats and other fairground attractions.

Despite its long history, the population has not changed much in size since the time of the Domesday survey, when it had some 120 residents. Being so small, there are virtually no amenities, but the Community Bus Service from Stanford-in-the-Vale does provide a means of transport into the nearby market towns of Faringdon and Wantage on certain days of the week. There is no shop in the village and no pub, although there was an off-licence, until this received a direct hit from a German bomb in September 1940. One Hatford girl was killed and, ironically enough, two little boys from London, who had been sent to stay with their grandparents, in order to get away from the Blitz! Behind the site, now occupied by the aptly named Phoenix House, is a bakehouse, which has its shop in Faringdon but still supplies the villagers with bread and cakes to order.

Because Hatford lies mainly on sandstone soil, it is a rich source of sand and gravel. Sand has been extracted here for many years and it was during sand digging between 1937 and 1958 that an early Iron Age settlement was discovered. When the sand ran out in 1958 on that particular site, another pit was opened on the other side of the appropriately named Sandy Lane.

Agriculture features very much in Hatford and has probably done so since Neolithic times. There are ample springs of good clear water, even in times of drought, and the soil is rich. Hatford was one of the earliest places in the country to be enclosed, supposedly in 1577. The land is now farmed by one man, assisted by just three farm workers. Instead of a landscape divided up into strips or small fields, there are vast rolling plains, somewhat reminiscent of the prairies of the American Mid West.

Apart from a few relatively modern houses and bungalows, the basic layout of the village has changed little over the centuries. To walk through Hatford is, indeed, to walk back through time!

Headington Quarry 🌿

Headington Quarry village is situated on the north-eastern outskirts of Oxford city. Its name originated from the stone that was quarried there. It is now a suburb of neighbouring Headington and no longer a village in its own right, though it still keeps its individuality. One of Quarry's assets is its close proximity to Shotover. Until the advent of the eastern bypass, footpaths led directly to Shotover Plain.

Visitors can easily lose themselves among the steep, winding, narrow roads and the network of walled paths and alleyways that run behind houses and between streets. The alleys are still very much as they were in days past and it is only in recent years that they have been given names, most of them after well known Quarry people such as Coppock's Alley, Vallis Alley, Cox's Alley and Mason's Alley.

Years ago stone was quarried here and transported to nearby Oxford to be used in building the colleges for the University. The whole village, according to records, is built on a vast rabbit warren of old quarries and tip heaps. The survival of these quarries in a residential area is of great archaeological interest. Nowadays the village is a mixture of small stone cottages and modern brick houses.

Quarry boasts three public houses, the Mason's Arms, the Six Bells and the Chequers. In the 18th and 19th centuries the Chequers was the centre of the village. The first school was started in a room next to the Chequers by Catherine Mather. Later in 1864 the present school buildings were opened by Bishop Wilberforce. The school of course has been greatly improved over the years and it still teaches infants and primary children from Quarry and the surrounding neighbourhoods.

Quarry has two places of worship, a Methodist chapel and Holy Trinity church. The church was built in 1848–9. It is in the style of a 14th century church, which deceives many visitors into thinking it is much older than it is. The stone for the church was quarried from a nearby farm and was the gift of Mr Thomas Burrows, a churchwarden of St Andrew's church, Old Headington. C. S. Lewis, the famous author and his brother are buried in the churchyard.

The Methodist chapel was started when the teachings of John Wesley were felt in Quarry and a few men got together in a house near the Six Bells for prayers. For some years they continued to meet at the house but on Easter Sunday 1830 the first chapel was opened in Trinity Road. In 1860 a new and much larger chapel was built in High Street.

The village hall was not built until 1933. In 1900 a pavilion was erected by voluntary labour on land adjoining the Quarry Road. At that time this became the centre for all village activities, but as it fell in disrepair the need for a new hall was discussed and some land adjoining the recreation ground was purchased. In 1929 Oxford City extended its boundaries and took in Quarry village, and a new road linking Quarry Road and Windmill Road interfered with the site. After three years of negotiations, in 1932 on a new site in Quarry Road the Mayor of Oxford, Alderman Bennett laid the foundation stone and in 1933 the new hall was opened by a local MP, Sir Gifford Fox.

Morris dancing has been associated with Quarry for hundreds of years. Several dances originated in this area including many well known favourites. Tunes were handed down from fiddler to fiddler and the steps and figures to each younger generation. They were never written down until Mr William Kimber, with the help of Cecil Sharp, set about recording them. Nowadays the Morris dancers dance outside each public house on Boxing Day and at Whitsun.

Sadly the shops have all gradually closed and the post office is housed in a supermarket in Gladstone Road. The village bakery closed its doors in 1989.

The Friends of Quarry was formed in 1970 and has done much to keep Quarry as an exceptional place of interest. In 1971 Oxford City declared it a conservation area. This has helped to keep the stone walls and the narrow pathways intact for future generations and above all to retain the village atmosphere.

Hethe 🪶

On the west side of the little stream which runs through this village the ground rises steeply to form an upland ridge. This English settlers named Hethe, ie a high place, and the first dwellings were built alongside the stream. In the 15th century a family built a house on the high ground and slowly this became the main part of the village as it is today.

Like all villages, Hethe has suffered from the removal of industry to factories in the towns. The census of 1851, besides listing 50 agricultural workers, names 20 house servants, eight grooms, two coachmen, four carpenters, four tailors, four laundresses, three bakers, three dress-makers, three masons, two brewers, two sawyers, a pig dealer, a cooper, a glazier, and a straw bonnet maker. Hethe is still famous for its builders,

130

decorators and carpenter, plumbers, florist, welder, and antiques restorer, but with the disappearance of other trades, and the halving of the agricultural workers through mechanisation of farms, the village has steadily declined.

After the Second World War the decline was reversed by the building of 34 council houses down Hardwick Road. However, the village still lost its school, its grocery/general store and its Methodist chapel, and of the two public houses, only one remains.

Besides the delightful views afforded by the hills on either side of the brook, there are several attractive buildings round the village centre. There is the Manor Farm, Hethe House (the old dower house), the rectory, and a delightful selection of thatched cottages, including the round house, the newer part of which dates from 1752.

Hethe's community spirit goes back a very long way. It is something for a small village to maintain two independent but friendly churches: Church of England in the centre of the village and the Roman Catholic church on the edge in the Hardwick Road.

Shellswell Park estate makes up part of the parish, though sadly the magnificent Shellswell House became derelict and was demolished in the early 1980s. Since then freak high winds have destroyed hundreds of the fine trees on the estate.

A village character was Miss Catherine Palmer, who died in March 1989 aged 90 years and was then the oldest resident. Her father was a tailor and had only one leg. She stayed at home and helped him with his business, and used to cycle to Finmere station to collect cloth off the train. She lived in the same house for over 80 years and it had hardly changed since the day her parents moved in.

In 1948 the then local squire, John Dewer Harrison, who had high regard for the village folk, gave the ground floor of the dower house, Hethe House, to the village to use as a meeting place. This was used regularly until it was sold in 1986, with half the proceeds going towards building a new village hall, opened in May 1987.

Heythrop ✒️

Heythrop is a windswept village high up to the north-east above Chipping Norton. It is at its best in early February when the verges which border the village street are carpeted with snowdrops, or on a warm still July afternoon when the lime trees are in full flower and the only sound is of a distant lawnmower. The chances are that walking along the street you will meet nothing apart from an occasional tractor, for Heythrop is still, as it has always been, off the beaten track and its inhabitants are few. Rarely has its population, even with the people from the surrounding farms, reached 200 persons.

The village mentioned in the Domesday survey has left few traces today apart from the chancel of the old church, into the arch of which has been rebuilt the Norman doorway of the nave pulled down in the 19th century, and faint indications of the ridge and furrow cultivation of an earlier age traceable when the light is favourable. Substantially it is still the model village built in 1873 by Albert Brassey. His estate, centred on Heythrop Hall, was the wedding gift of Thomas Brassey the millionaire railway contractor, to his third son. As in other Oxfordshire villages wealth made in industry in one generation contributed to agricultural development in the next.

Before 1873 the village seems to have consisted of one or two cottages at most, a farmhouse and the church, and had been described as decayed or depopulated at intervals since the 14th century. Heythrop Hall, built in the early 18th century by the 12th earl of Shrewsbury, was one of the great houses of the county with its park laid out to the south-east in the Italian manner, but when the earldom passed to a Catholic branch of the Talbot family the owner of the house withdrew from public life and the village languished. Finally after a disastrous fire in 1831 the house was abandoned as an empty shell.

Although the golden age of English farming was already coming to an end, Albert was able with the resources inherited from his father to set out to rebuild the interior of Heythrop Hall, to restore the gardens and great stands of trees stretching down to the Banbury road, and to build his model village. There was no shop lest it should tempt the women to stand and gossip and no inn for fear of drunkenness, but the houses, constructed with stone from the local quarry, were furnished with the latest conveniences of the time – damp courses, underground water storage tanks, fed from the gutters, and outside closets with nightsoil tanks vented with soil pipes. The houses were surrounded with ample gardens and shelter belts of trees were planted to protect them from the north and east winds. The new church, built just inside the park, was sited to be the focus of the village. It was constructed to the design of A. W. Blomfield on a massive scale, with stone from the nave of the old church and from the Catholic chapel in the grounds of the Hall, in the popular Victorian Gothic style. Behind it a rectory of equally generous proportions replaced the old farmhouse. A school with an attached schoolhouse and a new lodge completed the building.

From the Hall the Brasseys overlooked village affairs. Mrs Brassey took a special interest in the cultivation of the village gardens, the best efforts being rewarded with the prize of a sovereign, quite a sum when wages were low. Forty indoor staff were needed to run the Hall and the park and gardens employed the services of a large force of gardeners, woodmen and gamekeepers. Many of these people must have come from Heythrop, others being recruited from villages around. Entertaining at the Hall was on a grand scale – one local farmer tells of a thousand guests expected in 1876 for a dinner to mark the first public meet of the Heythrop Hunt. Hunting took up a good deal of Albert Brassey's time after he took over the Duke of Beaufort's North Oxfordshire pack of hounds in 1873. He also played a prominent part in local affairs, sitting on the local bench and board of guardians, serving as president of the Oxfordshire County Agricultural Show and becoming mayor of Chipping Norton. A caring employer, he was in the last years of his life supporting the scheme for a memorial hospital there.

With his death in 1918 the economic foundation of all these activities collapsed. The Hall had to be sold to meet death duties, was eventually taken over by the Society of Jesus as a seminary and in 1969 was bought by the National Westminster Bank for a Management Development College. The link with the Hall broken, the village changed its character as the 20th century brought mechanisation to farming and decreased the demand for labourers. As in many Oxfordshire villages today a number of the houses are second homes or have been bought by retired people; the school has gone and the rectory is a private house.

Holton ❦

Holton is a small parish, little more than a hamlet, situated five miles east of Oxford. It was mentioned as far back as 1086 in the Domesday records, when it was known as Eltone. The area was inhabited by the Romans, but it was the Anglo-Saxons who gave the village its name. The population has fluctuated over the years and in 1987 there were 425 resident in the parish, as well as 300 students living at the Oxford Polytechnic.

There has been a castle or manor house in Holton Park since medieval times. The original was surrounded by a moat which was hand-dug, involving the removal of 24,000 cubic yards of rock. The present house was built in 1808 probably using stone from the original, but situated in the grounds and not on the moated island. The Biscoe family built the present house and it remained in the family until 1910 when it was sold and the estate broken up. The manorial rights had by now lapsed and in 1948 the house became a girls grammar school.

During the Second World War an American field hospital was built in the park. It was later taken over by the RAMC as a hospital for head injuries. It closed in 1961 and some of the wards were converted into classrooms for what is now Wheatley Park school and the rest were demolished. The 18th century stables have also been converted into classrooms.

To the right of the school entrance is the headquarters of the Oxford-shire Library and near to this is the John Watson school for mentally handicapped children. This school is very progressive, having integrated some of its children with the primary school in nearby Wheatley and also at the Wheatley Park Comprehensive School.

In 1985 a sports hall was built on the school campus by South Oxfordshire District Council which is for school use during school hours and is open to the public at all other times. The Park also accommodates the campus of the Lady Spencer Churchill College. The teacher training college which opened in 1966 is now part of the Oxford Polytechnic.

Holton church is dedicated to St Bartholomew and dates from the 12th century. The chancel was rebuilt in the 13th and 14th centuries. The whole church was extensively restored in the 19th century, the western gallery being enlarged and the stairs moved from the inside to the outside of the tower. The first organ was built in 1860, until then the music was provided by an orchestra consisting of a fiddle, a cello and a clarinet.

There are three bells including one medieval example and one made in 1662.

Holton has its fair share of ghost stories. The ghost of a lady is said to walk through the park and down to the village hall. She was apparently a nanny who worked at the manor house and who dropped the baby she was looking after down the stairs, killing it. She appears in the early morning and late at night and has been seen by many people.

A few years ago two headstones from the graves of dogs were discovered on the island in the park by workmen. Pets' graves were quite common in Victorian times. This discovery probably led to the stories of headless dogs roaming the island.

The other story is of a young boy dressed in dark blue velvet with a wide lace collar who owned the manor house. He was looked after by an uncle. The boy's governess fell in love with the guardian and killed the boy, hoping to marry the guardian and get the estate. They buried him in the garden south of the moat. Years later a new house was built over the grave. When the Biscoe family lived in the house a guest was standing at the foot of the stairs one evening at about 10 pm and saw a boy run towards him, but as he went to grasp him he disappeared. The boy was also seen on the stairs and in the billiard room. It is believed he still haunts the house.

Holton today tries hard to produce a village community atmosphere. The three farms in the village, Old Park Farm, Pond Farm and Warren Farm are still being worked, but a fairly high proportion of the inhabitants are commuters. A new village hall was built in 1975 after a great deal of community effort to raise the funds. It has a licensed bar for functions and opens every Friday evening for the use of the villagers. However, there is no longer a village store or post office and the younger children have to go out of the village to school. The Old School House and Old Post Office are now residential properties.

Horspath ✍

Nestling on the slopes of Shotover one mile outside the Oxford City boundary, Horspath is proud to remain a village. The parish boundary, along the Roman road, encloses Bullingdon Green, where gentlemen used to sport and Civil War battles were fought.

Shotover was once one of England's smaller Royal forests, and is now a conservation area and country park. The old bridle-path joining the London Road through Wheatley gave the Anglo-Saxon name Horsepadan, which became Horsepath, but in 1912 the parish council reverted to the unique form, Horspath. Medieval evidence suggests two distinct hamlets, Upper or Old Horspath and Nether, Lower or Church Horspath.

Three Oxford Colleges, Corpus Christi, Magdalen and Brasenose have owned land and property in the parish. A connection with Queen's College comes from the 15th century when student John Copcot, walking in Shotover Forest reading his Aristotle, was attacked by a wild boar. He thrust the volume down the animal's throat and 'the boar expired'. The college ceremony of carrying in the Boar's Head at Christmas resulted from this, as did the stained glass window in St Giles' church, presented in 1740 by the President of Magdalen to commemorate the Copcot Legend.

In the 19th and early 20th centuries laundresses stretched their lines across the green and market gardeners tended their vegetables for Pembroke College. Farmers also reared pigs for the college tables. In the census of 1871, showing a population of 373, 93 were employed on the land, 14 were craftsmen and there were 30 other trades, a curate and two publicans. There were 12 farmers in 1841 and only two in 1990, but the village still has its two publicans.

Horspath is not a pretty village, but it has character. It boasts 15 listed buildings including farm outbuildings and a cowhouse, the manor house, the church, and two thatched cottages, of which there were once 17, but fire has destroyed most. In 1936 the Queen's Head public house caught fire and sparks from the thatch destroyed two cottages opposite. The pub was restored with a tiled roof, as was Shepherd's Cottage, this thatch being burnt in the mid 1970s. The Chequers Inn, although dated 1624, was built in the 19th century.

The manor house, part dating back to 1513 and with a Tudor staircase, is mainly 17th century with a 19th century addition. Its ghost, 'The Grey Lady', is reputed to wander the landings and garden. Killed by her husband in a quarrel, her body was placed in a priest's hole. Several sightings have been reported and in December 1878 a first-class shot claimed he had fired three times at the figure, and found two bullets embedded in the wall. The present owner has done much to refurbish and restore the manor to its former glory.

The church of St Giles, dating from the 12th century, is dedicated to the patron saint of beggars and cripples, whose ceramic statuette, made by a local potter in 1988, may be found in the south chapel. The church is the proud possessor of an Elizabethan silver chalice, a pre-1740 faceless blacksmith clock, a carved late Jacobean pulpit, six tuneful bells, medieval stained glass windows and interesting memorial plaques. One of these to James Salisbury of Bullingdon Green, who died in 1770, is elaborately decorated. Another is to the five children of Thomas and Esther Herbert, who died from a recurrence of the plague between 1686 and 1688. Esther, whose family founded New College, died also in 1688 aged 33.

In the early 20th century there was much change with tarmac roads, housing developments and mobile homes replacing farmland and manor grounds, the loss of the elms, the village pond and the railway. The population is now approximately 1,500, and includes people from all walks of life including those employed at Rover car works.

Iffley ✤

Iffley's undoubted jewel is her famous Norman church of St Mary with its richly carved doorways, magnificent tower and tower arches. It stands on the brow of a hill overlooking the river, close to the mainly 16th century rectory, with parts dating back to the 1300s.

The large chestnut tree by the church gate is a magnificent sight when in bloom. The glebe field, in this part of the village, together with several stone cottages and the old village school, presents an attractive and unspoiled corner.

Iffley was mentioned as early as AD 941 in the Chronicles of Abingdon and in the Domesday Book in 1086 and its name is derived from the Saxon word 'Giftelege', which means the field of gifts.

At one time, the greater part of the population was employed in agriculture and there were several farms in the village, but these no longer exist. After 1946 at least 53% of the village population were on mechanical work with no farm workers, tilers or building labourers. Many sons followed their fathers into mechanical jobs, but today there is a great variety of occupations including the professions, with a fair number of retired people.

The river and lock are great attractions to Iffley visitors who often walk along the tow-path from Oxford and pause to see the keeper operating the lock and to admire his colourful garden.

The college eights start from just above this point for their Torpids and Eights Week races.

At one time there was a toll which was paid to Lincoln College to cross the bridge to the lock but this was discontinued in the mid 1950s. There was a tradition that if ever a corpse was carried through the toll it would be broken for ever and when an attempt was made to do this the toll keeper refused to let the party through and the corpse had to be taken across the water by ferry.

The old mill, featured in many old pictures of Iffley, stood nearby but, sadly, was burned down in 1908 and all that remains are two grindstones outside Grist Cottage and an inscription on a piece of wall.

The fields near Iffley lock were once rich in spring with purple fritillaries. They still bloom there, though in less profusion, and are now guarded by public-minded citizens when in flower.

The village has its fair share of ghosts and apparitions. The figure of a stately abbess has been known to appear in the old churchyard and the Rev Clarendon on his last night in the rectory heard a procession of monks as they passed through the corridors – a fitting tribute to the incumbent who had spent the longest spell of duty in the parish. Late one night in 1947 many residents were disturbed by the sound of a wooden-legged visitant clanking chains and stomping its way down Tree Lane!

Court Place, where the old manor courts were held, has housed many occupants. Admiral Nowell lived here for many years, and his widow, Mrs Sarah Nowell, made provision for the Sarah Nowell School where charity scholars were taught between 1822/54.

The *Warsaw Concerto* was written at Court House by Richard Addinsell who was the guest of John Bryson, after his London flat had been bombed. The last owner of Court House, before it was sold to the University, was Sir Alan Gardiner, the Egyptologist, who was a member of the team when Tutankhamen's tomb was discovered.

Iffley has two pubs, the Tree and the Prince of Wales, and the Priory Hotel, formerly the Elms. The village still has its shop and post office which, under the genial care of Hilda and Cyril, provides personal service and a welcome social focus to those fortunate enough to live in Iffley.

Ipsden 🌿

Ipsden lies in South Oxfordshire, a part of the county surrounded by a deep bend in the river Thames. It is in the foothills of the Chilterns, and is really a collection of scattered hamlets, rather than a village.

Its 13th century church stands on one of the approach roads to the village, and despite the ravages of the years, still has examples of early wall paintings within, and a very attractive brick and flint exterior.

'The Street' could be described as the centre of the village, running from the post office and stores at one end, past the Old Post House and Old Vicarage, down to Ipsden Farm with its huge tithe barn, onto the A4074 Reading road.

The Church of England Aided village school had been in existence for over 100 years, but finally closed its doors in July 1989, due to a continued decline in numbers.

Ipsden has had its share of characters and ghosts – only to be expected with a history which pre-dates Roman settlements in the area. Some of these have their names intertwined with village life, such as Janet Lindsey, a former postmistress whose name lives on in Janet's Grove, while Ben Remnant, killed in action, gives his name to Ben's Cottages at Newtown.

Stones and monuments abound. Two stones in the hedgerow opposite the school commemorate two farm workers killed by lightning while sheltering. There is also a mini-Stonehenge – a comparatively recent innovation by a member of the Reade family generations ago, and also a monument at the Mere (almost opposite the tithe barn) which was erected on the spot where the ghost of John Reade (d1827) was seen coming to tell his mother of his death in India.

Modern innovations have always been slow to take hold in Ipsden. Electricity did not arrive until 1954, and apart from a few modern houses, the village appears much the same now as it did then.

Islip 🐾

Islip is a 'working' village, where there are farms, two shops, two pubs and, above all, a good number of inhabitants who take part in helping to make the village live, not just a place to have a dwelling. The river Ray is a great attraction. In the Domesday Book, Islip was Githslepe, a muddy crossing, so the river was always important.

The pre-Conquest kings hunted in Oxfordshire, and had several hunting boxes in the area. In one of these, at Islip, Edward the Confessor was born, c1003. His will states, 'I have given to Christ and to St Peter in Westminster the little town of Islippe wherein I was born with all the things that belong thereto.'

Abbot John's heraldic device at Islip

So began the enduring connection of Islip with Westminster Abbey. The living is in the gift of Westminster, and the farmland is all owned by the Abbey. In 1464 a boy was born in Islip who attended Westminster School and became Abbot John of Westminster, also known as Abbot Islip. He built the little Islip Chapel in the Abbey, and his rebus, or heraldic device, was a little man and an eye, slipping down a tree. There is a version of this on a banner in Islip church.

In 1678, Robert South became rector of Islip. He was a great scholar, but never reached high office at Westminster because of his controversial views. He built a fine rectory, with a lovely tithe barn attached to it, but his greatest benefit to Islip was the school which he built and endowed in 1710, with a house for the master. The school flourishes in modern buildings, and Dr South's School and the village still benefit from the provisions of his will. One of the happy traditions at the school is the crowning of a May Queen, elected by the children. The school's present to the queen is always a silver thimble.

The school is part of the life blood of the village. There are interesting records in its log books. In the early 1920s, Robert Graves and his wife, who preferred to be called Nancy Nicholson, lived in a cottage 'over the

140

bridge' called World's End. He played football for Islip and for a short time served on the Parish Council. Their daughter, Jenny, was a pupil at Dr South's, and for the 18th November 1925, the log book entry reads 'Head out of school for 15 minutes this afternoon, seeing Mr R. Graves, who objects to his daughter Jenny being called by his surname, and desires that she be known as Jenny Nicholson – her name has now been altered on the register by me.'

The most famous Victorian rector was Dean Buckland, Dean of Westminster, Canon of Christ Church, Oxford, and University Reader in Mineralogy. He spent much of his time at Christ Church, but lived in Islip during the summer months, and is buried in Islip because it was his wish to be buried in rocky ground. There are many stories of his insistence on tasting everything; the *Daily Telegraph* of 24th November 1962, has a letter from Viscount Harcourt with what is likely to be the true version of Buckland swallowing the heart of Louis XIV of France. He had dined at Nuneham and was shown a locket which contained what resembled pumice stone. He maintained that he could identify any mineral from its taste, popped it into his mouth and swallowed it by accident. It was the heart of Louis XIV which had been brought to Nuneham by one of the family.

Monks' Cottage is thought to have been lived in by the monks who prayed for Edward the Confessor's soul in a chantry chapel which stood till about 1760 on the site of the Red Lion yard. Not described by name, but by symbol, was a cottage which in the 1930s had antlers over the front door, and its present owner says that numbers are still discernible on its bedroom doors. The antlers were a sign recognisable to some!

Kelmscott ❧

The small, remote village of Kelmscott is the epitome of rural, agricultural England. It remains undeveloped, un-suburbanised and unspoilt for two reasons. First, it is at the end of a non-through road which peters out into the tow-path by the Thames. Secondly, in the main, it is in three self-perpetuating ownerships: the Church Commissioners, the National Trust and the Society of Antiquaries of London. The latter results in most unusual and remarkable social and economic circumstances. The total population numbering just under a hundred is accommodated in no more than 32 dwellings of which only ten are owner-occupied. The rest are tied, yet of these 22 five are large 'gentlemen's' houses, two being owned by the National Trust, one by the Society and two by the Church Commissioners, three of them appertaining to the surrounding farm lands. Thus where a preponderance of residential accommodation is rented, affluence is conspicuous by its absence and where almost all the land is in institutional hands and so to all intents and purposes inalienable, little is readily available for development.

The older buildings are of stone and so to say in the Cotswold style for Kelmscott lies at the south-eastern extremity of the Cotswolds. But this setting is totally at variance with the landscape of small hills, valleys and woodlands stretching away to the north-west. Here the country is totally flat as far as the eye can see and more or less devoid of woods and copses. It has nonetheless great character and charm, even if an acquired taste, with the great unbroken dome of heaven above.

The oldest building in the village is the parish church of St George, begun in the late 12th century. It was enlarged thrice thereafter before about 1550 since when it has remained virtually unaltered. William Morris, the famous poet, artist and craftsman, who lived in Kelmscott Manor nearby made sure that the late 19th century restoration of it was done with care and discrimination with the result that its medieval character was not spoiled. So it stands today, redolent of the Middle Ages. Morris himself was buried in the churchyard in 1896 under a gravestone designed by his old friend and associate Philip Webb, the famous late Victorian architect.

The second oldest building, the aforesaid Manor, Morris's home from 1871 to 1896, was finished in 1571. In about 1670 an elegant wing was added. Since then, again like the church, it has remained virtually unaltered. It is open to the public on the first Wednesdays of the months May to September and is well worth a visit. It contains many works of Morris himself and his circle, Rossetti, Burne-Jones, Ford Madox Brown and Philip Webb. The four other large houses in the village are of the 17th and 18th centuries.

The village hall is interesting for it was built to the designs of Ernest Gimson, though after his death. Gimson was perhaps the prime exponent of the Arts and Crafts Movement in architecture and furniture in England. Here everything is hand-crafted and of high quality. Again the style is the vernacular style of the region. The hall was opened in 1934 by George Bernard Shaw, and Ramsay MacDonald was present. The funds for the building were raised almost wholly by May Morris, daughter of William Morris, then living in the Manor. She incidentally founded the Kelmscott branch of the Women's Institute, one of the earliest.

142

Two other buildings in the village are of historical and architectural distinction: the Memorial Cottages and the Gimson Cottages (nos 3 and 4 Manor Cottages); each, though single and free-standing, contains two tenements. Both were paid for by the Morris family, the former by Jane Morris widow of William Morris in 1902 in memory of her husband, the latter by May Morris their daughter in 1915 in memory of her mother. The Memorial Cottages are recognisable by the carving on the front of William Morris sitting in the Home Mead beside Kelmscott Manor. Philip Webb was the architect. George Jack did the carving. The architect of the Gimson Cottages was, again, Ernest Gimson, the Arts and Crafts architect. These too are a remarkable example of building in the local vernacular style. Their traditional character suggests much greater antiquity than 1915.

For the rest, the cottages built since the First World War by the local Council and the Church Commissioners and the four post 1945 houses respect the local idiom and fit into the unspoilt village scene without offence. Moreover, the future is reasonably assured because the West Oxfordshire District Planners have regard for the character of the place and, in co-operation with the three major landowners, in particular the National Trust, are concerned that it remains unviolated by unsightly development.

Kennington ৡৡ৹

Kennington is a long, straggly village between Oxford and Abingdon and is pleasantly situated between the river Thames and Bagley Wood. It is thought to have derived its name from Cenigtun, or the place of Cena's people and was first mentioned in a charter of AD 821.

Floods have always been a feature of the district and some present residents can remember having to walk out of the village on duck-boards before the drainage was improved. It is reported that in 1852 a train carrying the engineer Brunel could not get through and he and the other passengers had to alight in Kennington and be transported to Oxford by horse and wagon.

In the early 19th century some members of the University used to keep horses in Kennington as they enjoyed driving them in tandem, which they were not allowed to do in Oxford. This is commemorated in the name of one of the popular pubs, the Tandem. The other pub, the Scholar Gipsy, is a reminder that this was the area described in Matthew Arnold's poem of the same name.

The philosopher and writer Bertrand Russell once lived in a house on Bagley Wood Road and a plaque on the wall records this.

Village life is enhanced by the facilities of the new village hall, a splendid building opened in 1989. Here one finds a libary as well as a sports hall. This is also used by many village organisations and for productions of the local dramatic society. There is a new Youth Club building and adjoining the car park is the Kennington Social Club building, as well as a modern health centre. Here, too, is a stone lintel with the inscription 'Sunday School 1809', reminding the inhabitants of the spot where one of the oldest Sunday schools in the country once stood.

Demolition of a war-time cold store provided space for the erection of some attractive new houses with views over the river. Otters Reach development has now pushed the number of inhabitants to over 5,000.

There are three churches in the village, Methodist, Catholic and Church of England. A great ecumenical spirit exists and many joint functions are held. Many musical events are also held, led by the Kennington & District United Church Choirs, all monies raised going to charity.

Kennington boasts an unusual open space in the delightful Memorial Field. This covers several acres of natural ground and is a tribute to members of the village who gave their lives in the Second World War. It is administered by the Oxford Preservation Trust with a local committee representing many of the village organisations.

Education is provided by an infant and primary school and Templeton College, the former centre for business management, is within the parish boundaries.

Open air activities are encouraged and devotees have two sports fields and the appropriate football and cricket clubs.

The new industrial estate in Sandford Lane is becoming a hive of activity with many units providing employment.

The warmth of the community spirit compensates for the change from a rural hamlet to a semi-urban development and Kennington is known as the friendly village.

Kiddington ✍

The village of Over and Nether Kiddington is situated on the A34 trunk road north of Woodstock, and the two parts are divided in the wooded valley by the river Glyme.

The village has not altered significantly since Domesday. There are only four new houses, built by the local council in the 1920s.

The population is also fairly static. In 1066 it was 173. In 1951 it was 100, and at the present time it is about 110.

The village was always on the toll road between Oxford and Birmingham. The largest house near the main road, still known as 'The Chequers', was originally a coaching inn, where the Worcester Coach, the London Mail and the Blenheim called. The building close to the house was the blacksmith's and wheelwright's shop.

In the 1940s this building was given to the village on a 99 year lease by the late Squire, Mr Henry Melville Gaskell. The village people raised the money, with the help of the Oxfordshire Rural Community Council, to convert the building into a very useful village hall. Unfortunately due to rising costs and essential improvements that were required, it is no longer used.

Close by The Chequers is a stone archway, which until after the Second World War housed 'The Tap'. This was the water supply for the village. The water was carried in buckets to all parts of the village, including the council houses. On the other side of the busy A34, opposite The Chequers, is the village post office and shop.

The village is composed of four blocks of typical Cotswold stone cottages, some dated 1844. On the right hand side is Gate Farm, possibly connected with the toll gate, and the only thatched cottage now remaining in the village.

In Nether Kiddington, Kiddington Hall is situated on rising ground and overlooking the river Glyme and the lake. It is a great house with dormer windows and lantern roof. The grounds were designed by 'Capability' Brown. The stable complex once housed broughams, governess carts and a dog cart, which were used to fetch and carry all things necessary to the running of a large house. A 1911 Daimler and various horses and ponies were also housed, while above were rooms for the stud groom and stable lads. These rooms have now been converted into a conference centre more suitable to this computer age.

145

Close by the Hall stands the strong square-towered 14th century church. There are stained glass windows to the memory of Henry Lomax Gaskell and his wife Alice. The Gaskell family lived at the Hall from 1855–1953. There is a brass of Walter Goodere, a 16th century rector of Kiddington, on the west wall. North of the church is a stone-built house which was once the priest's house, now converted to two workers' cottages. Until after the Second World War we had a rector of our own, who resided in the rectory near the entrance to the Hall. Outside the churchyard stands a very attractive 16th century dovecote.

Turning left at the Old Rectory you pass two modernised 18th century farm cottages. A little further on, at a spot known by the locals as Will's Grave, a cross used to be cut in the grass verge where the last man convicted of sheep stealing was hanged.

The estate village used to consist of the park and woodlands, Park Farm and seven other farms, farmed by tenant farmers. Of these only one, White House Farm, is still farmed by a tenant farmer, the others are now farmed by the estate.

Kidmore End

The parish of Kidmore End covers a very wide area. The name is derived from the Celtic, 'kid' meaning wood, 'More/Mawr' being great and 'End' a boundary. It was renamed Kidmore in 1894, but after representations the Council agreed in 1902 that its name should revert to Kidmore End.

Kidmore End encompasses Gallowstree Common. The tree which gave this hamlet its name was a solitary oak standing apart from woodland. It is said that the last hanging, for sheep stealing, occurred in 1825. The stump was removed at the time of the Enclosure Acts but for some time the gibbet and chains were left on a post nearby. There are, however, happier associations with Gallowstree Common. This stands with Kidmore End in the lovely part of South Oxfordshire known as 'Cherry Country' and within living memory the Methodist chapel at Gallowstree held annual Cherry Teas in July, when the tables groaned under the huge bowls filled with local cherries, from which one took one's fill . . . and all for 9d! Sadly, the cherry orchards are no more, and the chapel has closed, but a walk through the lanes and woods when the wild cherries are in bloom is a delightful reminder of former days.

Kidmore End village school was established in 1862 and within a year the average attendance was 70 – this was before education became free and compulsory. In 1901 there were 143 children on the register and in this year the Bronze Medal, awarded by the Canadian Government through Lord Strathcona, was given to William Long for the best essay on Canada – a great honour for the village school.

The church festival or Parish Feast evolved from the annual treat for schoolchildren consisting of tea and games at the vicarage. In 1891 it was decided to hold a Parish Festival. On 1st July, Evensong was sung at 3 pm followed by tea on the vicarage lawn for all participants. The Festival became popular and included exhibits by children of collections of flowers and was enhanced by the attendance of the Church Lads Brigade Drum and Fife Band. It is recorded that the year 1901 produced a 'memorable and record festival'. At tea it is reported that 140 lb of cake, 8 gallons of bread and 70 gallons of tea were consumed! Sports were organized and prizes were awarded to children for needlework, drawings and good attendance. These Festivals were the forerunners of present Village Days.

An ancient landmark is the Kidmore End Well, now disused but in an excellent state of preservation. Often in its lifetime it had fallen into disrepair and been threatened by demolition but public opinion and generosity saved it from such a fate, one thoughtful Parish Councillor reasoning, during war time, that 'it would be very useful should an air raid disrupt the public water supply'.

Kingston Blount

The village developed at the foot of the Chiltern Hills, on the spring line. The hills provided beech trees for feeding pigs, brushwood, timber and building material. The soil on the plain is both chalky and clay, being highly productive for farming. Newcomers pronounce the 'oun' in Blount as in 'round'. It is usually taken to be lazy speech but in fact 'Blunt', used by the people born and bred in the village, is the more correct because the village takes its name from the Le Blunt family, lords of the manor in the 13th to the 15th centuries.

The nearby Icknield Way carried a lot of sheep drovers and travellers who needed sustenance and lodgings during the Middle Ages. The village expanded in the 18th and 19th centuries and was self-sufficient. It was described in 1852 as a 'large and respectable town'. It had a number of pubs, a draper, grocers, wine merchants, a smithy, a corn merchant, a butcher, baker, post office and a school. Today there remain just two pubs. The shops have all closed. With the decline of farming the villagers mainly travel to work.

Even the telephone exchange has moved. In the early days of the telephone one of the local merchants knew the chief engineer. He felt that Kingston Blount would benefit by having the exchange. He heard that the decision would be made on a particular day according to how much use the telephone system had. The gentleman arranged for many of his clients to use it that day, thus making Kingston Blount the name for all the local village telephone numbers.

The school in the village was always small. The land had been given for the building by a local landowner whose wife took an especial interest in the attendance of the children. Elderly residents tell how she walked the village in a long black dress, a black walking stick with a silver top swinging as she walked. Whenever she found a child potato-picking or stone-gathering she gave several sharp slaps to the bottom and sent them off to school. Later she would stalk into school to check that the children were there. After the school's closure, the building became a village hall, and later when a new hall was erected, a private house.

The present village hall is run by the Hillwerke Trust and is situated alongside the allotments. Many years ago the villagers had rights to collect brushwood and fuel from a part of the woods called the 'Poors Hillock'. Village rumour had it that in the 19th century firewood was not the only thing to come down the hill, but that more appetising things came down too. In those days of harsh poaching laws, villagers were taking great risks. The rights were exchanged in 1864 for four acres of land to be used as allotments by the poor of the village. The new village hall was built on a field next to the allotments and it was fitting that the old medieval word 'Hillwerke' was used.

The railway line which ran through the village had a railway halt at Kingston Blount and was popular as a starting point for conveying agricultural produce to the towns.

Trains apparently never went very fast for there is a story of a keen horseman challenging the train driver to a race to Chinnor from the halt at Kingston Blount. The rider won.

Kirtlington 🌿

Visitors to Kirtlington today will see an attractive village, with two greens, thatched cottages and a pond with ducks and daffodils in the spring. A walk round the village can take you through 'Tinkers Ditch', along 'Molly Minns' lane and to the church via 'Betty Bulls' lane. The track from South Green leads into Kirtlington Park with its many fine trees, including three ancient cedars bordering the sports field. From North Green, Mill Road passes a disused quarry where the bones of a dinosaur were discovered and where once stone was quarried and cement manufactured. At the end of the track is the Oxford Canal with Pigeons Lock, Flights Mill and the river Cherwell. The working narrow boats of the past have been replaced by holiday barges. The floodgate near Flights Mill has an eel trap incorporated in its structure.

The village is listed in the Domesday Book as a thriving community. Centuries later, in 1742 workmen began clearing the site to build the house in Kirtlington Park for Sir James Dashwood and his family, then living at the manor of Northbrook. The Dashwood family moved into the completed house in 1746 and many generations of the family lived there until the beginning of the 20th century.

The school log book started in April 1887 records the tea parties given by Sir George and Lady Mary Dashwood for the schoolchildren, which were the highlight of the school year. The old school, which had been converted from a barn, had 156 pupils in 1894 who paid sums varying from 1d to 4d per week for their education depending on their father's occupation. Holidays included half days for blackberrying and for the Church Temperance Fete. This building was used until 1966 when staff and pupils moved into the new school built on the same site. There are at present over 50 pupils who take an active and lively role in village life.

The church of St Mary the Virgin has been used by worshippers for centuries, the Norman arch and chancel being the oldest part. An interesting church 'character' was James Sandford who was appointed Parish Clerk in 1702 at the age of eleven and held office for 54 years, recording the births of his five children in the parish register in capital letters. At 19 he was appointed schoolmaster and taught in the village for 45 years.

Two events, one traditional and one started in recent years, take place in the village each year. The Lamb Ale Festival has been recorded in many contemporary writings of the past. A piece of land was set aside to

Polo in Kirtlington Park

150

grow wheat to make a cake and barley to make beer. Early writings tell of the maids of the village, on Trinity Monday, running after a fat live lamb with their thumbs tied behind them and the maid 'that with her mouth takes and holds the lamb' is declared Lady of the Lamb, which was later cooked and eaten at the Feast. Later accounts describe 'the dray with the load of ale' being escorted into the village by the Morris dancers. The lamb was carried on the men's shoulders to different farmhouses where, after a dance, beer and money was given to the dancers to help pay for the feast. Today the Lamb Ale Festival is a weekend of celebrations with a procession and dancing, with Morris sides from many parts of this country and abroad taking part. The 'Feast' is held on Trinity Monday and there is a fair on the South Green.

The second event held in September started in the 1980s. This is the Oxfordshire Triathlon where competitors swim, cycle and then run a cross-country course around the village to finish exhausted but triumphant on the sports field. This event raises money for the building of a new village hall.

Another sporting activity which takes place in the village is polo. The Kirtlington Polo Club was started in 1926 by the Budgett family. In the beautiful setting of Kirtlington Park matches are keenly contested, with the ponies skilfully guided and controlled by their riders. Prince Charles is a frequent visitor, playing for the 'Cambridge Old Blues' team.

A study of the 1881 census shows the many changes that have taken place in village life. Then the majority of villagers worked in the village, which was well served with five bakers, two of them Master Bakers, five dressmakers, a tailor, five wheelwrights and many other tradesmen. Today most people go out of the village to work in Oxford or other neighbouring towns. Despite this, village life continues and the community looks forward to a thriving future.

Leafield 🍂

The name Leafield comes from 'La Felde', French for 'the field', though it was usually called Feld or Field Town until the 19th century. It was probably given this name because the site was a natural clearing within Wychwood Forest. The ancient core of the village centres round the greens to the south of Leafield Barrow, on a small island of very infertile gravelly soil, which, in contrast to the surrounding area, is probably incapable of supporting fully-developed woodland. This would have made it attractive to settlers and, together with the presence of water from ponds and wells in the Oxford Clay around Leafield, no doubt explains the siting of the village.

For much of its existence, Leafield remained remote. Two themes which recur throughout Leafield's history are the strong links between the village and the surrounding Wychwood Forest and, secondly, crime. The two are closely related, partly because the forest in its legal sense of an area under Forest Law, gave scope for punishing many minor offences, but also because in its literal sense it provided hiding and protection for wrongdoers. By the early 19th century, the district had a very bad name. Arthur Young, writing in 1813, said: 'The vicinity is filled with poachers, deer-stealers, thieves and pilferers of every kind: offences of almost every description abound so much, that the offenders are a terror to all quiet and well-disposed persons; and Oxford gaol would be uninhabited, were it not for this fertile source of crimes'. It was only after the deforestation of Wychwood in 1857 and the attendant changes in social and economic conditions that Leafield's reputation for lawlessness diminished.

Leafield had a number of customs associated with the forest. On Palm Sunday, the children went with bottles and liquorice into the forest to the spring known as Worts Well, or 'Uzzle', and drank the liquorice dissolved in the water. This seems to have been a continuance of an ancient custom, based on the supposed healing powers of the spring. According to John Kibble, a local historian who wrote in the 1920s, prayers were said at the spring:

Hast then a wound to heal
The wych doth grieve thee?
Come then unto this welle,
It will relieve thee:
Nolie me tangeries,
And other maladies
Have here thyr remedies
Pray'sd be the Lord.

The local clergy did not approve of the custom. One Leafield villager has a crucifix given to her grandmother by the vicar, as a reward for being the only child to attend church on Palm Sunday, instead of going to the forest!

In the 18th and 19th centuries Leafield was an important centre for pottery manufacture, though the industry was probably established here very much earlier. The pottery was known as 'Field Town Chiney' and was crude, everyday earthenware, with a treacly orangey-brown glaze. Broken pieces are frequently found in the village gardens.

The main landmark in the village is the church, built, together with the old vicarage, in 1859 by the eminent Victorian architect, Sir George Gilbert Scott. It is the third on this site. The first, built sometime before 1533, and the second, which replaced it in 1822, were tiny chapels of ease. Communion and other regular services were held here, but for baptisms, marriages and burials the villagers had to go to Shipton. There was a handful of exceptions, as when in 1606 Robert Jeferie was baptised in the chapel because he was 'sicke and weake'. In 1831 a local farmer, Peter Harris, gave land for a churchyard, but marriages were not celebrated in Leafield until 1853.

Across the road from the church is the village cross. It is not known when or why it was first erected, but by the 19th century it was in a ruinous state. It was restored in 1873 as a memorial to Leafield's deliverance from a smallpox epidemic.

Letcombe Bassett ✒

Long before the Norman Conquest, here, in this small village, Saxon families lived and worked, establishing a settlement at the foot of the Berkshire Downs, close to the 'lede in the combe' – the 'brook in the valley', so that in the Domesday survey the name became Ledecumbe. In 1158 came the addition of Bassett, from the name of Richard Basset, who by that time held the manor.

In Saxon days the population was possibly 150. It is now 174. Although most people today work outside the parish, there are still three farms which recall those early cultivators of ridge and furrow. Sheep are kept and most arable land is used to grow grain. Footpaths and bridleways surround the fields. The old names such as 'Apple Pie' and 'Pitchpole' are still used. The houses are of various ages and designs. Many are thatched and of interesting construction.

On the east side of the village is Whites' Farm House, which has Norman associations – the lovely gardens here slope away to the watercress beds. The marketing of the cress was once a thriving industry, the springs rising from the hills providing the necessary pure water for cultivation. 'Bassett Cress' was one of the cries of old Covent Garden market in London.

The Old Rectory, of 17th century origins, with its large thatched barn dating from around 1400, has in its garden the mulberry tree under which Dean Swift sat while writing some of his famous satires.

Another literary association with Letcombe Bassett was made by Thomas Hardy when he wrote *Jude the Obscure*. The cottage where Jude first saw Arabella can still be found down by the brook.

No description of the village would be complete without mention of Capt Tim Foster's racehorse training establishment, which creates employment for many people and has reached fame on three occasions when Grand National winners returned home to a tumultuous welcome.

The little church of St Michael and All Angels stands, as it has done for some 850 years, on high ground near to Gramps Hill, which rises to the ancient Ridgeway. It has two features of special interest: the ornamentation on the Norman chancel arch and the Norman doorway on the north side of the chancel. The bells are Elizabethan, cast in 1576. They were made by William Knight II of Reading and are the only known dated examples by him in existence.

In 1774 land was set aside for the cutting of furze, to be divided amongst the poor as fire wood. In 1977 the land was sold and the money invested. The interest still provides pensioners with vouchers for electricity every winter.

The community shop is run by volunteers, so that there is a very useful village amenity as well as a meeting place for the exchange of news and ideas.

The village hall was once the school, designed by William Butterfield. Today the children go to Letcombe Regis for primary education.

Letcombe Regis

Letcombe was first recorded as 'Regis' in the reign of Richard II, but hundreds of years earlier it had been a Royal manor of the kings of Wessex, passing to William the Conqueror in 1066. King Stephen granted it to the Abbey of Cluny in France in 1136, and later kings had a hunting lodge here. The Old Manor was the original manor house.

Antwicks Manor, once an ancient moat house, was rebuilt at the end of the 19th century. 'Boss' Croker, who had made his millions in New York, turned it into a neo-Elizabethan mansion and headquarters of his racing stables. He also invented its name. One Bonfire Night in the early 1900s, a blazing effigy of a later owner of Antwicks was carried on a cart up to the iron gates. The crowd tried to tear down the gates and, from the steps of the Greyhound Inn, the Riot Act was read for the last time in England.

The third manor house in the village is more recent and houses the Letcombe Laboratory, now owned by the international firm of Dow Elanco. There used to be a story that another owner, an Edwardian lady, was so shocked by two naked statues in the grounds that she ordered them to be sunk in the lake. In 1982, when the lake was dredged, the 6 ft high white marble statue of a man was found – a 2nd century Roman statue of the hero Hercules, which was later sold for £28,000. His female companion could not be traced, but there used to be tales of a woman in white who haunted the banks of the Letcombe Brook after drowning herself for love. The Letcombe Laboratory is visited by a ghostly but friendly nun.

St Andrew's church stands on a mound at the centre of the village, near where the two streams meet. An earlier church is mentioned in the Domesday Book, and parts of the present church date from the 12th century. The east window contains fragments of 14th century glass which have recently been reassembled. An obelisk in the churchyard records the death of George King Hipango, a Maori chief who came to England to train as a Christian minister. He died here of tuberculosis when he was 19 years old, while staying at the vicarage.

There are many interesting buildings in the village, from the church with its partly 12th century tower to the late 19th century Old Bakery, and including thatched cottages such as Regis Cottage with its carvings of angels, the thatched Manor Farm, the two dovecotes, the Gothick gatehouse to the Letcombe Laboratory, the Georgian 'Hollies' and the Victorian vicarage.

Letcombe Regis is still an agricultural and racing village with four stables. Visitors find they need to drive carefully along the winding roads as they meet strings of horses, promenading ducks, occasional flocks of sheep, and even a sleeping dog in the road, as well as numbers of parked cars. Many people work away from the village at Harwell and the Rutherford Laboratory or in nearby towns. The village school is very much part of the community. The Cricket Club, the Gardening Club, the WI, bellringers and the Letcombe Singers, are some of the clubs and societies.

Up on the Downs above the village is the Court Hill Ridgeway Centre, a new youth hostel made out of five old barns. A few hundred yards to the west stands the Iron Age hill fort of Letcombe Castle, also known as Segsbury Camp. The story is still told of a great battle fought at Letcombe Castle. The blood from the slaughter came pouring down Castle Hill and the villagers shouted 'Let the blood come! Let it come! Let come!' – and so the village, according to legend, was named.

Little Milton ꧁

Little Milton lies along the A329 Thame to Stadhampton road, but a number of its oldest and most attractive dwellings are on the Haseley Road – a turn left immediately after the Lamb Inn. Along this road are the Old Post Office and thatched cottages with gardens a profusion of colour in the spring and summer.

Visitors today will find only one shop, the village post office stores, but in the census of 1851 Little Milton was a very active village with five shops, four stonemasons and three dealers of livestock.

Farming was the main occupation of the village with prize flocks of Downs Cotswold sheep recorded in 1934. Also recorded in the 17th and 18th centuries were wheelwrights, carpenters, cordwainers and blacksmiths, with quarries providing employment. Many of the aforesaid occupations were still carried on well into the 20th century.

The present church of St James was built in 1843/44 and has a full peal of six bells. Set on high ground the church commands a fine view over fields. A footpath beside the church will lead you down through fields and spinneys to the river Thames at Cuddesdon.

A wealth of information is passed on today through the children and grandchildren of those who lived in Little Milton during the mid 1880s. During that time the village school had around 100 pupils. When attending church services the girls had to curtsy to the vicar on entering and leaving the church. Evening classes were run for the men of the village to learn to read and write as many of them had little or no schooling prior to the mid 1880s.

Cattle and sheep were a common sight being driven through the village on their way to Thame market, and the carrier's cart was a useful means of transport for shoppers as an alternative to walking the round journey of 12 miles.

From about 1920 means of transport changed. There were few cars, but bicycles had become very popular and the young people of the village could cycle to such places as Oxford, Thame, Wallingford and Abingdon to visit cinemas and friends.

Village life was far from dull and listening to villagers who were children and teenagers during that period, they had a happy and full life, every season bringing some kind of celebration in the village to look forward to.

On Christmas Eve the bell ringers rang the midnight peal and then collected their Christmas boxes. This was followed on Christmas Day by family parties and on Boxing Day the Mummers would perform around the village followed by an excited band of children. Primrose Day on Good Friday was the only day on which people were allowed to pick primroses from Haseley Cover. These decorated the church and were given to the old people as Easter posies.

On the 1st of May the children would get up very early and with their garlands and head-dresses would go from house to house singing. It is recalled that provided the men of the village went to church on May Day they were then given the day off and went home to plant their vegetable gardens.

Feast Sunday was the highlight of the year, always held on the first Sunday after the 5th of August. It began with an open air service at the Cross accompanied by the Chalgrove Brass Band, the Feast followed and an afternoon of fun at the annual fair. When in conversation with people who live, and have always lived, in Little Milton it would appear that this day was the one most looked forward to.

The village has altered little in appearance, although small developments have appeared. At Old Field, off Thame Road, houses were built and reserved for servicemen returning from the Second World War, and bungalows for the elderly and retired. Other more recent homes are mainly occupied by people who have come to the quiet of village life, and commute daily to their work or are retired.

Annual events today are still looked forward to, such as the village Fete, held in mid-June in the grounds of the manor house, by kind permission of the owners, a day which can only be described as a continuation of the old Feast Day.

Little Wittenham ✍

Little Wittenham is a hamlet of some two dozen houses at the foot of the Sinodun Hills, better known as Wittenham Clumps. The Clumps are a favourite place for walking and kite-flying, and there is a splendid view over the Thames valley as a reward for the climb.

They are historically important too: Castle Hill is the site of an Iron Age hill fort and pottery from the early Iron Age has been found there. Unfortunately some of the trees on Round Hill had to be felled a few years ago but new ones are growing and will in time restore the well-known outline. The Clumps are now part of the Northmoor Trust. This was established in 1982, primarily for the conservation of wildlife. The public have access to the grassland and Clumps by agreement between the Trust and Oxfordshire County Council. The Council pay the Trust a 'rent' of one red rose annually for allowing this.

Little Wittenham was formerly known as Abbot's Wittenham because of its connection with the Benedictine abbey in Abingdon. It has no school or shop; the only central meeting place is St Peter's church. This little church with its 14th century tower is well worth a visit, especially in early spring when the churchyard is full of aconites and snowdrops. The nave was restored in 1862 and contains some fine memorial brasses. There is a marble and alabaster monument of Sir Walter Dunch, his wife (an aunt of Oliver Cromwell), and nine children.

Below the church, the steep path leads to the Thames. On the left the Trust are restoring a field to its original state as a water meadow. A newly rebuilt bridge over the Thames brings you to Days Lock. Here you can picnic, swim (if you dare) and watch the boats go by. The present lock-keeper works tirelessly for the Lifeboat Association organising fetes and sales. He has established the World Pooh-sticks Championships, held around New Year's Day. Competitors from near and far drop their stick into the water on one side of the bridge and rush to see whose is the first to come out the other side, just as Winnie-the-Pooh did in A. A. Milne's book.

Littlemore ❧

The first thing that comes to most people's minds when Littlemore is mentioned is Littlemore Hospital. There has been a mental hospital at Littlemore for over a century. It was founded in 1846 as the Pauper Lunatic Asylum, but it became a well known and highly respected psychiatric hospital. It is a teaching hospital and its fame has spread so that people from many parts of the world come to train there.

If the hospital should spring to mind, so also does Cardinal Newman, for he was vicar of Littlemore for 18 years. In 1828, when he first walked the three miles from Oxford, Littlemore was a hamlet, with only one street but plenty of scattered cottages, mainly occupied by farm workers. There was no church. Newman's fight for a church at Littlemore took seven years, but in 1835 the foundation stone was laid by Newman's mother.

Another vicar, Dr Bloxham, got the first school started, but a Baptist chapel had been built in 1807 and there was a flourishing Sunday school run by the Baptist movement.

Cardinal Newman was a good and sincere man and people flocked to hear his sermons. He wrote the beautiful hymns *Praise to the Holiest* and *Lead, Kindly Light* and he made the rather bleak hamlet green by arranging for trees to be planted. He loved Littlemore and inadvertently made it famous, for he turned away from the Church of England and joined the Roman faith. In 1848 he became a Catholic priest and served in Birmingham until he died in 1890. He was made a Cardinal and Catholics from all over the world come to Newman Hall in Littlemore to pay their respects.

Littlemore appears to have been based on religion, for there was a priory here as early as 1120. It was called The Minchery (meaning 'nuns') and even today part of Littlemore is called Minchery Farm.

The priory was not large. There appear to have been about six nuns and the prioress. By the 16th century the building was very dilapidated and the nuns afraid to sleep there. There was little space and they were sleeping two to a bed. The priory began to have a bad reputation. The young nuns were becoming rebellious, particularly one Anne Marcham, who refused to take her final vows and complained of poverty.

In 1517 the prioress, Elizabeth Welles, was taken for trial. She was accused of letting the building go to ruin, ill-treating the young nuns and stealing goods from the priory. She was also accused of having a lover and a baby. The baby died, but Elizabeth said that she loved the man and was making a home for him. To join him she walked to Oxford, accompanied by a seven year old boy, the son of another nun.

The prioress was deposed and the nunnery dissolved in 1523. It fell into ruins but was later restored and is now Minchery Farm Country Club.

There are reputed to be two ghosts at Littlemore. One is a monk, which is quite understandable with Littlemore's past history. The other is of an old, very disabled man, who used to live in the village. He rides a tricycle and, because of his facial deformities is unable to speak clearly, but he is said to have a deep chuckle as if something in life is amusing him deeply.

In 1873 there was cholera in Oxfordshire and it was felt that something should be done urgently, so a sewage plant was constructed on the outskirts of Littlemore. It was open-land treatment and crude sewage was systematically poured out on to the fields. When the fields were resting normal farmwork was carried out. The vegetables, it is reported, were terrific, especially the Brussels sprouts, but the smell was terrible, particularly in the evening when the valves were opened. The mosquitos and flies, too, were numerous. For some reason, the smell was stronger on frosty mornings.

However, with this sewage farm, Littlemore became noted for its bird population; lapwing, snipe, corncrake and wild duck crowded the fields. Even today, there are many birds at Littlemore, including the reed bunting, and seagulls during the winter months. A new sewage system was installed in 1920 and the bird population dropped, as also did the smell, although even today on a warm evening the pleasure of sitting in the garden is sometimes spoilt by the odour!

Littlemore is today a large, prosperous village, far different from the poor hamlet of the 19th century. Its rural character has gone, houses have been built on the farmland and there are many closes, avenues and squares. The car factory is probably the reason for the large population. Houses were also built for the employees at Littlemore Hospital.

There is now a modern-style Catholic church, The Blessed Dominic Barberi, named after the Italian priest who received Cardinal Newman into his church.

Long Wittenham ❦

Long Wittenham, a Thames-side village of a thousand people, sits on a quiet yet historic site. Archaeological remains ranging from a mammoth's tooth to an Iron Age shield, from a Viking age bracelet to a Roman brooch, have been found in the parish, in addition to a complete Iron Age village and a large Saxon cemetery. It takes its name from Witta, presumably a minor Saxon chief, who settled here with his people in the 5th century. The village cross, the base of which dates from the 7th century, by tradition marks the spot where St Birinus preached and converted the pagan Saxons to Christianity.

Walter Giffard, the 3rd Earl of Buckingham, rebuilt the church in 1120. Giffard built his church of white stone from Caen, in the Norman style; it was enlarged towards the end of the 12th century by the addition of the south aisle. The lead font, one of the few extant in England, was installed about the same time. The end of the 13th century saw the carving of the smallest effigy in England; that of a Crusader knight. This was possibly commissioned by Joan of Acre, second daughter of King Edward I, in memory of her husband Gilbert de Clare – 'Gilbert the Red' – Earl of Gloucester and Hertford, who had died in 1295.

There is a legend that during the Civil War Cromwell sat under the mulberry tree in the Old Farmhouse (the tree still stands); what is true is that the churchwardens, fearing that Cromwell's soldiers would melt down the lead font for bullets, surrounded it with a wooden packing case. There it remained hidden for 200 years, when it was rediscovered and restored in 1839. The wood from the case was used to build the small table which now sits just inside the church.

From 1322 Exeter College, Oxford had the right to name the vicar of St Mary's church, which included the right to gather the tithes. From 1554 the lord of the manor was St John's College, Oxford. Over the succeeding centuries more and more of the parish was purchased by the college, and certainly it is only in the second half of the 20th century that the majority of the residents of the parish have owned their own homes.

The two colleges, and other large landowners, forced the enclosure of the parish in 1809–12, and the remainder of the century saw the agricultural labourers suffering chronic poverty. Respite was apparently found in the pubs, the church and importantly, the Primitive Methodist chapel, founded sometime before 1829.

The chapel became the village shop and post office, and still flourishes today. There are now four pubs in the village, all of which provide accommodation and food. The Plough dining room was once a slaughterhouse, and the Vine was a butcher's shop. The Barley Mow enjoys fame as the venue for the writing of Jerome K. Jerome's *Three Men in a Boat*.

There are a number of cruck cottages in the village, notably Church Cottage and Cruckfield Cottage, as well as many other attractive styles of architecture. A fine old pigeon cote behind the church has now been restored and is used as an architect's office. A walk through the churchyard will bring you to the remains of the village cockpit and the manor house.

The present day village enjoys a few traditions and many activities. On 1st May a May Queen is crowned from amongst the members of the Girls Friendly Society, and village children dance around the maypole. The village also welcomes many visitors to the Pendon Museum, which specialises in model railways and a model of the Vale of the White Horse.

Longworth

Originally known as the village of Worth, the prefix 'Long' was added to describe its narrow shape. Situated on a ridge, the land drops away to the north where the river Thames forms the boundary. The soil is good sandy loam, excellent for growing most vegetables and flowers.

The oldest building in the village is the Anglican church, part of which was constructed in the 12th century. A leaflet on the table inside the south door describes the many items of interest, such as the brasses and the fragments of the monument to one of the Marten family. The monument was said to have been destroyed when Charles II came to the throne as Henry Marten had signed the death warrant of Charles I in 1649. Other distinguished persons to be born in Longworth were John Fell in 1625 and Richard Doddridge Blackmore in 1825, both sons of former rectors. John Fell later became Dean of Christ Church, Oxford and is recalled in the epigram

'I do not like thee, Doctor Fell,
The reason why I cannot tell
But this I know and know full well,
I do not like thee, Doctor Fell.'

Richard Blackmore was the author of the well known book, *Lorna Doone*.

Longworth village still has a few houses more than 100 or 200 years old, but during the 1980s many of the small cottages were 'developed' to make larger luxury homes. Still much of their character has been retained. None of the houses are open to the public but the gardens of the Manor, Haugh House and Martens Hall Farm are opened each year under the National Gardens Scheme and each September the village fete in aid of the church is held in the manor grounds.

In the early 20th century, Longworth became famous for its rose-growing. Though only a small village it boasted two rose nurseries, Prince's and Drew's. The two world wars interrupted the growing and breeding and now the specialist rose breeders are found elsewhere. Some of the Drew family still live in the village, and Prince's is still a garden centre under another owner and is called Woodbridge Nurseries. At Martens Hall Farm, Mrs Parker-Jervis grows and sells unusual plants and is a known specialist in varieties of snowdrop and other bulbs. Her nursery is normally open by appointment only.

Another unusual occupation in Longworth is that of the small family firm of Robert Longstaff, makers of high quality wooden toys and of folk and early musical instruments, which are sold in the UK and abroad.

Though a small village of some 550 adult persons, Longworth has two pubs, two churches, a primary school, a shop and post office, and a well run village hall. For many years the school was held behind the chapel, (now the United Reformed church) but in the 1960s a new one was built on land acquired by the council for the Bow Bank estate, many houses having been erected in the early 1950s. The school serves Hinton Waldrist as well as Longworth.

Lyford 🌾

About one mile from, and in the ecclesiastical parish of Charney Bassett, is the small village of Lyford. The name derives from a ford over the river and 'Ly' indicates a place where flax was once grown.

Lyford's link with history is bound up in Lyford Grange, the house where the Jesuit priest and martyr, Edmund Campion, in the reign of Elizabeth I, was captured after celebrating Mass in 1581. He has since been canonised.

The small church of St Mary is mainly Jacobean, and was built on the site of an earlier oratory or chapel of ease. It serves a parish of only about 70 souls. There is no shop or inn, but Lyford shares all the amenities of Charney Bassett.

Marcham 🌾

Marcham, or 'the place in the marshes', is perhaps better known these days as the 'Denman College village', and its many students can often be seen strolling around the streets in the afternoon when on courses there. Denman College is the National Federation of Women's Institutes' own independent residential adult education college.

For those who only pass through, however, it has to be 'That place with the awful bends!' Winding Packhorse Lane was simply not meant to take the cars and lorries that pass along its narrow way, sometimes scraping parts of the old cottages away and shaking the old trees.

There is, however, much more to Marcham than the twisty main road, and its ancient byways are always interesting.

Turn up North Street, between the Crown inn and the large garage, and you will see a selection of pretty cottages of varying styles, including a thatched house with a decorative thatched bird on the roof. St Nicholas' hall, built in the early years of the 20th century, is the village meeting place, and has a pair of splendid red brick lions, with shields, at its entrance. Adjoining it is an ex-servicemen's social club, replacing the old bowling alley. The road narrows past the 'Gap' and you can see part of the Denman College grounds.

New Road is over a century old, and was cut by Mr Duffield to make a better entrance to Marcham Park (Denman's former name). This road also leads to the church, which is a handsome 19th century building with a 12th century tower. The interior has recently been reordered and is impressively light. There are many interesting wall monuments, including the Fetyplace brass which shows a complete Tudor family at prayer. One of the monuments in the churchyard near the church porch is a 'listed building'. There is an active Baptist group in the village, with a small church on the main road.

To the south of the churchyard is the Tithe House, dated 1645, with its tithe barn and attractive dovecote. In this house at the start of the 20th century, the skeleton of a murdered newborn baby was discovered, following the hearing, over many months, of strange crying noises. Note the attractive porch with its twin 'bustle' seats.

Church Street is a quiet road to walk down, and has the old rectory on the right and the latest new buildings on the left, a small estate called All Saints Close. At the White Hart inn we arrive back on the main road and can see the second dovecote of the village, behind the war memorial.

Mill Road, to the south of the village, leads down to Marcham Mill, and it is here that 'green' Marcham is to be found, its quiet lanes and open fields being a haunt of butterflies and birds. Here also is the pound, where straying animals were impounded, and which is at present being restored by the Parish Council with WI help, as a quiet sitting area, with planting to encourage wild life.

Across to the east, two old buildings can be seen. The Priory, which would have been a weekend 'retreat' for the abbot of Abingdon Abbey in medieval times, and Hyde Farm, a very old (and haunted) small manor house with a history that suggests that it was given as a gift to one of the signatories to the death warrant of Charles I. James Hyde is later said to have thrown himself from the tower of Marcham church in remorse. At Hyde Farm there is an adjoining nursery which also sells caged birds and tropical fish.

This village has a post office and stores, a newsagent, a small super-market and a carpenter. Coal is delivered, as are fish and milk. The village doubled in size in the 1950s when a new school was built, and has been increasing in size ever since. A small estate called Farthings was built on land previously owned by Denman College.

On the outskirts of the village there is a vineyard and nearby is the Doghouse, an attractive restaurant and hotel. The Ark restaurant and bar lies to the south of the village.

The two hamlets of Frilford and Garford are included in the parish and are worth a visit. Frilford has a large 'pick-it-yourself' farm and garden centre, with a restaurant, and Garford has an interesting small chapel of ease almost hidden in a farmyard.

Marston 🦢

The parish of Marston, as distinct from New Marston in the city of Oxford, includes not only the old village but many new houses to the north, south and east, built since the late 1930s. Before then things were very different and access to North Oxford was by path along the river Cherwell or by the hand-operated Marston Ferry, and to Headington by an ancient footpath along the line of Saxon Way. In fact Marston was almost as isolated as it had been for hundreds of years.

The present lines of the village street and Back Lane indicate the layout from earliest times. Each copyholding tenant of the manor had a strip of land running at right angles to the village street, many with still-existing stone-lined wells which collect water from below the gravel. Mains water did not come till the late 1920s and main drainage in 1933. Beyond Back Lane each copyholder had strips of land in the communal fields – Colterne, Sutton and Marsh, and the use of the Cow Pasture. Brookfield, where the allotments now are, was attached to the demesne farm, Court Place. In some places the ridges and furrows can still be seen.

The Civil War and siege of Oxford put an end to the open field cultivation. Parliamentary troops under General Fairfax were billeted in the village. Earthworks were made in the fields and some time between 1646 and 1674 the fields were divided and enclosed by quickset hedges into pastures and closes. The surrender of the Royalist forces was arranged in the Mansion House, then owned by Unton Croke, a lawyer. This had been built about 1622 on the site of a previous house belonging to his wife, Anne Hore. It stands at the north end of the village in Mill Lane. After a period of decay in the late 18th and early 19th centuries, when it housed Napoleonic War prisoners and then paupers, it was altered and divided into the two present houses, Cromwell House and Manor House.

The yeoman farmers who took over the newly enclosed fields in the late 17th century, built, along the village street, substantial stone houses of the 'long house' type, probably thatched. Each had its original strip or strips of orchard and garden and one or more of the outlying fields where they reared cattle, to a lesser extent sheep, and grew hay and corn. The cows would be brought back to the farms in the village for milking, along the wide grassy, very muddy street with its bordering ditch and ponds. This was still happening in the 1950s though the road was better and the ditch was underground. There were also many very small thatched cottages of one or two rooms which have disappeared in living memory, but some later brick and slate of the 'one up, one down' variety have been modernised and fetch high prices. These used to house farm labourers, often with large families. The five pubs nicely spaced through the village must have provided social life, at least for the men.

With the decline in farming and the improvement of roads, Oxford people who valued the countryside peace moved out, a process which has rapidly increased. More new houses have been built and residents now include many professional people, including university dons. One of the very distinguished was Lord Florey of penicillin fame, who shared the Nobel prize for Medicine in 1945 and whose memorial is in the church porch.

There are still builders, plumbers, a picture framer, an upholsterer, a tailoress, a printer, and until recently the famous Vardoc tie factory, and the Unicol office equipment factory.

St Nicholas' church has had a succession of splendid vicars, notably Rev John Hamilton Mortimer 1904–1952, and later Rev Paul Rimmer 1959–1990. Mr Mortimer was a great benefactor to the village. He bought John Honour's builders' workshop to make the village reading room, where the Mortimer Memorial Garden now is with its trees, bulbs and wild flowers. He also gave land for the recreation ground beside the Mortimer Hall.

The present beautiful church building includes a transitional Norman nave, 15th century additions, a 17th century pulpit and memorials to the Croke family. In 1989, a Queen Anne Royal Arms was revealed above the chancel arch.

The village, now regrettably divided by Marston Ferry Road, still keeps much of its old coherence and is lucky to have a post office and shop, a great meeting place and convenience. It has become a conservation area and the fields and the Victoria Arms belong to the Oxford Preservation Trust. Hard work and vigilance try to keep the character of the village compatible with the inevitable change which time brings.

Minster Lovell

Domesday Book records two manors, Minstre and Parva Minstre (Little Minstre) separated by the river Windrush, the connecting bridge once being a toll bridge. In the first half of the 19th century the land on the higher ground towards Brize Norton was chosen by the Chartist Land Company for one of its housing allotment developments, and from the 1930s up to the present day the housing in this area has increased.

Ruins of Minster Lovell Hall

In early days the sheltered valley, with the river Windrush for fish, marshland for gamefowl and thatching reed, the Wychwood Forest for protection (villagers often disappeared to live in the forest in troubled times), timber and fuel, and plenty of quarriable stone, made it an obvious place for continuous habitation. Roman Akeman Street passes through the north of the parish, there are names of Celtic derivation and a jewelled brooch (thought to have come from the same workshop as the Alfred Jewel) was found here. There have been at least two manor houses on the same site and two churches, together with a chapel and an alien cell, for the church and land in Minster was once given to the abbey of Ivry in Normandy. The name Minster acknowledges the fact that the church here was of some significance in this area.

St Kenelm's church, named after the Cotswold prince, was completed in about 1450 and is very little changed except for the removal of the chancel screen and the minstrels' gallery. Cruciform in design and Perpendicular in style, it has an unusual central crossing where minor arches support the tower, which is narrower than the nave.

William Lovell, whose effigy is to be found in the church, rebuilt the manor house and the church. The family came to full eminence with William's grandson, Francis, Viscount Lovell, who was Lord Chamberlain to Richard III, and Richard is known to have stayed at Minster Hall, as did his successor Henry VII on three occasions. After the death of Richard at Bosworth field, Francis supported the pretender, Lambert Simnel, the Oxford baker's boy, and escaped again after further defeat at the battle of Stoke to disappear, which was the occasion for various legends, one being that he was incarcerated in a secret room at Minster Hall where he perished. John Buchan makes use of the legend in his fine historical novel *The Blanket of the Dark*. Later the house passed into the Coke family, sometime Earls of Leicester, but they rarely lived here and Thomas Coke dismantled much of the house to sell off the materials to raise money to build his great house and 'museum' at Holkham in Norfolk. The remaining romantic ruins show what a fine house it must have been.

Little Minster manor became the home of the Heylyn family at the time of the Commonwealth, when, after supporting King Charles in the Civil War, they were forced to find a quiet country retreat. Peter Heylyn was one of the great intellects of those times and in Minster he extended his great book on geography into a *Cosmography* published in 1651. He was buried in Westminster Abbey.

The Chartists' housing development, called Charterville, was designed to rehouse city dwellers in the countryside, to make them more self-sufficient and to qualify them for the vote through the ownership of land. The development of 78 bungalows, each with land of from two to four acres, a school and school house, took only ten months to build in 1847, but the newcomers did not settle to the rural life and soon most of the allotments were sold off. Although it could be called a failed experiment, the bungalows remain a token to good craftsmanship.

At the turn of the 20th century Minster Lovell was famous for its rushes and river crayfish. Rushes were used for caulking barrels and the rush cutter, Mr Greengrow, who came every year from Kent, declared this rush to be the best in the south of England.

The village once had three mills. There remains only one and this has been converted into a beautiful conference centre. However, there are three pubs. The Olde Swan is widely known and contains many features of its distant past. The White Hart was once a busy coaching inn serving coaches on the London-Gloucester-Cheltenham route. The New Inn, formerly called the 'Garibaldi', was only licensed at the end of the 19th century and was formerly a Charterville bungalow.

Moreton ⚜️

The hamlet of Moreton lies one mile to the south-west of Thame and forms part of its parish. It has been in existence as long as Thame, being mentioned with it in the Domesday Book.

In the past the main occupation of the inhabitants was farming – there being at least seven farms and more than 30 cottages, the majority housing the farm labourers. A decline in agriculture greatly reduced the size of the village and eventually led to the closure of the Methodist chapel, the school and the shop. The bottom of the decline came in the 1950s and today there are about 50 houses/cottages, plus two farms and a smallholding, all family-owned and run.

The majority of Moreton's older buildings cluster at the east end of the hamlet surrounding the green and the two ponds. They then trail thinly up to the war memorial which was erected in 1920. On from the war memorial is a small, but mixed, collection of houses, including the pub.

Although to car users Moreton is now a cul-de-sac, its roads were passable once. Until well into the 18th century, the main thoroughfare from Aylesbury to Tetsworth and Wallingford ran through Moreton. The needlemakers of Long Crendon made use of this road twice a year to send their goods via stage coach for sale in London. Before that, it was used by the Roundheads, who would have passed through carrying the mortally wounded John Hampden from the battle of Chalgrove to Thame in 1643.

Like many villages (and towns) in Oxfordshire, Moreton was troubled by pillaging during the Civil War. This era is the one that appears to have produced the 'troubled spirit' that haunts Brook Cottage. The various happenings have been recorded by Mr Ron Mott (now an inhabitant of Thame) who was born in the cottage. He remembers his parents occasionally referring to hearing the 'Old Man's' rat-tat on the door and heavy footsteps on the brick path outside.

Until early in the 20th century, Moreton was a two-pub hamlet with the Bell at one end and the Royal Oak at the other. The former was closed in 1908 but the latter (still going strong) was renowned in the neighbourhood as having the best beer, brewed on the premises by its blind but redoubtable publican, Mr John North.

Another local character of the early 20th century was Joe Honour who, with his wife and family, lived in a caravan on Lobbersdown Hill about a mile from Moreton. He earned his living by hedging and ditching for farmers round about. As well as this, he dug rose briars to sell to local nurseries to be budded into standard roses. He also dug and fashioned blackthorns which he seasoned in his chimney to later become walking sticks.

As a non-believer in education, Joe evaded the Education Officer (and the police) for some time, by moving his 'abode' frequently between the Thame and Tetsworth parishes. Eventually he had to comply with the law and his son was dragged unwillingly to school. On his first day, he successfully wreaked havoc on the football field, feeling that the object of the game was to nobble the opponents. Needless to say, Moreton won easily!

Murcott

Murcott, linked usually with Fencott, is the smallest of Otmoor's 'seven towns'. Separated by a straight mile of road, and green belt, the two villages barely support 100 dwellings, although Murcott has its own surviving public house, the Nut Tree, an Anglican church and a Primitive Methodist chapel dated 1847, both still in use. Only two small lanes off the main road provide access to the few houses.

Much of the customary winter flooding has been eradicated by the present Otmoor drainage schemes and the advent of mains water and sewage disposal to the village. It is barely 30 years ago though, that many of the householders moved upstairs with most of their furniture to escape the periodic flooding. Certainly when the roads flooded they became impassable, the waters ebbing and flowing like a tidal wave.

Because of its close proximity to Otmoor, and during the Second World War, the practice bombing ground, one cottage received a direct hit from a German bomb, killing a mother and child who had evacuated here for safety from London's bombs. There were several other bombs unloaded in the area, which left enormous craters.

Murcott House, dated 1803, would seem to have been the first cottage in the village in its original form. Many additions have been made during subsequent decades. Very few of the thatched cottages remain with any vestige of their original form. Most have succumbed to modern development.

The Nut Tree has been modernised and enlarged, but with the thatched roof and reflection in the village pond, still retains much of its rustic charm.

Fiveacres still retains its original cottage which until 30 years ago housed the village shop. Later another shop was set up, almost next door, but with modern ease of transport to the supermarkets it proved an uneconomic venture; both shops are now dwelling houses.

Murcott was essentially a farm village; apart from the three actual farms, every householder owned sufficient land to run a smallholding. The little paddocks still bear witness to the validity of the green belt area; there has been very little building off the main road. The lanes lead directly on to the moor and provide relaxing and delightful walks for the enthusiast.

Before the Second World War there was a fair amount of good natured rivalry between the 'towns'. The Charlton children would chant at their Murcott counterparts:

> Murcottites, Murcottites,
> What silly old fools they be
> Murcottites, Murcottites
> We'll drown 'em in the sea.

Probably with the influx of 'furreners' in the shape of London evacuees, the local folk welded together and now none of the old animosities remain.

One wonders how long Murcott will retain its identity as an Otmoor village as it gradually (not without some regrets) is made more habitable by developers from farther afield.

Nettlebed ᴥ

Nettlebed is one of the highest villages in the Chilterns, 211 metres above sea level, in an area of outstanding natural beauty. It stands on the Roman road between London and Oxford and Queen Elizabeth I is reputed to have stayed at the White Hart Hotel, a very old coaching inn situated in the main street.

Nettlebed was famous for its brick industry. Tiles and bricks were made here from at least the 14th century onwards. In 1365, 35,000 tiles were made for Wallingford Castle and they were also made for the roofing of a hall and chamber at Abingdon Abbey in 1422–3. Bricks were also made for the almshouses at Ewelme and for the chapel in Stonor Park. One bottle kiln remains, probably of 18th century date and it was restored between 1972–74.

The church of St Bartholomew has two stained glass windows designed by John Piper and interpreted by Patrick Reyntiens. The south window is in memory of Peter Fleming (1907–1971), a writer, traveller and soldier, and the east window is in memory of Robin Williamson, a much loved and respected doctor who served Nettlebed and the surrounding districts from 1946 to 1969.

The village hall was built in 1913 and presented as a gift by Robert Fleming. The Nettlebed Working Men's Club which uses the hall has recently changed its name to become the Nettlebed Village Club. The Fleming family lived at Joyce Grove, now a Sue Ryder Home. Joyce Grove was given to St Mary's Hospital, Paddington as a convalescent home and eventually sold to Sue Ryder in 1978.

North Leigh

The village of North Leigh has a particularly rich tradition of stories and rhymes. For instance, the North Leigh Enclosure Award is dated 14th April 1759. During 1760 and 1761 feelings were running high over the enclosures and when fences and hedges belonging to James Leigh Perrot were torn down by rioters the Berkshire Militia marched from Witney to North Leigh, where several were arrested. Thus this version of a contemporary verse –

> 'They was bad what stole the geese off the common ...
> But they was wuss what stole the common off the geese.'

The Sparks family lived in a farmhouse at East End where they brewed ale, and sold it at public houses they owned:

> 'Hit or Miss and the Golden Ball,
> The Leather Bottle and Shepherds All.'

There were many ways of 'seeing' your future husband. Throwing hempseed over your left shoulder, walking round the churchyard three times at midnight, or putting two pieces of cake under your pillow, then getting into bed backwards and saying:

> 'I put this cake under my head,
> To dream of the living, not of the dead.
> To dream of the man that I shall wed
> Not in his best or Sunday array,
> But in the clothes that he wears every day'.

A spring supplied the town well, which was situated near the Gospel chapel, and the pond which in the Enclosure Award was called Cucking Stool Pond. The name later changed to Cuckamus pond and is now Cuckamus Green. A certain Billy Wickson was blamed for the low level of water in the well and evidently the villagers were glad to see the back of him!

> 'Now grumbling Billy has gone away,
> There's plenty of water night and day'.

Northmoor ❧

Northmoor is a very small village, of about 70 houses, in the rough triangle of land bounded by the Windrush to the west, the Thames to the south and east and the gravel lakes of Stanton Harcourt to the north. Its position has meant that the area has been remarkably undisturbed by roads or development, with the result that recent archaeological exploration has been able to find signs of continuous habitation and land cultivation going back to the Iron Age.

The village lies very low, and until a system of drainage ditches was dug by prisoners of war during the Second World War, was liable to flooding. Not only does it lie hidden off the beaten track, on the way to nowhere, but its shape is so strung out and full of gaps that it is possible for strangers to whisk through in their cars without quite realizing that they have been through a village. This impression is perhaps assisted by the fact that the nucleus of architecturally interesting buildings, that is to say the church which dates back to the 14th century, the Elizabethan Rectory Farm close by, with its dovecote, and, a little further off, the 18th century Church House, all stand well back from the road, offering only glimpses to the passing motorist.

But to the inhabitants of Northmoor, it is a very real and vital community. The farm just mentioned is a working farm, with its bulging haysheds and barns full of cattle bordering the churchyard. On the other side of the road is Ferryman's Farm, still in operation, though part time now, its cow byres visited by local children whenever there's a newborn calf to be kept in the warm. The sight of a tractor trundling along the village road, or, at the appropriate times, of livestock being herded down the street is so common here that only a townee would comment. But modern farming methods require less labour than formerly, so what used to be primarily an agricultural community is now more diverse. The largest single substitute for farm employment is gravel extraction, carried out by the international conglomerate ARC on a very large scale.

Northmoor is not, on the face of it, one of those 'perfect' villages that attract the second-home buyer, and takes some pride in being a working, as distinct from a dormitory or week-end, village. It is true that, sadly, the one-room primary school had to close, and the village shop and post office is now a private house. But there is a continuing focus for village life in the form of the two pubs, and the church, with its crusading knight and his lady, the de la Mores, after whom the village is named.

North Moreton ❧

The manor of North Moreton is recorded in the Domesday Book of 1086, and a church existed then. The manor house itself no longer exists, its site lying east of the church and roughly identified by the remains of a moat.

North Moreton retains many houses from the 15th, 16th and 17th centuries, despite a fire in 1807 which destroyed one side of the main street. Important buildings include Stapleton's Chantry, where the chantry priests once lived, the Tudor vicarage and a tithe barn. The church itself has a 12th century tub-font. The glass in the chantry, dating from 1310, is regarded by experts as one of the finest examples of its period.

In 1550, the churchwardens reported that 'our church is in great decay for the lack of tiles, the which we will see it redressed against Allhallows-tide next'. In August 1603 'this little village' was visited 'with great sickness', ten people dying 'all out of one house where the plague did first begin'. 'It could never be known how it did first come' although the incumbent, far ahead of his times, made a reference to bad water being drunk. Thirty-nine people died in that month, the normal death rate for the 17th century in the parish being about five a year.

Later in the century, the village was a centre for marriages under the Protectorate of Cromwell – five times as many ceremonies taking place as in any comparable period in the 16th and 17th centuries. People came from as far as Wallingford and Abingdon to be married by a parson licensed to perform the ceremony, probably because of his Cromwellian sympathies. From an earlier period also survive records of two connected local 'incidents'. In 1598 a brawl at a football match led to loss of life and bitterness between two families which erupted, a few years later, when the one accused the other of witchcraft. Though the alleged witch was acquitted, the matter did not end there and the accuser was pursued in the Court of Star Chamber. Unfortunately the eventual judgment is not known.

The comparative remoteness of North Moreton ended in the 19th century. The coming of the railways provided both links and employment while the episcopate of Samuel Wilberforce, in the diocese of Oxford, encouraged the restoration of the church fabric in North Moreton in the 1850s.

In the following 14 years, North Moreton came under the influence of the Oxford Movement. The incumbent, Albert Barff, brought important figures in the movement such as Edward King, Henry Liddon, John Keble and Edward Pusey to preach on several occasions. Barff's visitation returns provide an interesting commentary on local events. He noted, for example, the relationship between agricultural depression and population movements. North Moreton's population dropped from 400 in the 1841 census to well below 300.

In the 20th century, among those who lived in North Moreton were R. G. Collingwood, described in the *Dictionary of National Biography* as 'one of the most learned men of his generation', and the pioneer women-educationalists Geraldine and Eglantyne Jebb. The village firm of Thames Valley Eggs Ltd was founded by A. G. Kingham. Beginning as a farmers' co-operative in 1934 it is now one of the largest organisations of its kind in Western Europe.

Today North Moreton is a typical commuting village although agriculture still remains the main source of employment within the parish.

North Stoke �

North Stoke is one of a handful of pretty villages between Wallingford and Goring. It has a population of about 200, which has remained stable for many years.

To reach the quaint village street, pass the modern buildings and former council houses on the B4009 and turn into Cook Lane, where in 1966 a few bungalows and chalets were built on what used to be allotments. After a sharp right turn, 'The Street' appears very much as it has for many years, a mixture of farmhouses and cottages. At the end of the street is the mill, over a stream called the Drincan, flowing from the spring-fed lake to the north-east of the village. Until the 19th century the mill ground corn and provided meal for the villagers' bread, but latterly it harnessed the force of the stream to generate electricity to light The Springs house. The mill later became derelict, but has now been restored and is a private home. Beyond the mill the Ridgeway Path, which passes through the village, leads along a bridle track towards Mongewell.

The old farmhouses, built mainly in the 16th, 17th and 18th centuries, have been restored or extended and are now the comfortable homes of business or professional people. How different from former times when all the inhabitants were employed in the village, either on the farms, in the big houses or in Robert Keen's North Stoke Wagon Works that was in production from 1936 until it moved to Wallingford in the late 1940s.

There are still a few original cottages, though some were demolished and others extended. Until the early 1960s, there had been virtually no new building for many years.

The largest house in the village is The Springs. In the early part of the 20th century the house was occupied by Sir John Wormald, who added to the house and improved the beautiful grounds. He was a generous benefactor to the village, providing it with a village hall and an excellent cricket ground. Unfortunately, years later a subsequent owner had the cricket field ploughed up! Sir John was said to be a man who liked, and usually got his own way. On Sunday mornings in church, while sitting with his family in his front pew, he would ostentatiously turn and scan the congregation to see who among his workers was missing! The house became an old people's home in the late 1950s and since about 1970 has been an hotel.

The village no longer has a shop, post office, school or pub. The nearest public house, the White House, stands on the A4704, a mile east of the village, up the hill towards Ipsden. At least it is downhill all the way home!

From The Street, a short lane leads to the 13th century St Mary's church. Inside there are interesting wall paintings and a Jacobean pulpit. On the west side of the church beneath the tower is a memorial to Dame Clara Butt, the singer, who with her husband Robert Kennerley Rumford, lived at Brook Lodge from 1922. There are still some in the village who remember, with pleasure, her rich contralto voice. When possible she entered into village life and was, in fact, the first president of the North Stoke WI. The lime-shaded lychgate at the entrance to the churchyard, was given by Dame Clara in memory of one of her two sons, both of whom died young.

The 17th century Rectory Farm House, next to the church, is one of several houses built on this site, thought to be originally that of a Roman settlement.

This village has had its share of interesting characters, but none so eccentric as the gentleman who in the 1920s kept lions at The Grange, and took them for walks along the village street.

Oddington 🌿

In the 1950s there were four farms with milking herds in Oddington, now all gone, and three outlying farms within the parish. There was a row of ten thatched cottages, although only three were inhabited at that time. They were pulled down and three houses built in their place, while 16 others have gone onto odd bits of land.

In those days the village was well served with tradespeople; a good grocer who called for orders and delivered the goods later, an excellent baker who came at odd hours – you hung a bag on the door if it was late at night, also a 'wet fish' man who sold fruit and vegetables once a week. There were weekly visits from the haberdasher and the hardware van, which also carried paraffin. There was no public telephone, and only about four in private houses.

In those earlier years one of the interesting events was the coming of the 'Blackberry Man'. Twice a week he appeared, to buy blackberries for dyeing, as many as he could get. Many local people picked hard for the weeks his visits lasted and in a good season you could pick a hundred-weight in a week.

Otmoor was a lovely wild place then with high uncut hedges partly composed of blackberries and the riverbank was a solid block of briars. Now the moor has been reclaimed, it grows heavy crops of corn but the mystery of the area has vanished.

The farmhouses are all large and old; one has a fireplace dated 1659, and one smaller one was originally the coach house of Rectory Farm, a private house for many years. The rectory, also large, is the only place with a suggestion of a ghost, though it has not been seen since the last rector to live there retired. In the churchyard is the grave of a Maori princess, Maggie Papakura, who lived at Oddington Grange as Mrs Staples-Brown. When she died in 1930 her grave was marked by a simple wooden cross but a few years ago it was discovered by some of her compatriots who put a bronze plaque beneath the cross. It has since been visited by many of her people including a group who came in native costume and sang a Maori lament.

It appears that the population (round about 100 over the years) has always been on the move. None of the farms were owned by the older generations – most of the village was owned by the Sawyer estate who sold it bit by bit. There is one young woman though, whose roots go back a long way. Her great-great uncle took part in the Otmoor riots over the Land Enclosure Act.

Old Headington 🖎

The impact created by Old Headington is one of inherited timeless character as a 'Village within a City'! So it was aptly identified by Leslie Taylor and Jean Cook in their book.

The polished axes of prehistoric man, found locally, can be seen in the Ashmolean and Pitt-Rivers Museums. There is also evidence of Roman pottery and kilns. Quarrying was a source of village livelihood, and many farms, dairy and agricultural, were scattered over the area, giving a mixed community.

Many beautiful houses, some dating from the 17th century and vernacular in character, lie alongside small attractive cottages. A feature of the village are the rubble-stone walls that surround the properties and line the crofts and lanes that criss-cross the village.

The manor house is now used as offices by the Oxfordshire Health Authority. It had previously been the preliminary training school for nurses. The old TB hospital and convalescent home have long since disappeared in a sea of laboratories, and a large modern hospital has brought social and visual dominance to the area. Undeterred are flocks of wagtails that gather on the roof garden to roost, and the song of the nightingale can still be enjoyed.

Bury Knowle Mansion, built in the 19th century, and set in an attractive park now open to the public, offers sports facilities and space to enjoy peace and quiet. The City Council acquired the property that now houses a branch library and doctors' clinic.

Granny Berry, who had twelve children, started baking bread in the farm kitchen when her husband died. The popular bakery was run by three generations, but sadly is now closed and a modern house stands on the site.

A pub rhyme, naming all the old Headington pubs goes as follows: 'A Black Boy rode a White Horse carrying a Royal Standard, shouting rule Britannia. He chased the White Hart which had a Bell around its neck. This disturbed the Fox which ran to ground at the Princess Castle.' The White Hart, the Black Boy and the Bell are still serving ale in the village, but the other public houses are now outside the parish.

The church of St Andrew, which may have originated as a small Saxon building on the same site, was founded by St Frideswide in 1004. Later rebuilt, it has had many repairs and additions, the most recent in 1977 when the 19th century roof was somewhat controversially redecorated in strong medieval colours. An underground passage is said to run from the church to the Rookery now owned by Ruskin College. The Fish Window in the baptistry marks the initiation of the Fish Good Neighbourhood Scheme, adopted world wide. New seating arrangements allow for religious plays, organ recitals and choral works to be performed.

From the original post office, telegrams were dispatched by horse and cart, and the shops selling fresh bread, fish, meat and vegetables have sadly disappeared. A large supermarket now supplies village needs, and a car park stands on the site of what was once a market garden. Mattocks, the famous rose growers, started their nurseries in the village.

Transport into Oxford was provided by the *Rocket*, a two-horse brake that needed two extra horses to pull up Headington Hill. William Morris, later Lord Nuffield, initiated the first double-decker buses. Now, ironically, the village has no direct public transport.

The Friends of Old Headington, now affiliated with the Oxford Preservation Trust, have been given three awards for watching over development proposals, thus helping to preserve the character of the village, which has been recognised as a conservation area. Many of the houses are designated as listed buildings, and several new projects have been sympathetically designed and screened behind the original rubble-stone walling.

Over Norton 🌿

The village is situated three quarters of a mile above the town of Chipping Norton. The first dated record, in the 12th century, is in connection with Cold Norton Priory, so called because of its bleak situation.

In 1559 some priory buildings were let, including the Chapel on the Heath, situated off what was then the main road from Oxford and signposted to Heythrop at the present time. A secret passage was known to exist, but was thought to have been used only until the last prior died. Legend says that goods from coaches robbed by highwaymen were taken underground, unsuspected by the sheriff. The chapel was eventually demolished and an inn named the Shakespeare's Head took its place. Although Shakespeare may have used this road from Stratford it is doubtful whether he stayed there.

Other roads, or dust tracks, came into use, including the 'Woolway' from Great Rollright. This route would be taken by Cotswold sheep, famous for their quality wool. The ancient 'Salt Way' also crossed Over Norton from the west to avoid the toll area.

The first mention of the Dawkins family in the early 18th century occurs when James Dawkins lived in the village. He was Member of Parliament for Woodstock from 1734–47. The Dawkins were local landowners and James, born in Jamaica in 1696, died, unmarried, in 1766 and is buried in the family vault in Chipping Norton church.

Over Norton Park was inherited by a nephew, Henry Dawkins, who was also a Member of Parliament. The house was rebuilt in Tudor style in 1879, standing in well-wooded grounds of some 90 acres. At that time the village population was 242 souls. On the death of Henry Dawkins in 1864, a memorial drinking fountain was built as a tribute from the family to Henry and his wife Emma.

Some considerable interest was taken in Over Norton Park in 1891 when geological exploration was carried out regarding the likelihood of a coal seam being present. A report for Lt Col W. G. Dawkins produced a suggestion for further investigation, but no more is known about the enterprise. Previously, records of quarrying in the area of Hit or Miss Wood mention a site where stone may have been obtained for the building of Chipping Norton properties.

Before approximately 1878 there were no ovens in the village as food was cooked above the fire. About this time the bakery was a welcome addition to the village, selling groceries and providing a cooking service for the villagers. Yorkshire puddings cost 1d, and 1½d for pies; these were sometimes delivered by the children. The population of the village was 440 in 1881. In 1887 the Great Western Railway Corporation opened a single line between Banbury and Chipping Norton, providing work for the villagers.

With the changing pattern of farming, the milking herds have made way for arable cultivation. A council estate has been established at Quarhill Close and private houses have been added in the beautiful setting of the surrounding countryside. As a sign of progress a cellular communications aerial is in the course of erection.

Pudlicote ᘓᕟ

Pudlicote is a small hamlet situated about two miles from Chadlington. The existing Pudlicote House is built on the site of a Roman villa. The present owner, Sir Frederic Bolton, has been researching the history of Pudlicote and has copies of leases dated in the 1740s which show that the present boundaries are more or less the same as they were then, and that the land was not affected by any of the local enclosure acts. There is also evidence that this land was afforested to celebrate the coronation of Henry II and according to the laws of the forests, if anyone was found shooting game they had their thumbs cut off.

A notorious owner of Pudlicote House was John de Pudlicote, who in 1303 attempted to steal the Crown Jewels from the Chapel of the Pyx in Westminster Abbey. He and his accomplices were caught and hanged.

A number of crooked sixpences have been dug up in the fields around Pudlicote and these apparently were luck tokens. Is there a connection here with the rhyme, 'There was a crooked man who walked a crooked mile, And found a crooked sixpence upon a crooked stile.'?

Sir Frederic also has in his possession a bill of sale dated 1878 which proudly boasted of 'two rookeries', obviously in those days considered to be an advantage to the sale of the farm, by supplementing the dinner table with rook pie. The rookeries are still in existence today, but there is a very different view of their value as they take their toll of the crops.

Radley ᘓᕟ

The village of Radley has a church and a college, a river and a railway and, centrally located, a post office and a pub. Modern village life is centred round the church, the school and the new village hall.

In the 1950s village boys competed for the right to earn sixpence carrying the 'Young Gents' trunks up to the college from the railway station. Since then the building of large areas of housing has increased the pre-war size of the village fourfold and the rural cottages are overshadowed.

Local people have access to the college's sporting facilities, and often walk in its pleasant, tree-filled, well maintained grounds. Many an elderly person has been grateful for the help of the 'Social Service' boys who visit them, and firm friendships have been formed. The summer

184

months are characterized by the daily stream of athletic looking young men running or cycling past the church and over the railway bridge down to the boathouse on the Thames.

St James the Great, a pretty 13th century stone church with a square tower, overlooks the timber-framed vicarage house believed to have been inhabited since the 13th century, but not always by vicars. In the church, beneath a gallery is a pictorial map of Radley, embroidered by members of the WI in 1971.

The railway bridge links the village of Radley and Lower Radley. Almost all the houses on the Radley side were built since 1920, and it is in Lower Radley that the picturesque thatched cottages can be found.

Railway and Thames run through Radley on their journey from Oxford to London. The station, which was originally built to serve the college, meets the needs of commuters, but local life turns to the buses, which give a good service to the towns on either side.

The passing year is marked by the church's Palm Sunday procession through the village, the Good Friday Walk into Oxford to raise money for local charities, the school's May Fayre, the Fete and Flower Show, the Football Festival, the Harvest Supper and the Christmas Bazaar. In all seasons tractors can be heard working late into the evenings and the sound of a train in the cutting is a herald of rain over Radley.

Ramsden

A clearing in an ancient Royal hunting forest, at the crossroads of a well trodden footpath and the Roman road from St Albans to Cirencester, was the humble beginnings of an attractive and well-loved, mellow Cotswold-Stone village called Ramsden. Early in the 20th century herds of cows were a common sight wandering down the high street for milking. The road was made of broken stone then and the village had its own stonebreaker who worked from a shed on the site of the top pub, the Stag and Hounds.

In the centre of the village at the crossroads is a recently cleaned and repaired war memorial which lists all the men killed in the two World Wars. Once there were three places for Christian worship, a Methodist chapel, a Roman Catholic chapel, and the parish church of St James. This was consecrated in 1872 and has a magnificent spire which can be seen for miles around. Now the only centre for worship, the large festivals have an ecumenical flavour and are well supported by villagers of many persuasions. The most popular service is the candlelit carol service on Christmas Eve when there is standing room only at the back of a packed church.

Most of the village community life takes place in the Memorial Hall which is a converted barn, opened in 1949, after a concerted effort by a handful of villagers to raise funds. This is now the meeting place of Ramsden Women's Institute which was started in the village school in December 1922. One momentous achievement by WI members during the Second World War is recorded in the minutes when one ton of plums was canned by hand in 15 hours, the last lid being sealed at midnight on the 1,010th tin!

The flavour of the village today is a happy mix of families who have their roots in the past, going back generations, and those whose work in Oxford, London, Witney or Charlbury has brought them to seek housing in a quiet, pleasant and friendly village, just off the busy main road between Witney and Charlbury.

Rotherfield Greys ✍

Despite the loss of the village school and post office over the years, Greys still retains its charm and attracts many visitors to see the beautiful cherry blossom in the spring, to watch the cricket matches on the village green and to visit Greys Court (the home of Lady Brunner) with its beautiful gardens set amid the ruins of a 14th century fortress.

The estate was given to the National Trust several years ago and is open to the public from Easter each year.

The village hall has recently been extended and modernised as a memorial to the late Sir Felix Brunner.

Three generations of the Barratt family owned and worked at the blacksmith's premises bordering the village green; the last smith died in the late 1980s. Much of his work can be seen around the village.

The interior of the church and the churchyard are tended by a band of willing helpers and the rector serves both the parish of Rotherfield Greys and Rotherfield Peppard.

Rotherfield Peppard 🌿

Situated on the southern slopes of the Chilterns, in that loop of the Thames that dips towards Reading, Rotherfield Peppard was long ago on the 'Pack and Prime' way from Henley to Goring, an overland route transporting goods to avoid the difficult navigation of the Thames around Reading. A settlement called Redrefeld is recorded in the Domesday Book. Later, in the reign of Edward I, Ralph Pipard was given the estate, whereby the area became known as Retheresfelde Pipard. Around that time the construction of All Saints' church began, consisting then only of the chancel which has three small 12th century windows. One of its three bells is a mid 14th century bell from the Wokingham foundry; another is 17th century, inscribed 'Henry Knight made mee 1621'.

The village is scattered on two sides of Peppard Common, a natural beauty spot deeply divided by a dry valley that in prehistoric times carried water as it wound its way down to the river at Henley. Indeed, this parish once extended as far as the Thames and had its own pump, in Mill Lane, Henley, for extracting water from the river in times of severe drought. Until the water main was laid in early 1900, people relied on rain water tanks in their gardens, although some were lucky to live near Spring Wood, from whose natural spring the local bakery still drew water a generation ago.

The common has always been the great meeting place for the villagers to celebrate, a place for recreation and enjoyment, for providing pasture and firewood, blackberries and crab apples. Many the bonfire lit here to rejoice at a Coronation, Jubilee, or end-of-war celebration. Many a winter's day spent tobogganing down its steepest slope, or a summer's day picnicking among harebells and heather. Generations of children have sat astride its 'wishing stone', isolated in the undergrowth – perhaps originally a marker stone for those packhorses of the Pack and Prime way that crossed the common here? Not far away, overlooking the common, stands one of the oldest houses in the village, Manor House, once a coaching house known as 'The Blue Monkey' which served those same travellers on the Pack and Prime road.

Centuries ago the villagers met here on fair days, as featured in Elizabeth Goudge's book, *The White Witch*, set in this village during the English Civil War. (This well-loved author lived in Dog Lane for many years). The Peppard Revels were held annually on Whit Monday, and appear to have been wanton and wicked!

In the 1950s an area of the common was donated by the lord of the manor to provide a sports ground and pavilion, in memory of those villagers who lost their lives in the Second World War. Earlier, in memory of those lives lost in the First World War, a fine village hall had been built. Here also is a flourishing bowls club.

Rambling over the common, through beech woods and over farmland one sees much evidence of pits from which chalk was dug, for spreading on the fields and for providing firm floors for cattle sheds and barns. Also sites of flint excavation can be seen in the valley, and fine use of this in the building of Peppard primary school and many farm cottages. There is also evidence of a flint mine worked during the early Stone Age in the aptly named Stony Bottom.

For generations this was a farming community with cattle, pigs and poultry grazing and rooting in patchwork meadows. Today, sadly, the small farms have given way to vast acres of cereals and oilseed rape, devoid of wildlife – no partridge, hare or lapwing on these antiseptic fields.

Most people now commute to Reading and London for work. Until a few years ago Peppard Hospital employed many local people, on its farm and market garden as well as the wards. Starting as a sanatorium because of the 'wonderful healing air' here in Peppard, it pioneered the valuable work in beating that one-time scourge, tuberculosis.

Once on the Pack and Prime route, hence pubs such as the Pack Horse and the Pack Saddle in a neighbouring parish, also on the old drovers' route from Bristol, hence the Butcher's Arms, Peppard is now, unfortunately, on the 'avoid Reading' route to the M4.

Although there has been considerable development since 1900 (population then about 500), luckily Peppard, perched on its common, surrounded by beautiful beech woods, has not spread alarmingly in recent years, with a population of under 1,400 today. Fortunately there is still a village stores, a DIY store and, most important, the village post office run by the same family that established it around 1900.

Salford 🌿

Salford is no beauty spot frequented by tourists. Nor is it on the way to anywhere, lying as it does off the A44 between Chipping Norton and Moreton-in-Marsh. It is a small village of just over 300 souls in the centre of the manor of Salford, which lies within the boundaries of the 1,500 acres forming the ancient parish. Small it may be, but it is today a very close-knit and active village. The school and the village shop have gone, but the church and pub flourish and the villagers run a dramatic society, a history society, a WI, a sports ground, an annual flower show, a pre-Christmas dinner for the over sixties, given by the village hall committee, and all sorts of other activities.

As a place name, Salford is relatively common, but this version is unique. The other Salford settlements take their names from the Latin 'Salix' or willow, and presumably mean the ford near the willow copse or osiers. This Salford means 'salt-ford' and the village may have been a stop-over on the ancient Salt Way linking Droitwich to the south coast.

So Salford is an ancient village and there are still families in it who have lived here for several centuries. Among these are the Fawdrys and the well-stocked churchyard indicates the continuity of the family within the parish. Fawdrys have been farming here – though not at the same farm – over the centuries. The first mention of the family occurs in an old document as 'Ralph Fawdry flourishing in Salford 1640'. They look set to farm and flourish here for some time to come.

Agriculture, of course, was the only livelihood of the majority of villagers until the Industrial Revolution, when workers drifted into nearby towns. Before the Second World War, the parish of Salford contained ten farms. Now, with intensive farming, there are four farms and a smallholding.

Salford is part of what is fondly known as 'The Five Parishes' – Salford, Cornwell, Chastleton, Little Compton and Little Rollright – and 13th century St Mary's church stands on a rise to the west of the village. It was considerably altered by George Street in 1856, but original windows, a Norman tympanum and Norman font speak of the past.

The most dramatic church event of late has been the removal on 12th September 1989 of the historic Bagley ring of five bells, all cast in 1687. Whites of Appleton joined forces with volunteer labour on that day and the tower became a hive of activity. By lunch time they had cleared all the wood, wheels and old frame from the tower, and the five bells were lined up on the church path. It was a beautiful moment, as sightseers and workers stood in the mellow September sun, gazing at these historic pieces of art. The bells were returned to their home in April 1990.

Since 1981, summertime has seen the Salford Flower Show engaging the attention of numerous people in the village. At lunch time on Flower Show day the Black Horse is packed with trade and a good number repair there after the show, too! The pub is a comfortable focal point for those in the village and surrounding areas who want company, a drink and good food.

Shellingford 🌿

Shellingford was first mentioned in Saxon times, when King Athelstan granted the monastery of Abingdon twelve hides of land at 'Scaringaford', in AD 931. The ford crossed Mill brook, one of the tributaries of Rosey brook. Drinking water was at one time obtained here from a spring and served the whole village, as well as a roadside pump. Various industries were also served by this water – as many as six malthouses, a mill, a laundry for the Kitemore estate, and an old smithy which existed from the 18th century until the early 20th century.

The largest house still standing was built in 1867 as Kitemore House and it still commands a fine view across the parish to the Ridgeway.

Several large houses in the village have served as rectory, four in all, the largest being a 16th century manor house known locally as Shellingford Castle. Sadly it fell into decay and was finally demolished. On its site the newest rectory stands, now in its turn redundant and privately owned.

St Faith's, the partly Norman, 12th century church stands nearby, and still provides services on a regular basis, although like many local churches, the rector is shared amongst other parishes.

One of the more noted rectors was John Morton, who went on to become Archbishop of Canterbury and Chancellor of England in the reign of Henry VII. He was noted as being the inventor of 'Morton's Fork', a two-pronged attempt at securing monies for the Church and Crown from the thrifty and spendthrift alike!

The local area is mainly agricultural, and as such the lifeblood of the village could be called the many farms – Home Farm and Church Farm within the village and Sands Farm and Little Newbury Farms on the outskirts, as well as Kitemore Home Farm. Many of the inhabitants of the village are agricultural workers.

Land over the centuries has changed a great deal, an enormous amount of woodland having disappeared, although there are still remnants of copses still remaining. In Fishpond Copse, attached to the village, there can still be seen the remains of medieval fishponds managed by sluices and banks to provide fish and wildfowl for the table at Kitemore estate and the rectory.

Although the village has now lost its shop and pub (known locally as the 'Hole in the Wall' as the customers had to stand in the yard to drink their ale, served from a literal hole in the wall!), there is still a very busy and thriving school, built on land given by one of the former inhabitants of Kitemore House. A school has existed in the village for a very long time, although it is now a far cry from the 'Penny on a Monday' for the week's tuition – no penny, no school!

Shilton ༄

A lovely little stream runs through Shilton, called 'The Shill', so it may be from this the village gets its name. It certainly owes its reputation for being a very pretty place to its setting in a valley with the pond in the centre, grass areas, red and white chestnut trees, a pump from which villagers used to get their drinking and washing water, and a pump-stack where water barrels were filled for farm use. Close by is a well complete with ornamental stone, a war memorial, and spanning the stream as it leaves the pond is a very attractive stone footbridge called 'The Arch'.

The source of the stream rises somewhere near Westwell and runs through Signett and Burford Bottoms (once called Mount Zion Bottom) before reaching Shilton.

In a dry season this stream almost disappears but a strong spring, called Wells Head, rises just beyond a beautiful water-meadow, and this ensures the village is never without a constant flow of water. Snowdrops and later kingcups grow in profusion here in the spring. This is one of a dwindling number of ancient unspoilt meadows. Luckily there are two 'common land banks', a small paddock and a water meadow in the middle of the village which give it 'green lungs'. Willow trees on the banks of the stream add to its beauty.

In medieval times there was a Cistercian settlement consisting of a grange, tithe barn, dovecote, fish pond and rabbit warren. The paddock is still called Conyger after the latter. The main building was used as a stable around 1910–40, and as a chick-rearing unit from 1948–51, and converted to a dwelling about 1970. The roof of the tithe barn was destroyed by fire years ago and replaced with corrugated iron. This was made into a house at about the same time.

Shilton was once very much a farming community consisting of six farms, with four farmyards right in the village. Cows were driven up the street and grazed the grass banks whilst ducks and hens wandered in and out of the rickyards. There was a baker, blacksmith, post office and for a time two shops, a band and also cricket and football teams. Alas they are no more!

There is a story that 'Silly Shilton' was an apt name – that people used to drive the fish under the bridge when it rained to keep them dry and put a pig on a wall to see the band go by. Also, that someone was seen, having left the Rose and Crown, trying to rake the reflection of a full moon from the pond believing it to be a cheese.

The Norman church sits squarely on a hill overlooking the village – the church of the Holy Rood. It has a notable font with beautifully carved scenes from the life of Christ on its four faces. There are several 'wool tombs' in the churchyard and a magnificent copper beech tree near the gate. On the opposite side of the lane is the old school which closed in 1970 – it is now a village hall fulfilling many needs.

Also in Church Lane is the Baptist chapel built in 1830. It has a small band of faithful worshippers.

A footpath linking Shilton with Alvescot passes through the churchyard, and a bridlepath from Shilton to Burford crosses the route of the old Akeman Street and is a lovely walk. People who know this small Cotswold village well have a tremendous love for, and loyalty to it. As the old jingle says –

> Bampton steeple wears a hat,
> Witney steeple looks at that,
> Burford steeple's ready to fall,
> Shilton tower beats them all.

Shiplake ✍

Newcomers often ask 'but where is the village?' It is true there are few houses on the main road from Henley to Reading but not many would grumble these days at having a built-in bypass.

It happened for historic reasons. The late 18th century owner of Shiplake Court, the manor house, gambled away all his money, and the house fell into such decay that it was pulled down in 1804. The estate did not support a thriving economy and little building took place for the next 50 years.

In 1858 the railway came through the parish, about a mile away from what had been the centre, near the Court and the church. It passed through a small settlement near the Lashbrook. In fact this was probably settled before Shiplake, as it is mentioned in Domesday Book, along with its mill. The mill, which was where the lock now is, existed until 1908. It is interesting that though Lashbrook Farm, the site of the Domesday manor, is in the flood plain, it occupies a small area of higher ground which becomes an island.

Gradually summer houseboats moored on the river-bank near the new station, and they acquired gardens alongside. The gardens were then built upon to provide luxurious homes. As commuting became common, more and more houses were built within easy reach of the station and although the long steam-engined trains have given way to one and two-coach diesels it is still this part of the parish which is the main settlement. It is here that the three shops, the hairdresser and the garage are. As in most of the south-east commuter belt the pressure for new houses is great and nearly 100 new houses have been built since the 1960s.

But it is a very mixed village – there is council-run sheltered housing, and a thriving Church of England primary school. A playgroup for the very small has its home in the village hall, which, recently refurbished, hosts many other activities. Cricket, football, bowls and tennis clubs flourish. The school and the hall and playing fields form part of another area of development on the opposite side of the main road from the station.

Shiplake Court was rebuilt in 1894 on its beautiful site overlooking the river. Now it is a boys public school which has flourished since its foundation some thirty years ago. They have had great success at rowing, and scholastically in teaching the dyslexic.

Modern estate agents like to call the village Shiplake on Thames. It's not correct but most villagers appreciate the beautiful tow path walk upstream from Shiplake Lock. The changing seasons bring fresh palettes of colour: the brash primary charms of summer hire boats, the delicate pastels of winter with bare trees tracing patterns against the cold sky. Time can be idled away happily at the lock, watching the expert and inexpert boat owners. A world away from the social accent of Henley Royal Regatta, Shiplake joins forces each year with Wargrave, the village on the Berkshire bank of the river, for a 'fun' regatta.

The historic parish, only a mile and half wide, stretched seven miles, from the river up to the fringe of the Chilterns. All the South Oxfordshire parishes were of this form, providing lush water meadows which flooded in winter, and the upland pasture necessary as a result. Small settlements occurred all the way along the seven miles, and one has grown to form another small village at Binfield Heath.

Shiplake has no great claims to a place in the history of the nation. Sir Francis Plowden, Queen Elizabeth's Chancellor lived at Shiplake Court, but as far as is known Queen Elizabeth did *not* sleep here. James Granger, vicar from 1747 to 1776, was famous in his day as a promoter of illustrating books by adding pictures cut from other books. His name has entered the dictionaries as 'grangerising'. Lord Tennyson was married in the attractive small church, and wrote a poem about the place. George Orwell lived here briefly as a boy. There has been a brickworks and a paper mill, though now there is little employment actually in the village: like so many rural places it is but a dormitory and retirement home. However, it is a happy community that few people leave voluntarily.

Shipton-under-Wychwood

Through the centuries Saxon, Norman, Plantagenet and Tudor hunters, all have pursued the hart, hind and hare in the now drastically reduced metes and bounds of the Wychwood Forest. William the Conqueror enjoyed such sport and set aside some 68 forests in England for his royal chases. Of these, the Wychwood was one of the four largest in the land. It is not surprising then that three neighbouring villages took the name of this mighty domain – Ascott, Milton and Shipton – all 'under Wychwood'.

Shipton is an ancient village pleasantly situated on the Evenlode river. It was a very important royal manor before Domesday and the church of St Mary the Virgin may have been a minster in Saxon times.

If calling at Christmastide, look up to the arches decorated with evergreen-covered battens, a custom still carried on from the early 1900s. Sadly, in the churchyard the gravestones now stand around the wall, or lie flat to form a path. Walk there in the spring and the snowdrops and daffodils will dance for you.

Adjacent to the church is the now restored and resplendent Old Prebendal House, which boasts as one of its 40-odd prebends John Foxe, author of *The Book of Martyrs*. The core of this fine mellow stone building is mid 13th century with later additions. It is now a beautifully appointed retirement home.

Shipton Court, which may have been the local manor house, is situated on the High Street across from the cricket ground. It was built by Sir Rowland de Lacy in 1603 and is one of the largest Jacobean houses in the country. An 18th century couplet pays grudging tribute to three Cotswold families who seem to have been 'to the manor born':

> The Lacies, Tracies and Fettiplaces
> Own all the manors, parks and chases.

A number of families now share the leasehold ownership of the Court and the houses and cottages within its confines.

The village green was allotments until the late 1960s, then was bought for the village by Colonel Stedall in memory of his wife. At the top of the green is the war memorial and the fountain in memory of 17 Shipton people who perished at sea on the *Cospatrick* in 1874 when emigrating to New Zealand. The beech tree was planted in 1974 to commemorate 100 years from the sinking of the *Cospatrick* and the closing of the post office, which had been in the Wiggins family since 1845. It was the oldest-established post office in England and now it is the Old Post House looking onto the green.

The beech tree is now a picture in spring and autumn and has grown big enough for boys to climb and hide. Few know of the hours of work spent watering the tree in the summers of 1975 and 1976 by Doctor Scott Senior, who first grew the tree from a local seed, and Mr and Mrs V. Avery, who suffered a much punctured garden hose as this had to cross Church Street to reach the tree, not to mention floods in the lean-to when the hose came off the tap as cars went over it!

Village scene at Shipton-under-Wychwood

Shipton-under-Wychwood has three fine, unspoiled pubs – the Lamb, the Shaven Crown and the Red Horse, as well as a cricket ground, a bowls club, and a late 19th century village hall which hosts the many and varied local activities. If Shiptonians cannot lay claim to a Cotswold home – the purists exclude us from that Area of Outstanding Beauty by some four miles – villagers are content. The houses and dry-stone walls are of the same golden oolite eggstone, the sheep are as fat, the river is as swift flowing, the valley is as green and the people – well, the people are the nicest mix of Oxfordshire natives, Home Counties' retirees and outright 'foreigners' that one could find anywhere!

Shrivenham 🪶

One of the most westerly villages in Oxfordshire, Shrivenham nestles in the Vale of the White Horse on the route from Swindon to Oxford. A bypass, built in 1984, ensures that Shrivenham's rural atmosphere is preserved. Elm Tree House, a gracious house built in the style of Inigo Jones, a village school built in 1863 and many lovely thatched cottages border the wide tree-lined main street. In *Tom Brown's Schooldays*, Thomas Hughes' hero set forth to Rugby school from Shrivenham station (sadly now defunct).

Recent archaeological excavations near Shrivenham, just before the construction of the bypass, revealed flint implements of the late Neolithic and early Bronze Age and also domestic debris from Iron Age settlements. Twenty four coins of the 3rd century reign of Allectus were discovered in an old well in Shrivenham in 1905.

St Andrew's church is impressively large for a small village, with parts dating back to the 11th, 12th and 13th centuries. Its many unusual features include the central tower, 18 large clear windows, Tuscan-like tapering columns, magnificent brass chandeliers and hanging pyx. There are many memorials to the Barrington family, important landowners locally in previous decades.

The ancient manor of Beckett, mentioned in the Domesday survey as Becote, was acquired by King John in 1204. One of the four Shrivenham manors, Fowersmill was held by the de Becotes in 1367 in service of coming before the King whenever he passed Fowersmill Bridge and offering two white capons saying, 'See here, Sir, these two capons you shall have at some other time but not now!'. Obviously, to have two white leghorns flapping round in one's coach was not conducive to a pleasant journey! The manor later belonged to the Barrington family and now, the house and grounds belong to the Royal Military College of Science.

Shrivenham possesses one of the finest village halls in the county, the Memorial Hall, presented by Charlotte, Countess Barrington and opened by Princess Beatrice in 1925 as a memorial to villagers killed in the First World War. Six houses for ex-servicemen border the adjoining recreation ground, which is large enough for a football and cricket pitch. In August, Shrivenham village fete is held here. The hall is a splendid edifice for a small village. The roof covering is Cotswold stone tiles supported by a massive hammerbeam roof of very large oak members, possibly the last of the great timber roofs to be built in the country.

Fred 'Gramophone' Knapp was an eccentric village character. After seeking his fortune in America, he returned to Shrivenham to make very large garden plant bowls in concrete, and he also cast a man to stand in the garden. A lorry driver approached this realistic figure at dusk, to ask the way! Fred could recite a long poem which he had composed about some poor soul's foot trouble and he also had the family history of Lord Barrington committed to memory. Considered one of the 'long-headed' of the village, he was often in demand as a letter reader or writer.

Fred's son Harold farmed the village farm and would 'accidentally' let the ram out into the street. This creature chased anything in sight and women dived into the nearest shop at the ram's approach. Harold would follow, waving his arms but enjoying every minute of it! He heard that the Duke of Edinburgh was visiting locally and painted RAF roundels in red and blue on the wings of several of his geese and paraded them in the street. He insisted on doing his own thatching with the resultant cottage looking like a rick and always managing to grow a lovely bright green crop of grass on it!

The definitive book about the history of Shrivenham was written by the Rev Edward F. Hill, MA in 1928. Frequently quoted, this volume is the most sought-after book in Shrivenham. Canon Hill Gardens, a beautiful short road of modern houses curving round a tree-shaded village pond, immortalises the name of this highly-esteemed former vicar of Shrivenham.

Sibford Ferris & Sibford Gower

Between Banbury and Shipston-on-Stour, just off the B4035, lie the delightful Sibford villages, known locally as The Ferris and The Gower, with the tiny hamlet of Burdrop adjoining the latter.

In the 12th century considerable land at Sibford was given by William Fitz Roger to the Knights Templars. Today's Temple Close, with its dovecote, and Temple Mill, bear witness to their Norman connections.

The two local inns are other reminders of the past. Dated 1610, the Bishop Blaize (patron saint of wool weavers) indicates that Sibford was part of the flourishing Cotswold sheep-farming area. The Wykham Arms undoubtedly derived its name from the Wykehams, lords of nearby Swalcliffe Manor.

The spiritual welfare of the Sibfords is cared for by the church, the small Methodist chapel and the Society of Friends. The church of Holy

Sibford Manor

Trinity, consecrated in 1840 when the modern parish was created, is unusual in having neither tower nor steeple.

The first Friends' Meeting House, a small thatched building dated 1680, was erected by an enthusiastic band of puritan dissenters following a visit from George Fox, the Quaker leader. This was replaced in 1866 by the present, much larger, building.

In 1839 Joshua Lamb walked to Oxford from Sibford, and resulting from his meeting with other Quakers there, the 'Great House' in Sibford Ferris, built in 1666 and later known as the Manor, was purchased for £1,200. Three years later 26 boys and 22 girls were admitted as the first boarding scholars. Girls assisted with household duties and boys worked on the 25 acre farm, from whence home-grown corn was ground at Temple Mill.

There has been a village school on the present site in the Gower since 1631. The mid-Victorian building was updated in 1957 when coke stoves, bucket toilets and high latticed windows gave place to modern amenities. With its panoramic views to the south, it is thought to be one of the most beautifully situated in the county.

The Sibford Gower and Burdrop Town Estates Charity was founded in 1560, the income from the bequeathed land being equally divided between 'the poor', 'pious and charitable purposes' and 'the primary school and school master'. Much benefit is still derived from this charity.

The Lamb family have farmed in the village for over 300 years. Unquestionably the best-known member of the family was Theodore, born about 1880. The youngest of a large family he attended the Quaker school and became a skilled watch and clock mender. There is no known explanation of why he spent his last 40 years living as a hermit; his home, on Sibford Heath, a shack of galvanised sheets and iron bedsteads; his transport a tyre-less bicycle; and his raiment mostly sacking. His sustenance was purchased from the village shop, supplemented from his own vegetable patch. A meagre income was derived from passers-by, often in coaches, who stopped to look and wonder, but Theodore never conversed before a coin had been dropped in his tin mug. Totally honest, completely harmless and immensely strong, he eventually contracted pneumonia and died, aged 70, in Banbury hospital, the nurses respecting his request not to cut his long matted hair – he said it would spoil his appearance! Money which he had entrusted to the vicar was sufficient to pay for his funeral, attended by many paying their last respects to a long-to-be-remembered Sibford character.

Another local man was Joseph Alcock, recalled as the last of the cottage weavers attached to the local plush industry. He wove part of the red carpet used in Westminster Abbey for the coronation of Edward VII.

Sonning Common ❧

Just over the border from Berkshire, Sonning Common today is a far cry from the few cottages, farms and beerhouses scattered on and around 200 acres of rough pasture, with cultivated areas and woods, that existed in the 1860s. Originally part of the manor of Sonning-on-Thames, the land was used for grazing cattle and sheep. When the rich water meadows by the river flooded, animals were driven up to the higher ground, often for months in the winter. Hog Lane (now Woodlands Road) in Sonning Common was so called because pigs were driven along it to the woods, to feed on the beech mast.

Widmore Pond, on the edge of the village, at one time supplied most of the water used locally. Dr Plot's *Natural History of Oxfordshire*, written in 1677, stated that when the pond was cleaned out, oak trees were found standing upright. In the mud at the bottom Roman coins and stag antlers were found, and the theory was put forward that it had originally been a Roman silver mine. Before 1940, local boys spent many hours sitting on the wall fishing – but the fish died out, and the whole area became neglected and overgrown. In the early 1970s members of the Parish Council organised working parties, and the pond was cleared of rubbish, landscaped, and a seat provided. Ducks and swans were installed, and the whole area has become a feature of the village, with some of the best-fed birds in Oxfordshire!

With the break up of the manor in the 1880s, much of the land was sold off piecemeal, and the slow building of an actual village began. Formerly part of the civil parish of Eye and Dunsden, it was afforded its own Parish Council status in 1951. With the building of three large housing estates in the 1960s the population increased from about 1,000 at the beginning of the decade to 4,000 by 1970.

Pressure from developers has been constant and house prices have soared. Recent attempts to incorporate the village into Berkshire, with the likelihood of it simply becoming a suburb of Reading, have been successfully repelled, and there is currently a strong move to build homes for first time buyers.

Sonning Common is an active, lively community, with 15 shops, three public houses, two banks, three garages, a library, health centre, dentist and veterinary surgery. The primary school has 260 pupils on the roll, and Chiltern Edge Comprehensive with about 1,000 students covers a considerably larger catchment area. The Community Education Centre attached to the latter runs a wide range of vocational and leisure classes, and the village boasts over 30 clubs and societies, including an active amenity group.

Main employers are the Johnson Matthey Research Laboratories (on the outskirts of the village), and of course the wide range of firms in Reading, which is five miles to the south. London is accessible from Reading in 25 minutes on a high speed train on a good day, so there are a fair proportion of commuters, for whom the village provides a rural retreat from the bustle of the city.

Souldern 🌿

Souldern is a small village of less than 200 houses situated some seven miles north of Bicester in the very north of Oxfordshire, and just half a mile from the Northamptonshire border. Being a cul-de-sac village it is fairly peaceful and quiet and has a close-knit community, some families having lived there for 200–300 years. In more recent years the character of the village has changed with the influx of commuters and retired people.

Souldern is an extremely pretty village right on the edge of the Cotswolds and overlooking the Cherwell valley. There are many keen gardeners, many of whom open their gardens to the public for a weekend each summer and divide the proceeds amongst several worthy causes.

In earlier times Souldern was known as Sulthorn because of the many thorn trees which grew there. The first recorded burial is that of William de Say in 1161, the parish church of St Mary having been built by the de Say family a few years previously. During the Civil War, when the king was stationed in Oxford, Souldern suffered badly from the marauding bands of Parliamentary troops, about 20,000 of them being camped in the area.

Most of the houses are built of stone, some being large family homes. There is a constant supply of spring water which feeds the village pond, formerly the old town well. There is also a second well known as St Chad's Well.

Souldern is fortunate in having its own village hall, which was largely built by public subscription and many local events take place there and on the adjoining sports ground.

In 1986 a group of residents, spurred on by the Parish Council, formed a committee to plan and organise the planting of a 'harmony wood' on the outskirts of the village. Since then more adjoining land has become available and extensions have been made to the wood. This is a favourite walk for local people, as indeed are the many public footpaths and bridleways in the area. With the planting of the wood an ancient custom was revived – 'Oak Apple Day'. On this special day in May the 'locals' picnic in the wood and the families join together and have a pleasant afternoon. Another annual event is the show organised by the Horticultural Society.

Souldern has two pubs, a post office stores and a garage as well as a church and a chapel. Whilst there is employment in the village, most of those who work do so in either Banbury, Bicester or Oxford. The M40 motorway now passes less than a mile from the village and can be seen down in the valley.

South Moreton 🌿

The parish of South Moreton was part of the Blewbury Hundred in the Domesday Book. It extends from the northerly boundary with Wittenham edge to Mill brook and its tributary Hakkas brook in the south, an area of approximately 1,350 acres. It was once part of Berkshire. Part of the parish boundary brook called Tibbald was once the sheepwash where local farmers drove their sheep for dipping.

From pre-Conquest times the settlement was a prosperous place supporting four manor houses. In 1199 Robert de Sanderville held the moated manor house on the north side of the village street. The manor house of Bray, with Tudor remains, has now been converted into two cottages near to the present-day Hall Farm. The terraces of the manor house of Adresham are traceable on the south side of the street. The hamlet of Fulscot, also mentioned in Domesday, lies to the west of the village and there is a manor house where a moat can be traced and buildings and cottages supporting a mixed farm.

Malting was a staple in Elizabethan times and there was a forge and a village pound. The village stocks, last used in 1838, were situated where Manor Lane meets the main village street, known today as Cross Tree. There were many small businesses such as saddler, baker, grocer, boot and shoe maker, blacksmith, wheelwright and carpenter, bricklayer, tailor and dressmaker.

There was a paper mill and a corn mill, which was possibly the mill valued at twelve shillings in Domesday. The (corn) mill house was hired out as a hospital during the smallpox epidemic of 1799. This mill was also used as a rag store where the rags were prepared and then sent down the brook in flat-bottomed boats to the paper mill, located near to the present railway arch over the Mill brook. There are few remains as the mill was burnt down in 1825, and although rebuilt, it suffered the same fate 13 years later.

The church of St John the Baptist was built on the site of a chapel which overlooked the causeway that connected the brook crossing-point to the village. The original chapel was a stopping-point for medieval pilgrims following the footsteps of St Birinus, who journeyed from Churn Knob near Blewbury to Dorchester, where he founded the abbey. This pilgrimage is revived each year on the first Sunday in July but the pilgrims now cross the brook by the bridge at the mill and stop for refreshments in the village. The church has a rare Saxon doorway, which is blocked up, and near the gate stands a mighty yew tree reputed to be 1,600 years old.

In 1850 the Great Western Railway was built and the main line from London ran across the parish north of the village street. Gravel and sand were extracted locally and used in its construction. Some local men worked on the line and at the important goods' marshalling yards in the west of the parish.

A nameless shepherd, who tended sheep by the wayside, left £10 to parish charity. This amount, together with £1,000 sterling given by Edward Sherman Esq of London in 1863, formed the South Moreton Consolidated Charity, the annual proceeds thereof to be distributed amongst the poor of the parish. Edward Sherman had lived at one of the manors with his uncle Sadgrove, who is reputed to have boxed his ears. He then ran off to London and later became the largest coach proprietor in the country with 17,000 horses at work in various parts. The Consolidated Charity still divides proceeds among the villagers during the Christmas period.

Anchor Inn, now a private house, was once the site of much merrymaking when the Whitsun Feast was held there, with swingboats, coconut shies and dancing on the barrel to accordion music.

Hilaire Belloc, the French-born writer, lived in the village and the name of his son Peter Belloc appears on the war memorial in the church.

Village legend recounts two interesting ghost stories from the past. In 1804 a local wheelwright hanged himself in a barn. Shortly afterwards an apparition terrified several people in the stackyard south of the barn. This alarming situation led to no less than eleven local clergy meeting together to exorcise the ghost.

The inhabitants of a cottage on the edge of the village invented stories of ghostly happenings, desperately hoping for a reduced rent. They said that candles would apparently go out, rekindle and then explode. A bible would suddenly tumble across the floor and gravel was thrown up at the windows. The story does not state whether they were successful with the rent reduction!

The parish has an abundance of footpaths and bridleways making interesting connections with neighbouring parishes, and the recent addition of the Moreton Ride, a licensed horseway which skirts the fields and links existing tracks, enables the horselover to enjoy traffic-free exercise.

South Stoke

The village of South Stoke is unusual in that three highways, which have done much to influence its history and people, pass through it. Two of these highways are ancient, the river Thames and the Ridgeway path, while the third is the Great Western Railway built by Isambard Brunel. These three routes converge as they cross the parish boundaries near Ye Olde Leatherne Bottle public house to the south and at the Moulsford railway bridge, known locally as the Four Arches, to the north.

Clearly the oldest of these is the river Thames which borders South Stoke to the west. Before the 16th century the lower land in South Stoke was marshy but then the river provided fish and the adjacent land brushwood, willows and osiers. Today one can still see, from the footpath between South Stoke and Little Stoke, remains of a series of fishponds which provided food for the medieval monks resident in the village at that time. These ponds were part of a much larger complex and were fed by drainage ditches connected to the river. During the 16th century a series of weirs was constructed along the Thames to control the flow and to ease navigation for the increasing barge traffic. The barges were towed by horses, the towpath crossed the river at the village at a point opposite Moulsford and the horses were transferred by ferry from one side of the bank to the other. As elsewhere river traffic declined with the advent of the railway and the ferry ceased activity in 1961/2.

The Ridgeway path is a prehistoric way which was part of a comprehensive communication system long before the Romans arrived. Evidence of ancient enclosures and burial pits has been found in South Stoke, together with Roman remains and coins. The Ridgeway now crosses land still owned by Christ Church, Oxford, before it passes through the village.

When the railway came in 1838 it changed the character of the village dramatically. It is built on a wide embankment with three low bridges over the only roads into the village and there is a small culvert, known locally as the bogey hole, which was constructed for the footpath to Little

Stoke. The Four Arches bridge, which crosses the river and the Ridgeway path together is, itself, a listed building.

Manor Farm, beside the church, has always been the largest farm in South Stoke and is still active. Parts of the present farmhouse date from the 16th century and it still has the original oak panelling, moulded beams and a fireplace from an even earlier date. Within the old brick and flint walls around the house are several old buildings and barns. These include a square four-gabled medieval brick dovecote, reputed to be one of the largest in the south of England, and a granary standing on staddle stones.

St Andrew's church incorporates several periods of architecture, with some of the arches on the north side suggesting Norman work. The font is Early English and a fragment of 14th century glass can be seen in the south-east window. The chancel is dominated by a memorial commemorating Griffith Higgs. South Stoke's most famous son was born in 1589, was ordained as a priest and became chaplain to King Charles I. The King sent him to be chaplain to his sister, Princess Elizabeth, when she married and became Queen of Bohemia. Later Griffith Higgs became Dean of Lichfield but during the Civil War, like his sponsor, fell from grace. He saved his head but was stripped of all his titles and returned to South Stoke. He created many charities and, in particular, an educational charity which still benefits the children of South Stoke today.

During the early 19th century the parishioners of South Stoke became increasingly disenchanted with the church vestry's conduct of local affairs. Twenty four dissenters who worshipped in Goring built their own chapel in South Stoke in 1820. Like the Goring chapel it came under the auspices of the Countess of Huntingdon's Connexion and flourished for over a century but this building has not been used for worship since 1976.

Today converted barges, other pleasure craft and energetic rowers pass up and down the river. Fishermen frequently line the banks, either in competition or just for pleasure. The public house, the Perch and Pike, still displays record catches of fish taken from the river in more recent times and large numbers of Ridgeway hikers stop here for refreshment. On their way they often meet tractors and combine harvesters, to say nothing of the Jersey cows from the two working farms. Some of the people living in the village work in it, others commute to work elsewhere. Thus the three highways are still very much a part of South Stoke's character.

Spelsbury ᪐

Spelsbury is a small village on the road between Chipping Norton and Charlbury (B4026).

Of the 50 houses in the village about a quarter are in the region of 100 years old, while over 25 have been built since 1920. There are four almshouses, built in 1689 by the land agent of the Ditchley estate – John Carey of Wilcote. There are still charities settled on the almshouses with Wilcote connections. John Carey was buried in the churchyard – his tomb, a substantial affair, is on the south side of the church.

Several of the old cottages had tradesmen living in them. The shape of the old bread oven can still be identified in the old bakehouse wall. There are a few thatched cottages which look quite picturesque. The village school ceased to be a school in 1958 and was turned into a house. It still retains the bell turret and clock. Some dwellings have been converted from farm buildings and stables.

There is a large water fountain under a canopy built of honey-coloured and pink stone. It was built in memory of Constantine Augustus Dillon (1813–1853), who was the 13th Viscount Dillon. Until about 1953 when mains water was laid on in the village, this was the local water supply. At that time the Hon Elsie Corbett had the village sewerage system put in – both must have been of great benefit to everyone.

The church is dedicated to All Saints. There has been a place of worship on this spot for about 900 years and there is evidence of Roman work in the pillars of the tower. Parts of the nave date from about 1300 but a great deal of rebuilding has been done over the years, particularly in the 18th century.

The church has many memorials, mainly to residents of Ditchley. Lord Rochester, the 17th century poet of Charles II's Court, is interred here in the crypt and his and a number of other coffin plates are now displayed in the baptistry. Another interesting memorial is to a daughter of Charles II and Barbara, Duchess of Cleveland who married Edward Henry Lee – they lived at Ditchley for most of their married life and had 18 children.

The policy of the Rural District Council is that this should be a non-growth village. There is a small estate of a farm and a number of the older cottages, but an increasing number of the dwellings are privately owned, including the original council houses. The village is too small to have a shop or public house but there is a post office in one of the houses every Tuesday morning.

From higher points around the village there is a very pleasing view over the Evenlode valley. The landscape is undulating and wooded with a truly rural aspect.

Stadhampton & Chiselhampton 🐝

Stadhampton was not mentioned in the Domesday Book, but a village existed at that time and the first mention of it by name came in 1146. Years ago, the majority of houses were round the green where the cattle and sheep were allowed to graze for a nominal sum. At the east end of the village, the 17th century manor house lies, approached by an avenue of lime trees. In 1845 the district was hunted by the Old Berkshire Hunt, and new kennels were built in 1884 to house the South Oxfordshire Hunt. Nowadays, their premises are private properties. The Oxfordshire Animal Sanctuary, run by a charity, is housed here.

Mill Lane leads down to the mill house and Cuxham brook. The mill was still working in 1939 and continued in a small way until 1948. Several years ago, a Brook Race was held each year, and this custom was renewed recently. For many years, 'Stadham Feast' was held on the village green, with the fair people setting up their roundabouts and stalls en route from St Giles' Fair in Oxford to Thame Fair.

The oldest house in Stadhampton is Doyleys Farm House and there are still a number of Georgian houses and thatched properties round the green and other parts of the village.

The church of St John the Baptist lies at the other end of the village green and the font is the only part that survives from the original building that existed in 1146. In 1744, the curate presented the church with an oak carving of the coat of arms of Queen Elizabeth I, painted in proper colours, and which now hangs above the door leading to the belfry.

In 1957, a row of houses called Malthouse Row was pulled down to make way for the entrance to Cratlands Close, at the end of which a new primary school was built. The old school, built in 1878 of the same type of brick as was used for a great deal of 19th century building in Stadhampton, was sold in the 1970s.

There are two public houses in the village; the Crown, first licensed in 1825, and the Bear and Ragged Staff. A third, the Black Horse, with a bakehouse adjoining dated 1685 and used as a bakehouse until 1914, is now a private residence. There is still a village shop and post office, a daily delivery of post, doorstep deliveries of milk and a very efficient newsagent who delivers daily and evening papers in all weathers.

Approaching Chiselhampton, one drives along a road which was used during the Civil War by troops, and it is reported that Prince Rupert rode through on his way to Tetsworth in 1643, and returned by the same route after the battle of Chalgrove.

Chiselhampton House was built between 1766 and 1768 from bricks made locally. St Katherine's church remains one of the few complete Georgian churches in the country, with high box pews and Georgian staircase leading to the Jacobean pulpit. This church now comes under the jurisdiction of the Redundant Churches Commission. Chiselhampton Bridge also featured in the Civil War and was made of freestone from Headington Quarry. One of the oldest historical buildings still existing in this district is Camoys House.

Standlake

Standlake is an appropriate name, one might think, particularly looking at the village from the air, as it is surrounded by at least eight lakes. In 1718 the diarist Richard Rawlinson wrote that Standlake was 'among streams in a moorish lakish soil' and 'situate on a dam'd standing puddle, long, deep and dirty'. In fact the old English meaning of Standlake is 'hill by a stony stream'. Three old hamlets form Standlake as we know it today: Standlake, Brittenton and Brighthampton.

In 1228 the living of the church of St Giles was presented by Lady Eva de Gray to John de Limesaya. The 750th anniversary of this event was celebrated in 1978, when a booklet *1228 & All That* was published by the Standlake History Society. From 1543 until 1947 the living was in the gift of Magdalen College and on one occasion the Duke of Windsor, who was then Prince of Wales, visited the rectory with the Magdalen College Beagles. Four Oxford Colleges owned a large part of the village until the end of the First World War when they sold off much of their property.

A large army hut, purchased in 1921, served as village hall until 1989 when a new village hall was opened. To mark the occasion a village map was made, incorporating pictorial contributions from all village organisations and the primary school children, and water colours of a number of properties.

The Mulberry Bush, a school for severely emotionally disturbed children, celebrated its 40th anniversary in 1988 and the village school still has 90 or so pupils, although the number of young families in the village is diminishing, partly due to the high cost of housing.

A light engineering firm and a family firm of builders provide employment for a small number of people, as do the garage, post office, schools and a residential home for the elderly. Standlake has become a centre for tourists and holiday-makers, with three caravan and camping sites and sailing, windsurfing, boating and water skiing facilities on many of the lakes.

Standlake has few village customs: primary school children receive a 'penny loaf' on Ascension Day and income from land bequeathed by the Rev John Chambers in 1721 provides book prizes; the crowning of the Rose Queen at the annual Church Fete was introduced by a rector to the parish in 1951; the Church Fete has been in existence since 1950, having superseded the Flower Show. Barrel rolling and a tug-of-war competition between teams from the local pubs have both ceased in recent years. Dr Robert Plot in his *Natural History of Oxfordshire*, 1705, mentioned that the parson, in procession on Holy Thursday, read a gospel at a barrel's head in the cellar of the Chequer Inn, which was once a hermitage and where there had been a cross. The Chequer Inn was on the main London to Gloucester road, now the Abingdon road, but ceased to be a public house in 1789 when other routes became more important. There is an old jingle:

'The Bell tolling, the Ball rolling, the black Horse kicking.'

These are the names of the three pubs remaining in the village out of eight in existence in the 18th century.

In the past 20 years or so the landscape of Standlake has changed dramatically; elm trees have gone leaving a bare skyline in many places, and gravel pits have been dug and filled with water, enriching the lives of water sports enthusiasts but causing the demise of many trees and hedgerows. The bird watcher will certainly see birds which are not normally associated with inland areas, such as shag which roost in winter in trees on islands in local lakes. One can still find a wonderful variety of wild flowers and fruits in the hedgerows; wine and jam makers can pick blackberries, rosehips, elderflowers, elderberries, sloes and bullace plums, while there are hops for the beer maker and hazel and beech nuts. Mushrooms have been found struggling through the gravel at the side of a haulage road.

210

Stanford-in-the-Vale

Stanford is a large village, with two large greens. The central one, with its many lime trees, is dominated by the tall, square tower of the church of St Denys and bordered on two sides by rows of ancient, picturesque cottages. Here too is the manor house, once occupied by Anne Neville, daughter of the Earl of Warwick. When she married the Duke of Gloucester (afterwards Richard III), to mark the occasion, they built the south porch on the church, bearing the Arms of Warwick.

On the other side of the green stands the rectory and the vicarage, once the home of Bishop Wordsworth who wrote many well known hymns.

Stanford was once a farming community, consisting of eight farms. Some sent milk to London every day by train from Challow station, the others kept sheep. There were two smithies, a carpenter and wheel-wright's yard, two sets of threshing tackle and a brickmaking yard. Corn was ground at the two mills.

General Cox, who commanded an army at the battle of Culloden in 1746, built a house in Stanford and called it Cox's Hall. Oliver Cromwell stayed at Penstones during the Civil War.

The population in 1913 was 300, now it is over 2,000. In the 1950s a new estate was built, part of which is called Huntersfield after the Hunter family who lived at the manor house from 1816 to 1935. There are also roads called Warwick Close, Neville Way and Wordsworth Close, named after the famous people who once lived here.

A modern village hall is available for entertainments. A smaller vicarage has been built, and the old one is now a nursing home called The Grange. In 1913 there were seven public houses, now there are only three.

At the present time there are only five farms, and many people commute to London, Reading, Swindon and Oxford or work at Harwell Atomic Energy establishment.

As you pass through the village you will see many attractive houses of different periods, many of them having lovely gardens. The Upper Green has been planted with flowering trees, and here you find The Old House, which was once three cottages.

Stanton St John

Up on the stony ridge of the saucer of low hills surrounding Oxford, only five miles north-east of that city, with all it has to offer, is Stanton St John – the Saxon 'stan-tun' meaning 'homestead on stony ground' and St John perpetuating the name of the family who held the lordship of the manor for 200 years from the 12th century. In the 16th century, after years of dispute, the lordship passed to New College, which still owns land in the surrounding countryside and many of the village houses.

Several dwellings date back to the 16th century, although 21 of the original dwellings were destroyed in 1793 in a fire which traversed the narrow village street, fanned by wind and setting alight the thatched roofs on either side. The unfortunate villagers were left destitute by the disaster and were sustained largely by public appeal. The devastation was rectified by building pairs of stone houses, slate-roofed and set well back from the road – some bearing the New College coat of arms. This crest is repeated in the church, the oldest and dominant building in the village, set in a beflowered churchyard. The interior has much of interest – carved bench ends of human heads or grotesque animals, 13th and 14th

Rectory farm house, Stanton St John

century glass, and further evidence of the link with New College through the crest carved in the Jacobean pulpit and set into a window in the chancel. Another window bears the arms of Robert Pinck, the last Warden of the College to be rector of the parish, though his successors to the end of the 18th century included Fellows of the College.

Robert Pinck DD was a devoted Royalist who suffered imprisonment in 1642 at the hands of the Parliamentary troops under Lord Saye and Sele. He is remembered today in the village because of a bequest he made in his will in 1647. He left £110 so that local children could be helped to take up apprenticeships with tradesmen living outside the parish. The money was invested and today young people may still apply to the charity's trustees for help with such things as books and tools.

The village also has reason to be grateful to Lady Elizabeth Holford who was born here in 1650. She married a rich London merchant Henry Harbin, and after his death married Sir William Holford. In her will, dated 1717, she left £500 to be invested until the sum of £750 had accumulated, when it was to be used to build a charity school at Stanton St John. Children from both Stanton St John and the neighbouring village of Forest Hill were to be given instruction and six boys and six girls to be provided with clothing and called Lady Holford's scholars.

Across the road from the 13th century church of St John the Baptist is Rectory Farm House. A plaque over the door says 'The birthplace of John White, 1575–1648, Fellow of New College, Oxford, and chief founder of the colony of Massachusetts, New England'. John White was the son of the tenant farmer, and 400 years later the house is still lived in by the tenant farmer of New College. In 1647 he was designated Warden of the College but declined the post because of ill-health. He became rector of a church in Dorset, where he became interested in sending out a colony to settle in Salem, Massachusetts. The first church was called 'Daughter of John White' and is known as such to this day.

The village today is still a thriving community. It is fortunate still to have a friendly shop and post office. The school closed in 1984 and is now called the Holford Centre: playschools, committee meetings and adult education classes are held there. The village hall was built with funds raised in the village, and opened in 1963. Next to the hall car park and opposite the church, is a children's playground. The recreation ground, adjacent to the B4027, just along from the two public houses, is still in use today for cricket and football.

There are many interesting walks that are accessible to the village, with extensive views of Stanton Great Wood and the Chilterns.

Steeple Aston ᘉ

Steeple Aston lies about nine miles south of Banbury and was an established market centre of 200 souls when, according to the Domesday Book, Henry de Estone was the non-resident rector. By the end of the 13th century the name had changed to Stepelaston, a steeple being the old name for an unfortified tower. It is not possible to know when the first church was built on the site used regularly today for worship, but part of the pillar now used for the hymns board is probably original. Additions and alterations have been made every century since and there is now an excellent organ and a peal of eight bells. There is also a memorial to Judge Page (the hanging judge) whose ghost, it is said, is put into a beer barrel every midsummer night and chased round Middle Aston pond by owls, who are the ghosts of widows of 100 men hanged by the Judge. Judge Page would not complete payment to the stonemason, Hendrick Scheemaker, who omitted the wedding ring on the finger of the Judge's wife.

The famous Steeple Aston cope, which was cut up at the time of the Reformation, is now in the Victoria and Albert Museum for safe keeping, but a photograph of it is at the back of the church.

Brasenose College was entitled to appoint rectors to Steeple Aston, as they do now, one of the earliest being Dr Samuel Radcliffe who founded a school and master's house in North Side. As the village grew a new technical school (now the village hall) was built, also an infants school with its inscription 'Feed my Lambs' which can be seen from the road.

Under Dr Radcliffe's will two almshouses were built (1663) near the old school. These have been modernised and are well maintained under the Radcliffe Trust. Until the Second World War a Sunday dinner was sent from the rectory to each house weekly but food rationing put a stop to that.

Over 30 Grade II listed buildings are in the conservation area. Most large houses have been subdivided, including the Grange, an ornate house with some doors and window tracery (visible from Water Lane) which may have come from Kew Palace. Most old cottages have been joined together to form single homes but old artisans' cottages in Harrisville were destroyed fairly recently and the occupants rehoused in council houses opposite Nizewell (Nine Wells) Head. The oldest council houses may be found at the end of Fenway. Later, Jubilee Close was constructed in the field named in honour of Queen Victoria's Jubilee.

Then Bradshaw Close was built on 'Meadowfold' and lastly Grange Park Road was developed on the beautiful gardens of the Grange. Other individual houses have been built as in-filling. Old coach houses, stables and barns have been converted into homes, often because their doors were too small for modern machinery.

The nine footpaths are well marked and include The Tchur which runs from North Side to South Side – the word Tchur is local and means a passage between two high walls. To complete the walk round the village centre is exactly one mile. Go down Cow Lane and follow the signs round Folly field to find the eye-catcher designed by William Kent (1740) as a feature of landscape for Rousham House. The remains of a Roman villa are hidden under a field, but for special pleasure see the huge sycamore tree in the late winter when snowdrops are out or walk down South Side at daffodil time; everywhere are young trees planted to commemorate Queen Elizabeth's Jubilee in 1977.

Buses run through the village several times a day between Oxford and Coventry. The Heyford BR station is only one mile down the hill by the canal and river Cherwell. Both the Red Lion and White Lion offer pub food and the Hopcrofts Holt Hotel, on the extreme south-west border of the village, has a conference centre. The Hopcrofts Holt has been a staging post for many centuries. When the old thatch roof was removed, lucky-charm mud-cats were found, still in good condition. The pub sign shows highwayman Duval, with the gallows behind him, on one of his raiding trips before he was caught and hanged at Tyburn.

Steventon 🐚

Five roads converge on one point in the village, directing the villagers to the little shop which sits there, a demure and unpretentious structure. The day starts quite early at the shop with the arrival of secondary school children requiring crisps and fizzy drinks to sustain them during their wait for the school bus.

After a while the next group arrives pushing prams and buggies. Older brothers and sisters have been deposited at the village school and there is time to take in the village shop in a leisurely walk to the playgroup. Only the walking is leisurely; the conversation is brisk, animated, vital; their actions alert, demonstrating an enviable command of logistics as, in addition to the babies in prams, they cope with wayward small children, some walking, some on bikes, some pushing doll's prams. Hardly any time elapses before the next group appears. Older people, women clutching purses and shopping bags, men, also with shopping bags, clearly enjoying the walk, purposefully heading towards the little shop. On pension day quite a large queue forms. Until the shopping is completed, concentration is unbroken; but that done, conversational little groups form in and around the outside of the little shop, and along the five diverging ways from the shop.

By this time more people are driving up to the shop, in much more of a hurry, but no less conversational, discussing Church choir practices, Parish Council concerns, out of village school run deliveries and collections rota, the times of village pantomime practices and dates for scenery construction and painting. After lunch mothers with pre-playgroup age offspring wend their way to the shop, among their number the mother and toddler group organiser finalising addresses for each meeting and working out who shall host the weekly music for babies meeting.

Teatime brings children from the village school. They buy icecream and share their excitement at having had senior citizens in school to eat lunch with them. After the children depart the shop is quiet for a while, then there is a final flurry of activity as villagers on their way home from work, reach the little shop before its door is shut for the night, and its lights shine out on to the silent empty space, and five roads leading off round the village.

Stoke Lyne 🪶

The stream that serves the village is the Bure, which continues on its way through nearby Bicester and eventually joins the river Thames. Stoke Lyne is a small village with a population of approximately 140. Employment is mostly found in the local market town of Bicester or in agriculture, the area being mostly arable and wooded.

In 1851 a fire destroyed a large number of the cottages and the school. A new school was built but has now been demolished to make way for new housing. The village pub, named the Peyton Arms, is also used for meetings, there being no village hall.

The church, dedicated to St Peter, is in the centre of the village. The vicarage, now a private house, was built in 1872. It has had many vicars but none so infamous as the Rev William Bryant MA who used to walk round the church tower calling his parishioners to worship. His daughter Emily Ermyntrude died an untimely death on 9th February 1906 aged 14

216

years. The Rev Bryant shot himself in the vicarage in 1914. His burial on 3rd November took place without the service of the Church of England, and the service authorised for use in the Diocese was said.

Swifts House on the edge of the parish was a stop for horse-drawn stage coaches, on the route from the North to London. Today travellers go north and south at much greater speeds on the M40 motorway not much more than a stone's throw from Swifts House, while overhead at still greater speed, fly the fast jet aircraft, taking off and landing at the nearby air base.

Stoke Lyne's oldest inhabitant, Mrs Kate Adams, was born in 1887. She was born in the local pub, the Peyton Arms, her father being the landlord. She recalls the village feast which was held annually at the beginning of July. This has long since been discontinued – but for one year in 1975 Stoke Lyne Women's Institute did revive it, which was a great success.

Stoke Row ❧

The map of South Oxfordshire shows Stoke Row at the epicentre of the Thames loop, equidistant from Wallingford, Reading and Henley. It is also at the highest point of the southern Chiltern hills (about 670 ft), reached along steep, deeply wooded roads. This high ground is poor for farming as it is exceptionally chalky with flints and has pockets of heavy clay and no natural sources of water.

Because of these inhospitable characteristics the area was slow to develop, although its name is traceable to the 1300s when it was part of the ancient Saxon parish of North Stoke along with Ipsden.

Although historically it is bound up with Ipsden, today the two villages have little contact. Until 1848, Stoke Row did not have its own parish church, all its affairs being recorded in the Ipsden registers. In that year it also became an ecclesiastical parish in its own right, but remained part of Ipsden parish until 1952 for civil affairs. At the opposite end of the village is the pleasing red-brick chapel built in 1815 to cater for a substantial non-conformist element in the district.

The principal landowners for some 700 years were the Reade family of Ipsden. Over the years they lost much of their land and influence in Stoke Row but their name has guaranteed the village a unique claim to fame via its world-renowned monument, 'The Maharajah's Well'. The well is

365 ft deep (twice the height of Nelson's Column) and was entirely dug by hand although only four feet wide from top to bottom!

The expenses of sinking it, building the honey-pot Warden's cottage and providing and planting the adjacent cherry orchard, were defrayed by the Maharajah of Benares in 1863 as a token of friendship with Mr A. E. Reade, who worked in India and who had told his Highness about the acute local water shortages. It is open to the public and has recently been beautifully restored, the Indian temple appearance and yew avenue being a source of quaint delight.

Stoke Row's brick, tile and pottery industry started up in the 1600s, probably about the time the majority of its oldest vernacular houses were built. The clay pits, where up to 30 ft of clay was hauled out, are still evident in the woods and fields and the industry continued up to the start of the Second World War. There are no kilns left on the yard site, which over recent years has been developed into units of small offices and workshops. Pottery examples can be seen at the Reading and county museums.

Besides farming and the clay industry, timber has always been (and still is) an important local pursuit. For generations it was mostly the provision of firewood in huge commercial quantities but craft industries obviously developed to meet specific demands. Many still remember the chair-leg bodgers and the tent peggers who in their scores made a hard living working in the local woods and barns.

Bodgers existed from circa 1840 to circa 1940 throughout the Chiltern Hills, making chair legs and stretchers from local beech for the emerging, mechanised chair-making factories at High Wycombe, until the factories there developed machine methods for the tasks.

Tent pegging, however, is unique to Stoke Row and its neighbouring villages. Like bodging it was almost obsolete in the 1930s but the threat of war revived it so dramatically that some five million pegs were made for the Forces in a period up to 1942. It carried on until about 1952 when it finally succumbed.

The outbuildings at the Cherry Tree and Crooked Billet pubs were much used for these wood-craft industries and bodging equipment is in the county museum. Today most people work outside the village but the community (electoral roll 505) is thriving and dynamic.

Sunningwell & Bayworth

The villages of Sunningwell and Bayworth, lying on the south-western slopes of Boars Hill, three and a half miles from the city of Oxford, were in Saxon times the original site of the Abbey of Abingdon. Historically part of Berkshire, of which Abingdon was once the county town, the area became part of the county of Oxfordshire and under the control of the Vale of the White Horse District Council after local government reorganisation in 1974.

The Stert stream, which rises in the vicinity of Boars Hill, flows through the two villages and eventually joins the river Thames at Abingdon Bridge. Legend has it that the stream first appeared as a miraculous spring in answer to the prayers of a Saxon noble named Aben when he was dying of thirst. In memory of this saintly man it was decided to build the abbey at the site of the miracle. However, any work completed on one day was found demolished the next, so the abbey was eventually sited at the mouth of the stream. The stream to this day causes much trouble at times by excessive flooding during its journey through the villages to the Thames.

At the dissolution of the abbey in 1538, the prior became rector of Sunningwell. John Jewel, a noted Bishop of Salisbury, was rector here in 1551. It was he who, to provide shelter for baptismal parties at the church, had the heptagonal porch built, in a mixture of Gothic and Renaissance styles unique in English church architecture. He also gave the church its finely carved Elizabethan altar table. Another rector of Sunningwell was Samuel Fell, the famous Dean of Christ Church, who was in the village from 1625 to 1649, and with his family lies buried in the chancel of the church. His illustrious son Dr John Fell was born in the village.

Sunningwell church is an interesting example of medieval building, with its mixture of Norman, Tudor and Jacobean styles and artefacts. Tablets on the south wall of the chancel dated 1688 commemorate the Baskerville family, who were lords of the manors of Sunningwell and Bayworth from the late 16th to the 18th century. The glass mosaic floor of the chancel is 19th century and depicts Revelations Chapter 4. The walls of the nave are 13th century although the windows were reglassed early in the 20th century. The distinctive poppy heads of the pews are 15th century, and the font is also 15th century. It is said that Roger

Bacon conducted his scientific experiments into magnifying glass and gunpowder in a room in the original tower.

The manor house at Bayworth, built and occupied by the Baskerville family, was almost a ruin by 1722. During a dig on the site local secondary school pupils found a number of old wine bottles which came from the Crown Tavern in Abingdon, and this find was thought to indicate the cause of the fall of the house of Baskerville! Materials from the old house were put to good use, for when the present Manor Farmhouse was built 200 years ago beams and woodwork from the old manor were used. The Manor Farmhouse is occupied today by Mr R. G. Deane, whose family has farmed in the area for some 500 years.

Sunningwell still has its manor house, built by Benedictine monks; it was occupied by the abbot and used as a hospice and resthouse, the monks themselves living in cells in the grounds. After the Dissolution, Elizabeth I frequently stayed there when collecting monies from her Treasurer, who also lived in the neighbourhood. A former owner, Mrs Una Duval, was a companion of the redoubtable Mrs Pankhurst in the Women's Suffrage Movement.

Today Sunningwell parish is part of the joint benefice of Sunningwell and Radley. In 1972 a new school was built in Dark Lane to replace the original church school which had stood for some 100 years next to the village pond. The original premises now house the very popular Sunning-well School of Art.

The village pub, the Flowing Well, was originally the home of a bachelor rector of the parish, and is named after the source of the stream which flows into the pond opposite the church, and from which Sunning-well gets its name.

Cricket is played on a recreation ground presented to the village during the First World War, and a new pavilion was built some years ago by the efforts of villagers.

The parish of Sunningwell and Bayworth used to be mainly agricultural, consisting of five farms, Blagrove, Beaulieu, Church, Long Furlong and Manor Farm. These have now amalgamated and the majority of the working population of the area finds employment in the industries and businesses of Oxford, or travels even further afield.

Sutton Courtenay

Sutton Courtenay is situated three miles south-east of Abingdon. Most of the finer buildings lie in the area around All Saints' church and the well preserved village green. A pleasant walk is along the footpath from the church to Culham village, by the weirs and over the river Thames beyond. This causeway is reputed to have been constructed in about AD 1000.

It is possible to leave all traffic behind by taking the lane behind the church and walking the entire length of the village as far as the boundary with Didcot power station by footpaths and bridleways.

The Liberal Prime Minister, H. H. Asquith, was the longest serving Prime Minister in the 20th century, until his record was taken by Mrs Margaret Thatcher. He made his home in Sutton Courtenay at The Wharf and now lies buried with his wife, Margot, and his son Anthony, in the local churchyard. Anthony, often known by his nickname 'Puffin', was a well known film director. Asquith's daughter, Lady Violet Bonham Carter, was a frequent visitor to the village.

Also buried in the churchyard is George Orwell, the author of *Animal Farm* and *1984*. His tombstone, in his real name of Eric Arthur Blair, bears a simple inscription.

The manor house was formerly known as Brunce's Court when it was the home of the Brunce family, one of whom became Bishop of Norwich. It is a five-gabled, two-winged house which has had many additions over the centuries but originated as the great medieval hall of the Courtenay family, who gave their name to the village.

The Abbey, actually the rectory house, dates from c1300. The 15th century Great Hall has an oak roof on arched supports.

Norman Hall is one of the oldest buildings in the village. It was built c1190, in the reign of Richard I, Coeur de Lion. All Saints' church also dates from Norman times. The brick-built south porch has a room above reached by a narrow stairway from inside the church. The clock on the church tower is unusual in that it is one-handed and dates from about 1700.

A healthy community life flourishes despite the fact that the church lies at one end of the village and the school at the other in the centre of the housing estate.

Cocky, a white cockatoo, is a very popular character in the village. He is often to be seen perched on the fencing, bouncing up and down calling 'Cocky, Cocky' to passers-by in the High Street.

In the past, agriculture, a local paper mill and domestic service were the main sources of employment within the village. Now the prime employers include local scientific establishments and Didcot power station. There are many commuters using Didcot railway station, London being a mere 35 minutes away.

The outer area of the village has become scarred with gravel workings, and the nearby trading estate creeps ever closer, but this still remains a most pleasant village.

Swalcliffe ❧

The ancient village of Swalcliffe lies astride a ridge six miles west of Banbury; its name is said to mean 'the cliff where swallows nest' and has been spelled and pronounced differently over the centuries. It is still sometimes called 'Swayclye'. It has an Iron Age fort and evidence of Roman occupation within its boundaries.

The church of St Peter and St Paul has stood on a mound overlooking the village since Saxon times, having been altered and enlarged around the 14th century and 'improved' by the Victorians. It still needs costly restoration and care. William of Wykeham is thought to have been responsible for the former work and also some of the ancient manor house to the west and the great tithe barn standing near to it. The family of Wykham were great benefactors and of considerable influence, as their monuments and gifts in the church show. One descendant sailed on the *Mayflower* to the New World.

The surrounding farms provided work for men and women until about 50 years ago and servants were often recruited from the bright pupils leaving school, by the mistress of the 'big' house. Wages were low, but most people managed to keep a pig; rare fresh meat for a few days when it was killed, and the rest for curing, to be hung on the strong hooks in the beams and walls, which also served to hang the spring balance and net when the visiting nurse weighed the baby.

The wooden village hall was built by voluntary work and public subscription in 1924 and equipped with a billiard table, games and cards etc. There was also a well-used reading room before the 'wireless' was so common.

Electricity arrived in 1930, but not for all. Most people relied on oil lamps and candles for light and cooked on open fires. Wood could be collected from the common after a year's residence, or from the hedge-rows for firelighting.

Water came from springs, piped to the larger houses, but mostly carried by buckets from one of the communal taps or 'lion's heads' and there was usually a rainwater barrel by the door.

The village carrier, given a note, a bag and a charge of about 6d, would pick up shopping in Banbury on Thursdays and Saturdays. The village shop sold almost anything – food and hardware. The post office was at the other end of the village.

After the Second World War, and the evacuees had returned home, the number of children dwindled and the school closed in 1948. Mains water came about 1954 – not so nice as spring water but less work; then in 1970, mains drainage, long overdue.

Today there are 90 dwellings, some new or conversions, mostly on the edge of the village. There are 250 residents, 40 of them children, but no school, shop or post office and a very poor bus service. It does not look very different. The green and cottages still slope down past the Stag's Head and the now disused bakery, where Sunday dinners could be cooked for a few pence whilst the housewives attended morning service, and a house where Dick Turpin was said to call. The school is now a house, as is the shop though the window has not been changed. The telephone kiosk is drab and modern. The tithe barn stands empty and awaits development, the stackyard tidy. The Swalcliffe Park House, with its ancient remnant of a former building is now a residential school.

There are not many 'old' families left now to remember the past. However, the seasonal festivities continue and Swalcliffe is still a quiet and peaceful place when the traffic will allow. People get on well together and help each other in difficult times as they have always done.

Swinbrook ❧

Swinbrook is a delightful village, with its houses spread along the roadside for over a mile beside the little Wenrisc stream, that joins the river Windrush here. As you approach from the Burford road there is a lovely view of the stream tumbling into the river and the pond, scene of a wartime landmine crater, where there are swans, geese, ducks and moorhens enjoying life in and around the meadows. The cricket field with its beautiful trees is situated here, where all through the summer on Sundays and some Saturdays the local teams enjoy their games.

The bridge crosses two rivers, the Windrush on its way down to join the Thames at Newbridge and the mill stream which rejoins it in a few yards. The old mill has not been used for many decades for milling, but the house has a lovely garden, especially in springtime, with thousands of daffodils, which visitors to the Swan Inn next door fully appreciate.

The name Swinbrook conjures up a time some hundreds of years ago, when the swine from Wychwood Forest came down to the brook for their water. Many small woods and copses still grow to the north of the village, from Beech Grove in the north-west to Stockley Wood in the north-east, with Furzy Lees, Widely, Hensgrove and Fosgrove somewhere in between.

St Mary's church contains some very interesting figures, 16th and 17th century effigies of members of the Fettiplace family who lived at Swinbrook in a large house to the west of the church. There is now no trace of the house, which was destroyed almost 200 years ago, but the fishponds and formal terraces lie on either side of the footpath to Widford. The Redesdale family lived at Swinbrook House to the north of the village. Besides Lord and Lady Redesdale, two of their daughters are buried here, Nancy Mitford the authoress and her sister Unity. For many years they owned the estate, which included most of Asthall, Swinbrook and Widford, and all the houses and gateways were painted Redesdale Blue. There are very few houses with blue paint today, if any.

To the east of the Hall the little Swin Lane goes up Lime Kiln Hill towards Asthall Leigh, Fordwells and Leafield. On the left upstream, the Old School House is a reminder of the days when the school flourished here. As the numbers of children dropped after the Second World War and the evacuees returned home, the school was closed.

Passing the school house you come to the 'splash' where the stream crosses the road. On the side there is a small bridge for walkers or cyclists. Now the houses are spread thinly, three on the right, where a raised path shows where the stream used to come down the road. It now crosses and recrosses under two little humps. The 'Old Forge' stands on the corner of Blacksmith's Lane. It ceased to be a forge some 50 years ago.

The houses and large gardens through the narrow valley continue to be quite a distance apart until you get to the building which was a Primitive Methodist chapel. Here several homes are set into the steep hillside.

Almost at the end of Swinbrook a turning goes off right, up the New Road through the woods to Fordwells, but bearing left towards Shipton

224

under Wychwood you will pass the 'Hit or Miss', formerly a public house used by foresters, farm hands and poachers. Among them were the Dunsden brothers, whose bodies were hanged on the gibbet tree on Capps Lodge Plain. They had been found guilty of various crimes at Gloucester Assizes and their bodies brought back to the scene of their crimes.

The lane to the left leads on to Paynes Farm and four cottages and then becomes a farm track up on to the downs, but on the corner is a very attractive pond which attracts lots of visitors to see the ducks, geese and other water fowl that live there. The bank below the farmhouse is full of bulbs in spring and trees and shrubs lean over the water.

Sydenham ෨ℒℴ

Sydenham is a small village with a total population of around 300. A large part of the village is designated as a conservation area and there are many listed buildings of timber framing, brick, flint and wychert under thatch and old tiled roofs.

The place name Sydenham means 'by the wide river meadow' and the Crowell brook has played an important part in the village's economy throughout its history. It was already settled by Anglo-Saxon times and Domesday Book records that there was land for 14 ploughs and 60 acres of meadow land. There are still meadows supporting sheep and cattle, many bearing the mark of the medieval open field system. Only a few villagers are employed in agriculture now.

Robert Monday was a prosperous yeoman farmer. He died in 1662 and left a house and 'three and twenty acres of arable land in the common fields of Kingston Blount to the poor of Sydenham for ever' together with an annual payment of £1 for the upkeep of the church. The land was exchanged for a field and allotments in the Enclosure Award and the rents are now used to help pensioners with heating at Christmas.

Times were very hard for agricultural workers in the first half of the 19th century. To help alleviate the poverty a number of families from the village were assisted to emigrate to Australia in 1843 and 1844. Five families went on the barque *Wallace* in November 1843 with 18 children. Four more went on the *United Kingdom* bound for Sydney in December 1843 with 14 children, two single girls and a young man. Farm labourer William Quainton, and his little daughter Charlotte aged one, died on the arduous voyage which took five months. Others went on ships which included the *Elizabeth*, the *Francis Ridley* and the *Kate*. That they worked hard and prospered is evident from stories told by many of their descendants who have written or come to Sydenham to trace their roots in the past few years.

Baroness Wenman of Thame Park gave land and money towards the building of the National school in 1849. It was enlarged in 1886 and catered for all the village children. In 1929 it became a junior and infant school, when the children over 11 years old walked or cycled to Chinnor. The school closed in 1949. The old school room has been repaired and renovated and serves as a well-used village hall.

A village fair has been revived over the past few years and is held in the centre of Sydenham at the beginning of June. The proceeds are given to charity and towards the restoration of the Early English church of St Mary, which is a picturesque centre-piece for the village.

Tackley ✤

The village of Tackley is situated in the north of Oxfordshire, ten miles from Oxford and twelve miles from Banbury. It is reached by turning off from the A423 at Sturdy's Castle public house.

This attractive village has an 11th century church, St Nicholas', 17th century fish ponds and two Elizabethan arches, one of which reads 'Deus Industriam Beat', meaning 'God Bless Industry'.

The lord of the manor once lived at Tackley Park, which has a lake and used to abound with wildlife. At Easter time it used to be opened for the Sunday school children to pick a bunch of daffodils to take home to their mothers.

Several poor families from the village were sent to Australia in the year 1848, but sadly their ship was wrecked in a storm, just a day or so before they were due to arrive, and all lives were lost.

It is still the custom (which was only suspended during the years of the Second World War) to carry on the tradition of maypole dancing. The village school chooses a Queen and King and then they dance on the village green.

What is known as 'Tackley Club' takes place on the second Thursday of each July. These days it consists only of an amusement fair for three nights, but before the Second World War it was celebrated with a village feast and silver band parade through the village.

View of Tackley village

The local primary school is situated by the playing fields and is tucked in close to the old spring brook which provided the villagers with collectable drinking water in times gone by. Originally there were three 'Town Wells' as they were known, apart from a large number of private wells – totalling about 80.

There are two public houses in the village, apart from Sturdy's Castle on the main Banbury Road. They cater for villagers and visitors alike.

The population has increased enormously since 1945 with many new properties being built, but they all blend in well with the old stone cottages from centuries ago.

There is a village post office and stores, plus a modern self-service shop called the Apple Stores, which stocks almost everything. There is also a thriving furniture workshop which provides almost anything you can think of made of wood.

The main industry in the village used to be agriculture, sheep farming, game keeping, hedge-laying, etc as well as the local cement works. However, in this modern age, apart from some work on the land, most people go out of the village to the towns to work – even commuting to London.

Tadmarton

More than a hundred years before the Norman Conquest, Tadmarton is recorded as a royal estate belonging to the Saxon king, Edwy. Go back another 1,300 years and there is evidence of human habitation at the Iron Age camp on Tadmarton Heath. Situated at 641 ft above sea level on quick draining sandy soil, near to the ironstone which they needed for their tools, the camp must have been a place of refuge for people and their livestock in times of danger. The two barrows which are known to have been nearby have disappeared, but golfers enjoying a game at Tadmarton Heath Golf Club still have to skirt around the spring-fed pool near the site of the Holy Well.

The road over Tadmarton Heath, which bisects the Iron Age camp, follows a prehistoric way which was used by Welsh drovers up until the 19th century. As the motorist speeds along the tarmac he can distinctly feel the bumps as he goes over the banks and ditches engineered before 300 BC. Roman coins, a spearhead and human remains have also been found in this area.

It is likely that the hamlet of Lower Tadmarton, with its favourable location by a ford over the Sor brook, was an earlier settlement than Upper Tadmarton. It may be that the name derives from 'the place by the frog pool' – there still are quantities of frogs in a pool at Lower Tadmarton.

Some of the parish boundaries can be recognised as being the same as the boundaries of an estate granted to Abingdon Abbey in the 10th century– and which the abbey held, throughout many legal disputes over the payment of rent, for the next 500 years. The parish church of St Nicholas in Upper Tadmarton was built and added to during these centuries, also the manor tithe barn. These two buildings still stand in a good state of repair and are in constant use.

During the 19th century, three generations of MacDermots held the manor. The Manor Farm and house were let to tenants for most of this period. In the 1890s John Charles MacDermot reduced his family to penury through his gambling. However, the MacDermot family are remembered with gratitude by the older people in the village who receive benefits each year from a charity set up by the family in 1864.

Another landowner of the 19th century was Capt W. L. Lampet who built The Highlands, an imposing mansion on a hill between Lower Tadmarton and Bloxham. This also was let as the Captain certainly did not want to live surrounded by 'all those sheep'. He gave his family name to the pub, the Lampet Arms, which he may have built as a railway hotel when it was thought that the line would run along the Sor brook valley. The name of The Highlands was later changed to Tadmarton House.

Another large house in Tadmarton is the old rectory, now called the Grange, mostly rebuilt in gracious early-Victorian style in 1842.

The village and its hamlet still have many of the 26 stone, thatched houses built in the prosperous farming years of the 16th and 17th centuries, which were registered for the Hearth Tax of 1665. The population reached the high number of 450 in the census of 1851; the number of people registered to pay the Community Charge in 1990 was 326.

But there are now far more houses: council houses each end of the village spread out along the B4035, and a housing estate has been built on the last of the glebe land. This makes for a lively community, no longer dependent on the ups and downs in farming. The village shop and post office provide an excellent service as well as a cheerful meeting place; and the 19th century building which was once the village school has been transformed into a lovely village hall.

A memorial plaque in the church to someone who lived in Tadmarton for only three years sums up the sentiments of many who live in the village to this day: 'He lived in Tadmarton only a little while but loved it much'.

Tiddington & Albury

Tiddington lies midway between Thame and Wheatley, astride the busy A418 road. Drivers passing quickly through the village might see a garage, the Fox public house and a large caravan sales and service centre, as well as a few houses along the main road. Much of the village lies on the north-facing slope of the valley of the river Thame, south of the A418.

The village street has a number of cottages dating from the 16th to 18th centuries, with Tiddington House on the hill-top built in the reign of Queen Anne. There has been a steady increase in building in the village, from the Airey local authority housing of 1947 to the estate houses of the 1960s and 1970s. Other post-war dwellings, including a small estate built in the late 1980s, extend along the Ickford Road towards the water meadows of the river Thame.

To the west of the village, Sandy Lane links the main road to the M40 London/Birmingham motorway junction at Milton Common. On the south-eastern boundary of Tiddington lies Fernhill, a wood which has bluebells, a muntjak deer and badger sets. A quarter of a mile to the east, along the Oxfordshire Way, is the hamlet of Albury, once a much larger community than Tiddington. Here stands the parish church of St Helen together with the Old Rectory, the Grange and Church Farm. The original church was demolished in 1828 and the present church was built in the Perpendicular style by Thomas Rickman in 1830. The Romanesque font with zigzag ornamentation is all that remains from the original building.

Although the population of Tiddington has grown considerably since the Second World War, these years have also seen the disappearance of many of the amenities which were important to the village. The school, the general stores with post office and the forge have all become private dwelling houses and the railway line, once a useful link to Princes Risborough, Thame, Wheatley and Oxford, has become a haven for wildlife.

In earlier times the villagers worked on the many farms in the area or for the large estate of Rycote Park to the east. At the end of the 18th century there were nine farms. Now only Manor Farm in the centre of

St Helen's church at Albury

230

Tiddington and Sandy Lane Farm exist as working farms, where modern machinery replaces farm labourers. Church Farm at Albury, which had for some years been a teaching farm, was closed in 1988. People now travel away from the village to work in nearby towns or even as far afield as London. The extension of the M40 motorway, scheduled to be ready in Spring 1991, will bring Birmingham within easy reach.

The village hall is the community centre of the village. Built on the recreation ground in 1953 by the villagers to commemorate the Coronation of Queen Elizabeth II, it provides a meeting place for activities organised by several clubs and groups. Coronation year also marked the beginning of the annual tug-of-war between Oxfordshire and Buckinghamshire, represented by Tiddington and Ickford respectively, and contested from opposite banks of the river Thame, which is the county boundary at Ickford Bridges. The tug-of-war is held on the first Friday in August when junior and adult teams compete to avoid a ducking in the river.

Uffington

Situated in the Vale of the White Horse, Uffington is dominated by the beautiful 13th century church known as 'The Cathedral of the Vale'. It is a large cruciform building with an octagonal tower, and has eleven of the original twelve consecration crosses, the most complete series to be seen anywhere in England. The iron chandelier which hangs in the church was made by the local blacksmith in memory of the master craftsman, churchwarden and chorister, from whom he learned his trade. St Mary's has a modern font with a cover designed and made some years ago, by a local carpenter.

In the early 10th century the village was granted to the Abbey of Abingdon and it was mentioned in the Domesday survey of 1086. In 1620 it passed through marriage into the Craven family and until 1959 most of the land was held by the Craven estate.

Uffington was a thriving agricultural community. The Wilts and Berks canal, used as a means of carrying cargoes, contributed to its prosperity. Coal, wheat, bricks (made at the village's three kilns) and salt were all transported by horse-drawn barge; the salt house still remains at the wharf farm. The opening of the Great Western Railway caused the death of the canal. The railway provided transport and employment, but with the closure of the station in 1964 work became limited, as it did on the farms after mechanisation. Today, as in the majority of villages, most people commute to work. Since the Second World War a number of houses have been built and so the population has increased considerably.

'The Scouring of the White Horse' and *Tom Brown's Schooldays* both have their origins in this area. The games and merriment held on the hill, rolling of cheeses into the manger, the backsword play and the beer that flowed were all stories told by the old 'uns of the day, and recorded by Thomas Hughes. In *Tom Brown's Schooldays* he gives a colourful picture of 'Veast' held in the field behind the present school. He describes cheapjacks and penny shows, men in white smocks and women in red capes. People came from miles around to join in the fun. Strangely, history does repeat itself and people by the thousand still descend on the village each year for the well known White Horse Show.

In 1972 the Thomas Hughes memorial hall was built and is in constant use by the numerous organisations. The 17th century reading room known as Tom Brown's School is now a museum where remains of Roman pottery can be seen, found during the building of Craven Common housing estate. Having both a sports field donated by the Craven estate and a recreation ground, Uffington people are fortunate in being able to enjoy many sporting activities. Three shops have now been reduced to one, this being a general store and post office, and where there were five public houses only two remain.

A character from the past called 'Snobby' was the last of the shoe makers. A model of his thatched cottage complete with sewing machine, can be seen at the Pendon museum at Long Wittenham. He was a reputed drinker and the story goes that when he ran off in the middle of the night, villagers had to go to his house to retrieve their shoes.

There are still a number of chalkstone and thatch cottages in the village, although many of the old homesteads have been enlarged and modernised. Upper Common was once a joy to behold with its old cottages, country gardens, and wild flowers in spring and summer growing by the footpath. Now it is used by traffic and sadly there are no wayside flowers to be seen. However, the stream flowing round the village adds to its natural beauty, and there are many pleasant walks.

Warborough & Shillingford

The villages of Warborough and Shillingford lie approximately eleven miles east of Oxford, on the north side of the river Thames between Dorchester and Wallingford. Shillingford Bridge, with its three arches and balustrade, was built in 1827 to carry traffic between Thame and Wallingford on the road that had been turnpiked in 1764. Nestled in on the far side of the river is the Shillingford Bridge Hotel, a popular stopping place for both river and motoring tourists.

Beautiful scenery can be enjoyed from boat or foot between Shillingford and Days Lock, and if the climb to Wittenham Clumps can be made, a poem will be found carved into a beech tree in 1847 by Joseph Tubb, who camped up there for a fortnight so he could complete his work.

The Tubb family lived in Warborough and Shillingford between the years 1800 and 1984. Initially Benjamin Tubb, farmer and maltster, bought a house, and 20 years later in 1820 his brother James settled in the area too. James was a friend of William Cobbett, who among many other involvements was a radical reformer and later Member of Parliament, and he mentioned James Tubb in his *Rural Rides*. The Bodleian Library in Oxford have a number of letters from Cobbett to James Tubb and they also have the diaries of James Tubb's daugher, Maria Louise, telling of the events leading to the Reform Bill during the years 1831/2.

The charming village green in Warborough is off the main thoroughfare and has a wonderful outlook towards Benson and on up to the Chiltern hills. Throughout the year either football or cricket are played on the green. Records suggest that cricket has been played there for at least 130 years. The cricket club has at various times been associated with each of the five local hostelries, the Cricketers, the Nags Head, the Six Bells, the Kingfisher and the Shillingford Bridge, so it seems hardly surprising that their motto is 'Win or lose, we enjoy our booze'!

Up until 1987 Warborough and Shillingford's post office was situated in the centre of the village in a pretty black and white cottage. It had opened in 1840, the year the penny post was introduced by Rowland Hill and 15 days after the first issue of the penny black. Remarkably the position of sub post-master was held by a member of the same family for all that time. The last incumbent, Theo King, joined his aunt after his return from war service and took over as sub post-master after her death. He served the village in that capacity, and many others, for 41 years. Although now a private residence a plaque on the garden wall reminds us of Mr King's many services to the village.

Warborough post office

The parish church of St Laurence, was built in 1666, having a three-stage tower and, most unusually for Oxfordshire, a leaden font, similar to, but with a much simpler design, the one in Dorchester Abbey. Close to the church is the Georgian vicarage, a beautiful large building typical of that era, though no longer used as the vicarage. The village has two village halls, one being the St Laurence Hall, once the village Church school but now the parish hall. The Greet Memorial Hall was taken out of farming use by the Greet family, who used it for theatrical plays renowned locally and in London, and handed it over to the parish in 1930. The Greet Hall is a popular venue for many local activities and a wide variety of social occasions.

Waterperry ✣

The name comes from Pereium, probably meaning 'pear orchard'. Waterperry is on the Buckinghamshire border, with the river Thame for its southern boundary and the Holton brook for its western boundary. The ground is low-lying, generally about 200 ft above sea level, rising to 234 ft to the north. The soil is rich loam with a subsoil of gravel and clay, and it provides excellent meadow land and pasture.

Bernwood Forest is north-west of the parish, where rare butterflies can sometimes be found during the summer.

Waterperry has one street, with a mixture of new council houses and ancient cottages which are mostly of the 17th and 18th century. They are built of coarse rubble or brick and some are timber-framed.

Waterperry House owes its graceful Queen Anne frontage to Sir John Curson, who had it rebuilt in 1713. The Henley family bought the estate in 1830 and it was sold to Magdalen College in 1925. Seven years later Waterperry Horticultural School was opened by Beatrix Havergal, the principal, as a residential horticultural college for women. Miss Havergal was known as the 'Strawberry Queen' at Chelsea Flower Show, where for many years she won the gold medal prize for her exhibit of Royal Sovereign strawberries. She retired in 1971.

The house was then taken over by the Fellowship of the School of Economic Science. It is now run as a horticultural and garden centre. The school organises the annual 'Art in Action' festival in July, where craftsmen and women from all over the world exhibit their skills.

The church of St Mary was built in the pre-Conquest period. It comprises a nave of three bays, chancel, south aisle and south porch. The west tower with its weather-boarded bellcote is of wood, supported on oak pillars within the church. In the nave there are some high-backed pews on which the candlesticks remain and with the original hinges on the doors. Most interesting are the early 14th century windows with excellent tracery on the north wall.

The ghost of Waterperry is the Grey Lady, who walks the footpath from Holton to Waterperry House. Two people living in Waterperry in the past 20 years have encountered her while walking the footpath.

Waterperry is now within sight of the new M40 motorway and village life is bound to alter from the sleepy village it has been to a commuting village of the future.

Waterstock ❧

The little village of Waterstock lies in a loop off the A418 between Wheatley and Thame and is surrounded by farming land in a bend of the river Thame. The name, meaning 'waterplace', indicates Anglo-Saxon origins and there is much evidence to show it was a small medieval village. Many of the fields still show ridge and furrow strip cultivation. In 1279 there were probably about 200 inhabitants but after the Black Death the population decreased to 51 persons over the age of 14. Today there are about 70 inhabitants.

St Leonard's church is very much the hub of the village and as well as the regular church services, meetings and concerts take place there. There is no post office, pub or village shop. The earliest record of the church dates from about 1190. It was rebuilt at the end of the 15th century, the north aisle 'to be finished in as goodly hast as maybe'. Since then there has been much rebuilding with thorough restoration in the 19th century. The oldest part is the tower with its unusual little bellcote, recently restored.

Inside there is a canopied monument to Sir George Croke, a 17th century Justice of the King's Bench and lord of the manor. Notable, too, is the genealogical window in the north aisle, with its 43 shields showing the Ashhurst arms (from Adam de Ashhurst to John Henry Ashhurst 1848). Above, in the tracery, are the only remnants of medieval glass. In 1872 Mrs Ashhurst gave the painted reredos of the Last Supper which is flanked by panels of saints and prophets.

The manor house was finally pulled down, owing to the expense of upkeep, after the servants' quarters had been converted into the present substantial residence, but the stone-built stables are probably contemporary with the 1787 house. The whole village was a squirearchy owned by the Ashhurst family until the 1950s and most of the inhabitants were employed by them.

By the entrance to Waterstock House is the Pump House, dated 1898, a little building reminding one of a Saxon tower. From it many of the villagers collected their water until the mains supply came in 1951. Now the house and grounds are a renowned equestrian centre.

On the bridleway leading to Waterperry, Waterstock Mill stands on a small island on the river Thame. Originally a 15th century timber and brick house, it was rebuilt in the Elizabethan period and converted into a modern dwelling in 1957 when it was sold. By that date most of the other properties had been sold up by the Ashhurst family and the feudal system had released its patronage and its grip. Beyond is the delightful little Bow Bridge built by Diana Ashhurst in 1790 over Black Ditch. It is a single brick arch and curves outward with stone-capped parapets. It can be seen to best advantage from the riverside, much frequented by anglers. Swans and moorhens and the occasional flash of a kingfisher give added pleasure.

The single street is flanked by small cottages built of stone or local brick and some of the gardens have little buildings at the far ends – originally privies and pig-sties. The old school, tucked in behind and now a private house, still has the school bell hanging from the gable-end.

Home Farm is a 17th century timber-framed house with its ancient thatched barn and 17th century granary, and the 18th century Park Farm can be seen beyond.

The oldest buildings are the two thatched cottages, originally thought to be Elizabethan or Jacobean, but Orchard End has proved to be a cruck house of medieval origin and was a three-bay open hall. It is exceptional in its construction and believed to be late 13th or early 14th century.

Somehow the village retains a lived-in feeling, with many of the inhabitants self-employed and carrying on their work from their own homes. Waterstock is fortunate and relatively unusual among Oxfordshire villages, not being situated on a main through road, and much of the traffic consists of farm vehicles and horses. As you walk through this unspoilt village there is a sense of permanence and unity reflecting the presence of a strong community spirit.

Wendlebury 🍃

The village of Wendlebury lies in the north of the county, two and a half miles to the south of the market town of Bicester. There has been a settlement on or around this site since before Roman times. The remains of the Roman town of Alchester are just to the north of the village. The older houses are constructed from local stone, some of which may have been removed from the Roman ruins.

The village lies on the old Oxford to Bicester road, which was made a turnpike road in 1793 (in the 13th century the road south from Alchester was known as 'Buggestreet'). The village was bypassed in 1949 by the A421 trunk road. The aspect of the village has been changed recently as the M40 London to Birmingham motorway is under construction, bringing with it changes in the local population.

The only pub still open for business is the Red Lion, which stands in the centre of the village opposite the stream. This early 18th century building has been used over the years as the manorial court, the blacksmith's and a coaching inn. It is now owned by the Oxford brewers, Halls. The other pub, called the Plough, lay at the south of the village opposite where the village hall now stands. It is now a private home.

Until the late 19th century there were at least five farm houses and most of the men living in the village were employed on the farms. Many of the wives and children helped in the fields during the harvest and sheep-shearing time. The stream also provided income, the cress was harvested and sold in the local markets. All of the farm houses are now private homes, including the barns which formed College Farm, once owned by Christ Church College of Oxford.

The manor house in Church Lane is 17th century with an 18th century frontage. This has been divided over the years, with once as many as three houses. The smaller house at one end served the village as the washhouse and in the yard can still be seen the cobblestones that formed the draining area for the coppers. The old rectory is perhaps the largest building in the village, this has now been converted into flats. The field at its front, which is where Rectory Close now stands, used to be the playing field for the village where cricket matches were played and the May fair held.

The church of St Giles lies at the top of Church Lane. It is believed that it was built in the early 13th century. It has had a very chequered history, due mainly to the fact that it is sited on unstable foundations and a clay subsoil. By the middle of the 18th century it was evident that the church was about to collapse and, after morning service on Tuesday 24th March, 1761 the assembled churchgoers started to pull it down. The restored and rebuilt church opened again just over a year later, the cost to the parishioners was £400.

Unfortunately the problems had not been solved and by 1900 the tower was in such a poor state that the parishioners feared to attend church, as large lumps of masonry were liable to fall at any time. To add to the church's distress, during the winter a severe storm blew in the east window and great snow drifts partially filled the church. A great deal of the church was again rebuilt and the tower removed. The cost this time was £1,400. Three bells from the original tower, one of which is badly cracked, stand at the back of the church and on the wall, behind the

Norman font, is a picture of the church as it was with its tower. Just outside the door of the church are the remains of the village stocks.

The population of Wendlebury has fluctuated over the years. The present population is over 300. In 1981, when the village held a party on the day that Prince Charles and Lady Diana were married, every child of school age and under were given a commemorative crown; there were exactly 100 children. Unfortunately the village school was closed in 1959. The post office and shop was originally situated in what is now Post Well Cottage, Church Lane. It later moved to the Main Street but, recently, it too has closed.

Weston-on-the-Green

Weston-on-the-Green is not only 'on the green' but also 'on the road'. It is just south of Akeman Street, the Roman road from Corinium to Silchester. In later years the roads to Bicester and Northampton were both turnpikes, with a tollgate at Weston. In 1847 a William Marriott was fined five shillings and costs for preventing the Rev A. H. Matthews (the magistrate) from passing him on the turnpike by driving on the wrong side of the road. Nowadays the A43 is an extremely busy, dangerous main road, but with the building of the M40 extension, Weston hopes to become a peaceful place once more.

Weston is a typical English village of stone houses, many with thatched roofs, a manor house, a church and also a recently restored duck pond. The village school, which closed in 1984, was the only thatched school in Oxfordshire.

It has always been a farming community and in the 19th century many women supplemented the family income by lace-making. Some of their lace was sold by a splendid woman called Dinah Tuffrey, who acted as the local carrier and pedlar, walking to Bicester and then taking trains to places further afield where she sold local produce, and bringing back goods to the village.

Justice was dispensed by the magistrate aided by the village constable, whose account book gives a marvellous description of his arrangement of a marriage between Martha Coggins and Thomas Monk to enable Martha's baby to be born in wedlock. Summary justice for adulterers and other offenders was given in the form of 'rough music', where the villagers banged pots and pans to make a hideous noise at the offender's house, and even threw soot down the chimney!

In the 18th century the church had fallen into disrepair and was restored by the then lord of the manor. While on his Grand Tour in Italy he commissioned an altar piece from Pompeo Batoni – it is still in the church today. Sadly the Berties' tenure of the manor ended in 1918 when Richard Bertie was killed in Palestine four days before the end of the First World War. The whole estate was sold in 1919 and the manor house is now an hotel.

In addition to Weston Manor Hotel there are two pubs, the Chequers and the Ben Jonson. Both are thatched buildings and the Ben Jonson seems to have been the centre of activities at the annual Village Feast in September. As the *Bicester Advertiser* put it in 1879, 'a number of amusements of the itinerant kind' arrived at Weston either before or after St Giles's Fair in Oxford. In addition to this celebration there was the Weston on the Green Club Feast which took place in early summer. It seems to have been a savings club affiliated to the church and at the feast there was a service with a sermon and a sit-down dinner. The chapel, which was built by the Methodists themselves in 1838, still celebrates its anniversary with a splendid tea party.

North of the village on the A43 is Weston airfield, built in the First World War and now used by a civilian gliding club and by the RAF for parachute training. It is a common sight, in good weather, to see parachutes dropping from the sky, some of them free-falling from a great height.

Mad Maude, one of the village ghosts, in one story was a demented dairymaid who fell from the tower. Another version is that she was a nun who was burned to death as punishment for immoral behaviour. Either way, she is said to haunt a bedroom at the manor. There is also a ghostly coach and horses at the manor and one of the farmhouses has a 17th century serving woman who helps out at parties.

Weston today is a pleasant, friendly place, with a shop, several farms, a civil engineering plant hire firm, agricultural contractors, a sculpture casting workshop and an architect's office. There is also a new business park being built opposite the airfield.

Wheatley 🎐

Wheatley village lies six miles east of Oxford in a valley at right angles to the river Thame. A stream once flowed through the centre of the village and had to be crossed by stepping stones, but this is now contained in a culvert and covered with a road surface which forms the High Street, where most of the shops are to be found.

People have lived here since Saxon times and finds from a Saxon cemetery which was discovered in 1883 are housed in the Ashmolean Museum. A Roman villa was unearthed in 1845, and although nothing remains now, fragments of pottery, tiles and coins dating from AD 260 to 378 have been found. During the 13th century Wheatley was part of the property of the Abbey of Abingdon and in 1279 was described as a hamlet of Cuddesdon.

One of the main occupations for Wheatley people was stone quarrying and the stone was used for building Windsor Castle, Merton College, local cottages and ecclesiastical buildings, most of which were erected between the 13th and 18th centuries. Quarrying stone would have been thirsty work and gallons of ale would have been consumed at the ten public houses in the village. The quarry was notorious for its bull baiting and cock fighting activities and no doubt the men's meagre wages were squandered on placing bets on the unfortunate animals. Other occupations included faggot cutting and ochre cutting, the ochre being crushed at the windmill which is still standing today.

The manor house was enlarged and improved in 1601, and bears a plaque on the front stating 'T.A. 1601', which stands for Thomas Archdale, the owner at that time. It still retains its original appearance whereas most of the other old cottages and buildings have been restored. The George coaching inn stands opposite the manor and has been turned into a charming residence with courtyards and gift shop.

Stage coaches travelled from Oxford to London via the Old Road which crossed Shotover Plain, and the descent into Wheatley was a favourite haunt of highwaymen. Many of the inns had an upper entrance in Church Road and another in the High Street to accommodate the change of horses.

The railway arrived in 1862 and linked Wheatley with Oxford, High Wycombe and London. However, new roads were built, the railway closed and passengers are now served by local buses to Oxford, Thame and Aylesbury.

The village lock-up, built in 1834, is a pyramid-shaped stone structure standing near the edge of the old quarry site. It has a heavy padlocked door and the floor space is about six ft square with a headroom of about eight ft. During the 19th century it was used to lock up drunks overnight before sending them to the Oxford court. More recently it has been opened every May Day. For a small charge you can be locked up for five minutes or so, and given a certificate to prove it.

Shotover Park is an area of outstanding beauty and in its midst stands Shotover House, home of Lt Col Sir John Miller, who was Crown Equerry to the Queen. In 1888 his grandmother gave the building known as the Merry Bells to the villagers for use as a temperance hotel as she was saddened to see so much hardship caused by drunkenness. Today the building houses a new library and is the chief social centre of the village.

St Mary's church was designed by G. E. Street and consecrated in 1857. The Congregational church was built in 1842–43 and stands on the site of the old tannery. The village also has a Roman Catholic church and the Granary Hall chapel housed in the old mission hall.

During the past 50 years Wheatley has expanded and the population has risen from 900 in the 1880s to around 4,000. There are several shops, excellent schools, a post office, a bank and numerous village societies catering for everybody's needs, including the Wheatley Society and a Village Produce Association which holds a well supported annual show. Its future prosperity will be linked to the construction of the M40 London to Birmingham motorway.

Wigginton

Wigginton has always been a small village (the present population is about 200) and having no resident large landowner, nor at times a resident rector, has been and remains, rather independent. The church of St Giles is at least 600 years old, is well maintained and had the same resident rector for 50 years until the 1970s. There is a Roman villa which has been excavated on two occasions, but now sleeps under cultivated fields once more.

In the 19th and early 20th century Wigginton had a forge, a cart-wright, a cobbler, a tailor, coal merchant, undertaker, a working mill producing flour, and until the mid 1940s the baker cooked the villagers' Sunday roasts for 3d! Farmers and labourers made up most of the population and the children were educated at the village school built on land given by the then resident rector.

During and after the Second World War a small nursing home was run by Nurse Norton in one of the cottages, and at one time Unity Mitford was nursed there after her return from Germany. Evacuees from London were billeted in the village and a search light unit was based close by.

Water and electricity were brought to the village through the generosity of local landowners. The railway line from Banbury to Chipping Norton which called at nearby Hook Norton was used by villagers to shop in Banbury. Wigginton offered £20 towards the cost of a local halt for the use of villagers but this generous offer was refused. However, the line was one of the casualties of the Beeching Axe and part of it is now a BBONT nature reserve.

Many trees have been planted by both the village people and local landowners and the village is well maintained. Not being directly on a main road, traffic is not a problem and the village still likes to keep to itself, the people look after each other and the old are well cared for.

Wigginton still has three working farms, but the rectory is now a private house and the school is the village hall. Recently houses have been bought by townspeople but there are still old village families of long standing.

Wolvercote 🦢

The village, north-west of Oxford, was known as Ulfgarcote in Domesday after Ulfgar, the Saxon. The name Wolvercote came into being in 1185.

Situated on the edge of the wide expanse of its common and the open stretches of Port Meadow, the inhabitants have always jealously guarded their rights and stoutly defended their environment against the repeated efforts of Oxford City to enclose the land in order to meet the needs of its growing population. Even to this day the goose is their special emblem and the Women's Institute banner, permanently displayed in the village hall, shows a goose girl on the common. Some of today's older residents, when children, herded the geese back and forth across the common to the river's edge. Grazing rights continue to this day and at least once a year the Sheriff of Oxford rounds up the horses and cattle on Port Meadow and Wolvercote Common and impounds them. Those owners who have no right to pasture their animals there must pay a heavy fine before they can be released from the pound.

Wolvercote's location near to the city of Oxford also acocunts for its place in national history. Elizabeth I came through the village on both her visits to the city, in 1566 and 1592, travelling from the north on her way back to London. On the second occasion, a September day of heavy rain, the Queen, in her carriage, accompanied by courtiers in fine clothes, arrived at Godstow bridge, near the boundary of Wolvercote. Here she was met by the Vice-Chancellor, the heads of all the colleges and proctors, dressed in their best academic gowns, all on foot and accompanied by the beadles.

At the time of the Civil War, Charles I established his headquarters and Parliament in Oxford and during the siege required fodder for his horses. He made a written agreement (which is still in existence) with the tenants of land at Wolvercote and 61 freemen to provide hay for the King's stables. One of Wolvercote's two mills was used by the King's armourers to grind sword-blades. In the spring of 1644, when King Charles made his escape from Oxford by night, he and his 3,000 men took the unguarded track across Port Meadow and through lower Wolvercote to Yarnton and Bladon to the north. Wolvercote people showed their loyalty by keeping this move secret and the King was able to leave in safety.

The Walter family, whose tomb is in the parish church of St Peter, gave strong support to the King. Sir John Walter, Chief Baron of the Exchequer and Justice of England, was one of Wolvercote's foremost citizens and David Walter, his son, was Lieutenant of the Ordnance. David's loyalty to King Charles was so unstinting that he burned down his own house at nearby Godstow in an attempt to prevent it falling into the hands of Cromwell and his men.

Dominant over the village is the paper mill. There has been one there for three centuries and until recently it was owned by the University Press, its quality paper being used for bibles. At church harvest festivals, rolls of paper or paper sculpture are displayed in addition to fruit and vegetables. The river, necessary for the mill to function, has also played an important part in the life of Wolvercote. Its bathing place, near an old toll bridge, is one of the most beautifully-sited in England; to the south, across the meadow, one sees the magnificent skyline of Oxford with its ancient towers and spires.

On a summer afternoon in 1862, Charles Dodgson (otherwise known as Lewis Carroll) together with his friend Duckworth, Alice Liddell and

244

her sisters, came by in a rowing boat with a picnic basket on board. It was then that Dodgson began to tell the children a story. That was the start of *Alice in Wonderland*.

Wolvercote, described in 1817 as a 'rather extensive village', was never a place of wealth, most of its inhabitants living in simple hovels or earth-floored cottages, none of which survive. Nevertheless, a few finer houses of earlier centuries remain, much restored, and the village is now a conservation area. In the 19th and 20th centuries came extensive development and all of Wolvercote became part of Oxford City in 1928. The original, low-lying village, which was subject to winter flooding, grew up round the mill at the edge of the common. It is now separated from the church and school (which are situated on higher ground in Upper Wolvercote) by the canal and main railway line. The built-up higher area has no visible boundary between it and neighbouring Summertown in the north of Oxford and its large population has as its main focus the city rather than the village.

That there is no rift between the two parts of Wolvercote may partly be attributed to the well-placed village hall which acts as a focal point between the two and helps to nurture a sense of community.

Woodcote

Woodcote is situated on the edge of the south Chiltern hills, more than 500 ft above sea level. The air is fresh, even bracing, with no industry nearer than Didcot or Reading.

On the perimeter of the village there are still several farms, mostly arable, with some dairy herds and pigs.

Though not an 'olde worlde' place, proof of the existence of Woodcote for many generations comes from a map drawn by John Speede and dated 1605. Many trees and hills are drawn – done before the days of contour lines of a modern Ordnance Survey map.

There are still many trees, beech being the most prevalent. The beech woods are quite beautiful all the year round, but particularly so in the late spring when the bluebells are out and the canopy of leaves above is a soft pale green.

Small housing estates have been built in Woodcote since 1970, since which time the village has become a fast-growing community in danger of losing some of its rural identity.

245

Flint stones seem to 'grow' particularly well from the thin layer of soil above the chalky hills. In fact the local church of St Leonard, built in the Victorian era, is mostly of flint. It is now the centre of a parish in its own right, but originally was part of the ecclesiastical parish of 'South Stoke cum Woodcote' – South Stoke being a village about three miles distant bordering on to the river Thames with its rich wet pasturelands. St Leonard's now incorporates the Methodists, whose own place of worship (the Church in the Woods) had to close after more than 100 years of existence. Much newer is the building of the Catholic church of Christ the King, situated in a delightful spot.

Every year a traction engine rally held at Woodcote attracts steam rollers and veteran cars from many parts of Britain. The recreation ground is adjacent to the village club and the village hall and is home base for the local football and cricket teams. It is much changed since it was surrounded in pre-war days with gorse bushes. 'Lost ball' was often the cry.

There is not much open water in Woodcote but three ponds exist; one of which was the main source of drinking water, even within living memory.

Woodstock 🦢

Woodstock was a favourite hunting place for nearly all the Kings of England from Saxon times to the late Stuart Period.

It was Henry I who built a Manor House in what is now known as Blenheim Park. Edward the Black Prince, son of Edward III, was born here, Henry VIII was a frequent visitor with his first wife Katharine of Aragon, and Elizabeth I was imprisoned in the Manor for almost a year.

The story of Fair Rosamund is often told to visiting friends – she was a daughter of Walter de Clifford and mistress of Henry II. He brought her to Woodstock and built her a bower outside the walls of the Manor House and protected it with a complicated maze. The legend goes that Queen Eleanor, arriving at Woodstock unexpectedly, found a ball of silk attached to the King's spur. She followed it through the maze to the 'bower' where she found Rosamund whom she poisoned with a cup of wine. This has never been proved, but Rosamund did die in 1175 and she was buried at the Convent in Godstow. Traces of the Nunnery can still be seen on the bank of the Thames opposite the Trout Inn. Fair Rosamund's well can still be seen in Blenheim Park from the Grand Bridge.

Medieval Woodstock was a very small place with forests on all sides. The villagers were very poor – some were craftsmen but many scraped a living from the land. By the year 1450 Woodstock had become a Market Town having been granted a charter. The inhabitants became free burgesses and were allowed to send two representatives to Parliament, and the town was granted a staple for wool.

In about 1500 gloving became a Woodstock industry which gradually increased through Victorian times when there were many small factories producing gloves. Many were sent out to be hand-stitched by women and girls in their own homes. Gloving only started to decline after the last war when cheap Japanese imitations became readily available. It is still, however, a tradition that when a reigning king or queen visits Woodstock, a pair of gloves is presented to him or her, and when Queen Elizabeth II came here, the Mayor presented her with a pair of white kid gloves.

At one time families lived in the same house for generations, and all the shops were owned by local people, but today with high rents and properties fetching enormous prices this is no longer the case. One exception is the Banbury family who still have a drapers' shop in Oxford Street and have lived there for generations.

Many buildings are most attractive and date from the 16th, 17th and 18th centuries. Fletchers House is a notable example, a 16th century merchant's house which is now used as a County Museum. Lots of interesting exhibitions are held there.

The Church of St Mary Magdalene was badly damaged by Cromwell's army and very badly restored in 1877. It is worth a visit to see the attractive and colourful kneelers worked by many members of the Woodstock WI together with a group of 'Friends of the Church'. We are rather proud of them.

In the nearby village of Bladon is the church of St Martin where the grave of Winston Churchill still proves a place of interest to those who also visit his birthplace of Blenheim Palace. A small gateway close to the church leads to the grounds of the Palace and from here a very pleasant walk may be taken round the estate.

Woolstone 🐑

Overshadowed by the White Horse, the little village of Woolstone lies at the foot of the downs, its history going back into the Bronze Age.

Largely an agricultural area, the use of a steam plough led to the discovery of a Roman villa. Excavated in 1884, two mosaic floors were revealed.

It is known from Saxon charters that the Great Spring of Woolstone has been flowing for 1,000 years. Though it no longer supplies the whole population, it is still a great deal more pleasant to drink than the piped supply from the main source.

In 1195, the priory of St Swithun, Winchester built the church of All Saints. The walls, chalk and sarsen, have weathered well, and it possesses a Norman doorway and an unusual lead font. The Stations of the Cross, cast in fibreglass, makes a beautiful addition to the side chapel. The sculptor, Ulrica Seton Lloyd, lived for many years at Woolstone Lodge.

The village has a number of cottages dating from the 17th century and some very attractive thatch. It became a conservation area in the early 1970s.

The population has dwindled from around 300 in the 19th century to the present day when it is in the neighbourhood of 130. It is recorded that Mr and Mrs Breakspear had 21 children in a small cottage at lower town end, and all but one survived. Some of the cottages housed more than one family, so there must have been considerable overcrowding. Life cannot have been easy for the inhabitants. Water was supplied from wells, or the Woolstone Brook, and the first to pipe water were the Craven estate who owned the spring in 1862. It was brought to Manor and Woolstone Farms first, and to the Lodge in around 1910.

Before the Second World War, there was a shop in the village, a laundry, and even a cobbler. Now there is only the 16th century inn, which does a brisk trade.

The village school, given by Lord Craven in 1874, closed at the end of the 19th century. It became the parish meeting place and was at one time a lending library. Now it has passed into private ownership.

The arrival of George Butler in 1822 was a notable event in the village history. He saw action under Sir Robert Calder as a boy, and is listed on his memorial in Uffington church as Captain RN. It was he who converted the original corn mill to what is now known as Woolstone Lodge. His son William Butler became the tenant in 1871 until his death in 1917. The Lodge became the focal point of village life, and his four daughters, none of whom married, virtually 'ran' the village. They played the organ in the church, gave Bible classes, were responsible for the Girl Guides, and were in charge of the lending library. The Butler memorials are in Woolstone churchyard.

It seems appropriate to mention here William Noakes, one time tenant of the inn and churchwarden. Having a disagreement with the Butler family, he built the somewhat unusual tower to overlook their property. There he inscribed his initials and those of his brother and the date 1817. The tower is built in red brick, with coloured inlay, very much in the style of Keble College, and it forms a strange contrast with the thatched building next to it.

The sharp bend on the road to Uffington is always known as Miss Newman's Corner, after the old lady, once a court dressmaker, who lived there. A regular church attender, Miss Newman was a familiar and much loved figure with her dog. Miss Newman's spaniels were always black, and they were always called Tessa!

Wootton & Boars Hill ✍

The name Wootton derives from the Anglo-Saxon word meaning 'the township in the wood' – Wood-tun. The origin of the village goes back nearly 1,000 years, when a group of Saxon farmers made a clearing in the woodlands below Boars Hill, which in those days covered all the lower slopes of the hill and much of the valley below.

Until the 20th century, practically everyone in Wootton and Boars Hill made a living from the fields which stretched from the parish boundary with Dry Sandford to the foot of Boars Hill ridge. The heathland on the top of the ridge was used for grazing sheep. Hay could not be grown satisfactorily in Wootton, and had to be grown and fetched from meadowland near Donnington Bridge, and carted up Hinksey Hill to Wootton. At the time of Domesday (1086) the population was small, no more than 20 men and their families; even in the mid 19th century it was only 300–400.

There was no church in Wootton until the 14th century, when a chapel of ease to the mother church at Cumnor was built. This chapel, and the parish of Wootton and Boars Hill, remained dependent on Cumnor for practical purposes (eg burials) until 1735, and the old track northwards over the fields of Wootton to Cumnor (now a bridle path) is evidence of the route by which the people of Wootton once had to carry their dead to Cumnor. It was not until 1885 that Wootton became a separate parish.

During the 16th and 17th centuries there was a village pound for stray animals, near the present day Waterworks Crossroads, and Whitecross may have been named after the 16th century village constable, Thomas White. This was the era of prosperity for the yeoman farmers of the village – the families of Mayo, Richards, Bond, Badcock, Broughton and Busfield. The community was largely self supporting, growing their own food, making cloth from their sheep and the flax cultivated in 'Flexfield', and brewing their own ale in the farmhouses. The smithy was near the village green.

The turn of the 20th century saw great changes on Boars Hill, when many large houses and gardens were built. Residents like Sir Arthur Evans, the archaeologist, and Lord Berkeley transformed the appearance of Boars Hill with their tree planting and development.

Sir Arthur Evans became interested in the local Scout troop and in 1914 built a Scout hall within his 100 acre Youlbury estate, 70 of which were used for scouting purposes. The army and airforce used the estate during the Second World War and in 1947 the Scout HQ bought 36 acres.

The 1920s and 1930s saw the most startling changes in the village. Abingdon airfield became operational in September 1932, and this, together with the beginnings of the Amey Group development and the expanding motor car industry in Oxford led to a rapid increase in the population, resulting in new housing and shops on the southern and western edges of 'Wootton Village'.

Mike Buzzard, who with his wife runs the local supermarket, came to the 'new' shops in Besselsleigh Road when his parents opened a butchery there in 1938. This was before the Berrymere Road and Lamborough Hill estates were built, when a stream ran the whole length of the village street. Mr and Mrs Hatt kept the bakery next to the Methodist chapel and Mrs Thouless ran the post office from the front room of her cottage. In the early 1950s the community centre was built, within reach of Dry Sandford and the 'new' Wootton; a Roman Catholic chapel in the Cumnor Road was founded in 1952, and in 1959 Wootton school was rebuilt.

Wytham 🌿

Viewed from the embankment of the busy A34 bypass, Wytham appears an idyllic village. The Great Wood, once the haunt of highwaymen, is a splendid 'back-cloth' and also provides an indication of stormy weather to come, hence the old rhyme:

> When Wytham Hill wears a cap,
> Farmers all, beware of that!

The site on which the village stands has been inhabited since early times. The name Wytham is generally interpreted as meaning 'the dwelling at the bend of the river', the river being the Seacourt stream, which winds its way through the water meadows to join the Thames.

Wytham retains some aspects of a feudal settlement, for with the exception of the inn, the church, rectory, and two houses built on glebe land, the entire estate has one landowner, at the present time the University of Oxford. The estate was bequeathed to the University under the will of Colonel ffennell, the last lord of the manor to live in Wytham Abbey.

Before it was sold in 1920 to Raymond ffennell, Wytham Abbey was the seat of the Earls of Abingdon. Despite its name, the Abbey has no

The White Hart, Wytham

ecclesiastical connections, and until the middle of the 19th century was known as Wytham House.

It was the 5th Earl who had the old Norman church pulled down and in 1811–12 rebuilt the present church. He used materials from the ruined Cumnor Place, former home of the ill-fated Amy Robsart; the archway over the churchyard gate is one instance. There are some interesting examples of stained glass in the church from the late 14th to the early 20th century. Some of the old glass came from the earlier church, as did the 17th century altar table and chest.

Not all the residents of Wytham have added to its good name. In the early 18th century, the miller John Mauge murdered his sweetheart Annie Kite, and was hanged for the crime. The event is commemorated in a ballad, a copy of which is now lodged in the British Museum, entitled *The Wittam Miller*.

The University has brought many benefits to Wytham, not least the careful modernisation and maintenance of the 17th or 18th century houses, with their roofs of tiles or thatch. The wild life in the woods and surrounding fields is protected, and made the subject of careful research. For this reason, visitors to the woods must obtain permits from the University.

Despite the alarming increase of traffic through the village in the last few years, every effort is made to preserve the rural charm of this corner of Oxfordshire. For all such lovely places in which this county abounds, we echo the wish contained in the last two lines of a poem written by a local resident, –

> May those who hold the land in custody,
> Preserve such beauty, for all time to be!

Yarnton

To many people, Yarnton (or Eardington as it was once known) is a blur of houses as they speed along the A34 between Oxford and Woodstock, but to the people who call it home there is much beyond this stretch of tarmac.

The lovely manor house, originally built by Sir Thomas Spencer around 1611 and completely restored in 1897, is one of the largest Jacobean houses in the country and since 1973 has housed the Oxford Centre for Hebrew Studies. When there was a lord of the manor, villagers met in the grounds of the manor for fetes and celebrations, and the annual Flower Show, held in the Old Barn, was the cause of fierce rivalry between local gardeners.

Next door, and closely connected with the manor, is the 13th century church of St Bartholomew. Of particular interest are the two beautiful tombs in the Spencer Chapel to members of the family of Sir John Spencer of Althorp, also the stained glass, much of it English medieval, some of it Tudor.

The old vicarage, next to the church, has been taken over by the manor and converted into accommodation for their students, and one of the cottages nearby has been converted into a rectory.

The Lot Meadows down by the river, very rich in wild flowers and unusual grasses, have recently been adopted by the Berkshire, Buckinghamshire and Oxfordshire Naturalists' Trust to ensure their preservation. A unique custom, which lapsed only very recently, concerned the drawing of lots for the mowing rights of the meadows (hence 'Lot Meadows'). Thirteen wooden balls, each a little smaller than a golf ball and with a name painted on it, represented 'mowths' or thirteenth – parts of the meadow. The balls were drawn by the meadsmen to determine who had the right to which 'mowth' of the meadow's harvest.

All villages must have at least one ghost, and Yarnton is no exception. Christabel, forbidden to see the man she loved, threw herself from the bedroom window of her home at College Mead and her ghost is said to wander the lane outside the house, leaving a sweet perfume drifting after her. Poor Mary Ann, who lived at Home Close, was also forbidden to see her love and died there of a broken heart. Sad histories for two lovely old cottages.

The Grapes Inn on the A34 was once called the Turn Pike Inn in the days when the toll gate was in action and highwaymen frequented the road to Woodstock. The Red Lion, now a modern brick building, stands on the site once occupied by an ancient building with a very steep thatched roof. Following a serious fire the old building was demolished and the present Red Lion built in its place.

Yarnton is thriving today, with a modern village hall, a large garden centre and a local post office and shops. Many new houses have been built over the past few years, and although most of the population commute into Oxford and nearby towns to work, the various clubs and organisations flourish and grow. Community spirit is alive and well in this village as in many others. Yarnton is most certainly not just a ribbon of houses on a busy main road.

Index